For Au_

SACRED
PATH

All the best
my Friend

L. CONWAY

For Susie Sprite (the Bee Lady),
an angel of unconditional love

Sacred children,
Scott, Holly, Kerry, Hannah

My true friend and brother, Stephen,
the Barefoot Doctor, the kindest man...

Mad bad and dangerous
Chainsaw Maxie and his Angel Iris

My dear friends,
Mike Astley, Big Pete, John, Angie
and Jimmy Watts

Jenny Wren and Russ Tarrant

Kindred spirits and fellow compassion activists, Julia Honeebee,
Apple Amber, Alisha, Noranne, Manku, Martina
and all other soul brothers and sisters
who walk the Sacred Path...

SACRED PATH

MAN V NATURE
BOOK ONE

LEE CONWAY

Project management by whitefox
Designed and typeset by seagulls.net
Cover design by Madeline Meckiffe

Remember, remember the sacredness
Of things running streams and
Dwellings
The young within the nest
A hearth for sacred fire
The holy flame.

OMAHA AMERICAN INDIAN CHANT

Grandfather,
Look at our brokenness.
We know that in all creation
Only the human family
Has strayed from the sacred way.
We know that we are the ones
Who are divided
And we are the ones
Who must, come back together
To walk in the sacred way
Grandfather,
Sacred one,
Teach us love compassion, honour
That we may heal the earth
And heal each other.

OJIBWAY AMERICAN INDIAN PRAYER

ÍNDEX OF ROMANY
WORDS AND MEANÍNGS

Bar	One pound coin
Canni	Game bird
Chav/chavvy	Child/term of endearment
Chockas	Boots/shoes
Chor	Steal
Churi	Knife
Cushti	Good
Didiki	Not-true gypsy
Dik	Look/see
Dinlo	Stupid, idiot, retarded
Dordi	Register surprise
Hedge crawler/hopper	Tramp/vagrant
Juckal	Dog
Kenner	House/dwelling
Kitchima	Pub/alehouse
Livna	Beer/alcholic drink
Motor	Car/van
Pikie	Non gypsy
Rakli	Girl
Scran	Food
Shoshi	Rabbit
Toovla	Cigarette.
Trashd	Scared/frightened
Wongur	Money/cash
Yogger	Gun
Vardo	Caravan or trailer

A π
ÎΠ†RODUC†ÎOΠ

A sunny summer afternoon in 2001...

I sat alone, in a bungalow nestled high on a hillside in Cornwall, England, taking in the magnificent views out over a small harbour on the Helford River. It was here, in the small village of Gweek, that I began to write *Sacred Path*.

I had known for many years that I would write this book, my inner conviction of that certainty predestined by a higher force, although I had no clue how, or when I would start.

But today was the day... suddenly I felt compelled to write. It was as if a cosmic connection with the Great Spirit of Nature had arrived in the form of literary inspiration. I dashed for my old word processor and wrote the first chapter as fast as I could, so as not to lose the moment... When finished, I basked in the afterglow of achievement... At last! I had made the breakthrough. Overjoyed, I smiled, and leaned back in my chair, delighted.

Then all of a sudden... Bang! An ear-splitting crash and flash of lightning, followed by a tremendous thunder clap. The electricity supply was cut off, and I saw my first chapter, that (to me) oh so important intro, disappear into the ether, gone, literally in a flash.

Distraught, I raged and cursed at the cruel elements. After the initial shock, a period of calm, peaceful reflection brought forth a profound realisation... This was a cosmic test! It was as if Gaia were showing me that writing this book would be no easy street, and I should be prepared for setbacks and interruptions along the way, if

I, a former serial school truant, frequently suspended, and eventually expelled pupil (long story short: my sadistic maths teacher was shot with an air pistol... self-defence... honest, your honour!) with virtually no school education, and certainly no academic qualifications, college, or university, was seriously going to attempt such a monumental task. I did not attend any school until I was nine, and learnt almost nothing thereafter, except to read and write a little. I could barely scrawl my own name.

Then all of a sudden the power came back on... so I wrote the first chapter again, quickly, as best I could recall, and printed it out immediately. There! I let out a long sigh, as I gazed in satisfaction at the beginning of my book.

The result (eighteen years later) is *Sacred Path Book One*: Man V Nature, the first in a trilogy... or maybe quartet?

The tale is semi-autobiographical, and based on factual experiences and events, real people and places. Although, where necessary, the lines are intentionally blurred to respect the Sacred Path travel of the innocent, and also the guilty (depending on one's interpretation, or degree of adherence and obedience of Planet Earth law). Interwoven throughout is my interpretation and projection of the Universe based on my own spiritual and supernatural experiences and observations, based in great part on my interaction from an early age with the Great Spirit of Nature.

Sacred Path is the story of a young boy brought up in unconventional circumstances in 1950s England. At the age of two a profound connection occurs between the child and the omnipotent forces of Super Nature. Due to a lack of parental interaction during his early years he becomes drawn towards the unconditional love and magical teachings of Universal Cosmic Law, bestowed as blessings by Gaia, AKA the Great Spirit of Nature. This profound spiritual awakening subsequently leads to the boy's transition to veganism. It is the story of one free spirit's quest for supernatural enlightenment, an observational account of the superior power of Nature, and the potential karmic consequences of mankind's reluctance to coexist peacefully.

★ ★ ★

Wishing good fortune and safe passage to all those kindred souls who hold love, kindness and compassion in their heart for Planet Earth, Mother Nature, and all innocent life forms... May the Great Spirit be with you on your own journey of the Sacred Path.

Author Lee Conway, 2019

CHAPTER
ONE

Startled awake and frightened, Calum cowers in the cot that is his cage. The banshee wail of a furious storm wind screams through the dark forest, ripping and shredding leaves from swaying trees, bending and creaking, groaning in resistance against this awesome primeval force. Roots straining, trunks braced, muscular boughs flexing, branches scratching and screeching like desperate outstretched fingers against the rain-lashed windows of the old caravan.

Calum is afraid and alone, his mother sectioned, father out drinking. Weeping, trembling, and wide-eyed apprehensive, he peers through the wooden bars of his confinement, as darting shadows dash frantic from wall to ceiling, as if even the spirit world is spooked by the heavy rain pounding staccato rhythmic on the thin aluminium roof. Flinching, he gasps, terrified as thunder roars, super Nature, raging rampant, detonating bolts of fearsome fury, threatening to rent asunder the very fabric of the universe. Violent tremors reverberate, triggering seismic shockwaves, shaking up the forest floor, splitting dimensions, cleaving atoms, creating a cataclysmic cosmic hall of mirrors, momentarily distorting the molecular balance of time and space. Lightning enters the fray, this eternal energy, inevitably instrumental at the culmination of Nature's explosive orchestral crescendo. The voracious voltage illuminating a jagged descent of desire passionately propelled in anticipation of a lusty encounter with some metallic muse.

As suddenly as the storm began, so it abates, save for a lingering memory link of soft pitter-patter raindrops. Calum sobs and whimpers as great shudders of relief suddenly course through him.

A gentle voice whispers lullaby soft from the forbidding gloom. "Hush child, hush now, I visit you as the Great Spirit of Nature, the perpetual light within your soul. Please excuse the grand entrance, but my highly-strung offspring, the eternal elements, can be somewhat dramatic when heralding my arrival. I find you this night as a lost soul, a vulnerable creature of the forest cast adrift in my domain, so I deem it only fitting to bestow the healing love and wisdom of universal intervention."

Calum cries, tears of relief flooding forth, feeling as though a warm comforting cloak is being draped tenderly around him. At two years of age, he welcomes the powerful security of unconditional love for the first time.

CHAPTER
TWO

Moonlight filters serenely through heavy dissipating cloud, streaming in the small window, swathing Calum within an aura of magenta mist. The Great Spirit's voice resonates throughout the cramped confines of the caravan.

"Mother Nature can provide sustenance and healing for your soul, enabling you to grow and evolve spiritually, engendering knowledge, which if applied altruistically, can facilitate discovery of the hidden laws of Nature. When heeded and understood, this wisdom has unique potential to provide enlightenment and clarification with which to unravel the mysteries of the universe. These revelations are constantly evolving, and seamlessly integrated within the very structure and framework of said hidden laws, forming a living tapestry that hangs eternal within the cosmic corridors of infinity. This blessing can be the catalyst towards divine enlightenment at each and every stage of your journey upon the Sacred Path."

Calum sighs, accepting the tingling electromagnetic spark of pure intellectual illumination imparted to his soul through this profound connection.

"Your mother chose your name wisely," the Great Spirit continues, "the meaning of Calum, passed down from your ancient Gaelic ancestors is dove, messenger of peace. But you must always be vigilant, for your own self-preservation. When showing kindness one must be selective and on guard, and constantly aware of the premeditated cruel intent prevalent within a large cross-section of humanity, those dark souls contaminated by a defective rogue gene, a mutant malfunction abhorrent to the cosmic law of cause and effect. These perpetrators of crimes against Nature will suffer Divine Retribution, whereby universal justice is unleashed and a karmic lobotomy is performed, thus rendering the recipient dead inside. This irreversible operation will disconnect the criminal soul – in a spiritual sense – for all eternity. Of all the mortal dangers that you may encounter on the earth plane, my child, none are as grave as the evil intent from some of your fellow humans. However, should you, in your heart, remain loyal and true to the Great Spirit of Nature, then your soul shall forever frolic in the playground of immortality. The flora and fauna that coexist in peace and tolerance here on planet Earth can grant access to a level of spiritual attainment which will equip and empower you with the ability to visualise the one great truth.

These blessed gifts, if not abused for material or egotistical gain, will enable you to progress on your journey with love, compassion and tolerance, as your guiding light. From this moment forth you will possess the feral awareness of the natural world. The sensory aids of clairvoyance and premonition will become second nature. These blessings, if nurtured and cultivated, will bode well for your life journey upon this planet. Spirit guides in human form will interact with you. These spectral beings will appear before you as the reincarnation of Native American braves, who know me as Wakan Tanka, the Great Spirit. Be aware though Calum, should these divine gifts be used as a means of gaining entry into Man's maelstrom of material greed, then the power of Nature's blessing will diminish and eventually disappear. To feed the ego is to starve the soul. On occasion, whilst traversing the Sacred Path, you may wish to seek my direct guidance and advice. If you remain receptive to the hidden laws of Nature I shall always be close by, channeling sacred wisdom from ancient stones, crystals and the eternal elementals. You have been the recipient tonight of universal cosmic communication. There is no human explanation for this divine spark of knowledge. No scientific rationalisation exists to explain how you received and retained

Nature's wisdom instantly in this moment. The power of this love vibration travels faster than the speed of light from the birth of the very first stars to the present core of your reborn soul."

Calum peers into the darkness, trying to locate the exact whereabouts of his mysterious benefactor. "But... I don't see you... where are you?"

Just as he thinks the connection is broken the Great Spirit continues. "I know this will be difficult for you to understand, but an insertion of universal truth codes has now been completed, the first charge installed within your psyche. You are now an old soul in a young body."

Struggling to understand, Calum is somewhat perturbed by this revelation. "Uhh...? I don't mean to appear ungrateful, really I don't, but I'm not sure I like the sound of that."

"What's not to like, old soul, young body, that's a great combination, is it not? But the choice is yours, Calum. Please understand... you are under no obligation. Why not live with it for a while? If you find it's not for you, then you can always take your leave of the Sacred Path and follow your own way. But be warned, as with all divine blessings, if not used regularly for the greater good, they will soon atrophy and lose their power. It is, after all, your own free will choice that will dictate whether you are joyriding or on the road to redemption for the long haul."

"I understand, Great Spirit, but why have you chosen me to receive this ultimate wisdom?"

"Fate conspires to bring us together tonight, my child. Other humans have been selected by similar providence, but few can stay the course. The foundation of the seven universal galaxies was originally a floating love vibration, drawn inexorably to roaming karmic tentacles in the black swirling void that was all encompassing before the formation of stars and planets. This connection, known crudely as the 'Big Bang' in human scientific terms, was the catalyst, the sacred spark which created the beginning of existence, culminating in all life forms that now exist."

"Are you the divine ruler of these seven universes?"

"No Calum, I am the Great Spirit of Nature that is intrinsically linked with your closest universe. Some may call me Gaia, others Mother Nature. But whoever, whatever, let's just say I am your local representative. I shall not fill your head at this moment with machinations of other worlds. Your life is just beginning, you have precious little experience yet of planet Earth, so it would be rash of you to attempt to compartmentalise Nature, or to seek comparison with other intergalactic solar systems. Remember also, in terms of human comprehension it is unheard of in the history of mankind for a child of your age to be conversing as we do now. So be cautious when in the company of other humans, for your safety they must never know of our intergalactic connection. I must leave you now child, but follow Nature's way, and your soul shall forever be illuminated with spiritual enlightenment as you travel along the Sacred Path."

Calum is spellbound, as a magenta mist slowly manifests before him, transforming into a woman. Her beautiful facial features conveying a countenance of love and compassion. The word MOTHER infiltrates his soul. Although just two years born of this earth plane he is now blessed with an absolute understanding and comprehension of universal love and divine truth. This cosmic bequest, bestowed in a split second, is now a compassionate component of his soul. The knowledge transmitted to his psyche in a flash of inspired telepathic communication. A blessing of such magnitude and relevance – this instant information – comparable to a lifetime's study of the most learned spiritual sage.

Calum feels serene, calm, and strangely at ease with the magnitude of the moment as the Great Spirit fades into the ethereal vapour, shapeshifting into elongated blobs of pink ectoplasm floating slowly towards the open caravan skylight, before being sucked out with a loud *whoosh* into the great cosmic void of outer space.

He has a deep yearning to follow, but knows on this momentous occasion Mother Nature is advocating caution and patience.

CHAPTER
THREE

Calum slumps back in his cot, realising that to seek enlightenment at the highest level will be no easy task. Although in awe of the situation, he also feels invigorated and inspired by the possibility of escape from this lonely captivity. Gazing up through the small cracked window at the sparkling silver stars and pale yellow moonlight lulls him into a deep slumber only the innocent can enjoy.

This reverie, however, is short-lived as he's suddenly jolted awake by the caravan door being flung open. His father, Cormack, staggers in, followed by a dark-skinned woman with long jet-black hair. Her emerald-green satin dress shimmers and glistens phosphorescently in the gloom as they fool around, playing each other flirtatiously, laughing, teasing, and drinking beer from dark green bottles.

Calum rubs sleep from his eyes, looking on warily as the woman lights a candle. So absorbed in their lusty foreplay, they've taken no heed of the boy watching them from the dark shadows. The jokey sexual banter is instantly curtailed when Cormack grabs at her, pulling her hair, trying to kiss and fondle her.

She reacts violently, cursing shrilly, "Dirtee eengleesh bastart," swearing her vengeance, "I weell keel yuu bastart."

Her resistance serves only to spur Cormack on, and dragging her to him drunken clumsy, he rips the dress from her back. Struggling furiously, before breaking free, staggering backward, she snatches up a big bone handled carving knife from the tiny kitchen. Reflected candle flame flashes blindingly off the blade as she slashes and lunges at him.

"You two-bit Spanish whore," Cormack snarls, charging her in fury. Grappling, rolling on the floor, scratching, biting, slapping at each other, swearing and cursing before they are suddenly tumbling out of the caravan in a screaming frenzied tangle through the open door, landing heavily and rolling away in damp dark leaves, then scrambling to their feet and stumbling away, swallowed up by the dense woodland, their loud angry dialogue gradually fading to sporadic outbursts, until the forest is quiet once more, save for spooked resting birds, settling back, and the creak... creak... creaking of the caravan door, swinging slowly back and forth... back and forth... in the cold early morning breeze.

Although shivering uncontrollably with shock, Calum is absorbing and trusting the Great Spirit's blessed gift of understanding and enlightenment as a natural learning curve, accepting that this evening's dubious entertainment has been his first lesson on the earth plane.

Instinctively feral aware, he knows, going forward, it is imperative to be always on his guard, constantly alert, and forever expecting the unexpected where Nature and humans are concerned. 'Especially the humans,' he decides, as the gentle breeze caresses him, precipitating quick, deep sleep, his soul elevated to a dream dimension... where, emerging from deep darkness into daylight, he sits down on a fossilised tree trunk, patiently waiting, knowing he must, 'But why?'.

Eventually, a tall Native American, shrouded in grey mist, slowly materialises before him. The hazy atmosphere gradually clears... The man is standing on a solitary outcrop of rock in the midst of a barren sun-baked desert with sand as far as the eye can see. He raises outstretched arms towards a clear turquoise sky, and with a sweeping motion of his left hand ushers in ten white doves. The birds swoop about him before soaring away to glide high on sun-kissed warming thermals.

Calum is woken later that morning by the clattering din of his irritable father's kitchen activity as he washes up dirty plates and dishes at the sink. Cormack is broad, and heavily muscled, with sleek, short, coal-black hair and pointed goatee beard. So intimidating is he, that even the hangover-induced reluctance of attending to these mundane domestic chores charges his brooding presence with latent menace. Fumbling a frying pan with shaking hands, it slips through soapy fingers and onto his bare feet. "Arrrgh!" He cries out, hopping and staggering around, cursing bitterly, wincing with pain, "Fuck and bejasus! I'm gonna kill some bastard soon," sending a plate to go smashing against the wall, before turning to rage and shaking his scarred bunched fists at Calum, "Fuckin' wimin's work is this! What's the world comin' to? I ask yuh," macho beating his chest, "me, the hunter, the bandit, lookin' after fuckin' kids and doin' the poxy washin' up."

Calum looks around anxiously, wondering, 'Where's the woman from last night?!' Imagining her grisly fate… 'Probably beaten to a pulp by Cormack… and buried… somewhere… deep in the dark dark woods…'

Suddenly, incongruous, melodious birdsong mellows the malevolent mood within the caravan. Flighty sunbeams, sneaking through the rustling canopy of trees, link empathetically in penetrating the gloomy ambience. Calum is instantly calmed, comforted, gratefully appreciating Mother Nature's gift to planet Earth of this brand-new day.

CHAPTER
FOUR

Calum was born in Hertford, in the county of Hertfordshire, England, UK, on 11th February 1955. The son of Cormack Connor, a wild Irish Romany lumberjack from Connemara, who earned his living working for the Forestry Commission, travelling around England, felling and clearing condemned trees with his executioner's axe and cross cut saw, before selling on the wood and timber for firewood or mining pit props.

Calum's mother Ingrid – although of Scandinavian descent – had been born in Nottingham, England. Their family home is a beaten up old four-berth caravan, towed by a Second World War Humber army staff car, which had been purchased by Cormack from a military surplus auction.

Calum had lived the first two years of his life in the forest.

The populace of England, post Second World War, seemed to be carried along on a tide of optimism based on pretentious ideals. A hive of industrial activity ensued, as the UK doggedly shrugged off the dark cloak of attempted Nazi invasion. Many intellectuals and a handful of visionary academics believed this surge of positivity to be generated predominantly by a sense of hyperactive adrenaline-fuelled excitement, which consequently led much of the frenzied rebuilding of war-ravaged England to be carried out with indecent haste. The inevitable after-effects and consequences predestined to be repented at a later date.

Those on the breadline had a different priority and focused their attention on living in constant poverty. Politicians appeared to have learned little from past, or indeed, recent history. The main concern for them, and the top brass military, seemed to be feathering their own nests and engaging in even more destructive warfare. These men focused primarily on building large business empires and even larger bank accounts. Manufacturing advanced and high-powered deadly weapons was key to their materialistic personal goals. Meanwhile England's poverty-ridden lower class were suffering from malnutrition, rickets and tuberculosis, with many living rough or dwelling in slums. The poor and disadvantaged and any other unfortunate soul born on the wrong side of the tracks invariably endured miserable shortened lifespans within an environment of suffering and deprivation.

Despite these urgent social issues, much money was spent on this heavy weapon and armament development. The first helicopters were invented by the RAF in this decade, and used by the English armed forces in 1958 to capture rebels during jungle warfare in far-flung Malaya. "Millions on Malaya!?" Went the baffled cry from peace-preaching pacifists and the hungry homeless, "What the fuck are we doing there?"

One rule for the rich and another for the poor meant a hostile undercurrent was flowing through British society at this time. An atmosphere of cruelty and callous disregard ensued whereby a dog-eat-dog mentality prevailed. Racism and homophobia were rife, although there was a minority group of caring, compassionate, social reformers pressing for change.

After the initial euphoria and celebratory jubilation of victory in war, delayed shock reality hit hard. Many people were unable to cope with the loss of family and home, did not know who to turn to, and had no one to confide in. Many suffered severe mental breakdowns, some even resorting to suicide.

The class divide became even more pronounced than before. A callous indifference from the government condemned those lower down in the pecking order of society. The underprivileged were, ironically, even more vulnerable than during the conflict, appearing just as bewildered and shell-shocked by post-war civvy street as they were when German bombs were falling all about them, with many people left wondering if they would have been treated better under the rule of the Hun. The Nazis had been undeniably brutal and merciless in causing suffering and misery, but equally there seemed to be little government compassion on offer for the needy and downtrodden of Great Britain. The old Victorian workhouse values were still prevalent. Although it was claimed workhouses in England and Wales were abolished by the National Assistance act of 1948, it was just words on paper. The hard-hearted, ruthless overseer mentality continued.

As for animal welfare, this was a futuristic notion entertained and espoused by only the most liberal of far-seeing radical free-thinkers. The oppressive inhumane treatment of man and beast galvanised some of the public though, with strong-willed individuals showing renewed spirit, many looking to the exciting new phenomena of rock and roll in an attempt to escape domestic boredom and forget the war years... Elvis was king!

Calum's mother had been mostly absent in his life to date. Ingrid was prone to recurring bouts of manic depression. More often than not she was sectioned, incarcerated in the nearest mental institution. These leftover relics from the Victorian age were also known disparagingly as 'loony bins.' The buildings and standard of care therein had not been updated or improved by the 1950s. Condemned 'patients' were still locked in padded cells and straitjackets, and treated to experimental remedys, or 'therapy treatments.' These commonplace practices included a much-heralded supposed cure-all, the lobotomy, where a section of a patient's brain was removed. ECT (electro convulsive treatment) was another alleged miracle method, which involved administering heavy doses of electrical current to the restrained, conscious recipient, causing them to spasm and convulse like bulging-eyed, jerky rag dolls, whilst biting down on square wooden blocks rammed into their mouths just before the power was turned on. ECT was used to induce fits, and drugs that rendered patients in a continuous zombie-like state were routinely force-fed. Those locked away because of homosexual tendencies were subjected to their own specific medication and treatment for this crime. The use of sedative and potentially harmful drugs such as Lithium was widespread. Thorazine was introduced in 1954, proclaimed to be a better way to calm patients with schizophrenic disorders and manic depression. Millions of people were prescribed the drug as a way of taking pressure off hospital staff. Insulin comas were induced by injection, mostly just to keep the patients quiet. Half of all hospital beds were taken up by 'mental health patients.' Abuse was endemic.

When Ingrid was detained and Cormack was at work, the local child welfare authority would send female representatives – 'carers' – to 'look after' Calum. Cormack worked most every day and would, more often than not, spend the night away drinking, brawling and womanising. He was street-savvy though, and always made sure to be back in time for the carers' arrival, careful to be seen diligently attending to his youngster's needs while the welfare women were in attendance.

Calum grows accustomed to the isolation and solitude. Frequently left alone at night in the cold dark caravan, his only company the strange animal sounds emanating from the forest. The wild unpredictable resonance of the supernatural in the dreaded blackness of night, raging winds, lashing rain and thunderstorm, ravenous rats screeching and squealing, twigs and branches snapping under foot of skittish deer and snuffling boar, the assured wilderness cry of fox and owl, the frenzied rustling of badgers foraging through fallen leaves, and scores of hungry mice scurrying around in the caravan. This Nature noise, although at times scary and frightening, also engendered feral companionship. But Calum is still missing his mother, waiting long hours and lonely days, pining for her return.

The carers go through the motions, albeit in an impersonal robotic manner, providing the very basics of sustenance and warmth. There are few kind words or affection, no little treats or friendly banter. Calum thinks their title, 'carers', most ironic, as they obviously did not really care. Often he would catch them unawares, daydreaming of an escape from the monotonous day-to-day routine of their dreary mundane lives, fantasising of anything other than the self-induced drudgery they were locked into.

He recalls the Great Spirit's description of most humans, 'spiritually lobotomised', thinking this describes the carers perfectly. Sometimes, caught off guard, they would catch him peering intently at them, avoiding eye contact whenever possible, feeling unsettled and edgy in his company, whispering and pointing at "the strange child."

On Cormack's rare visits home, he would also on occasion catch his son looking at him in a knowing way, before demanding in his hostile tone, "What you fuckin' staring at young 'un? You're lookin' as if you ain't never seen I before."

If the carers were listening in, though, Cormack would make an attempt at humour. In one such mock-tender moment, accompanied by a forced nervous chuckle, he attempts to make a joke of Calum's cold scrutiny, jovially informing the welfare women, "Nosey little bugger, ain't he, means he's intelligent though, must get that from me." But Calum is well aware that his father's fake affection was just that; fake, and always synthetically enhanced by the copious amounts of alcohol he had previously consumed.

One morning, after returning home drunk at three am and sleeping off a particularly potent hangover, Cormack's slumber is disturbed by two carers arriving at breakfast time. They knock loudly and enter without waiting to be invited in, accustomed to him rising late.

"Morning Calum," a large red-faced woman leans into the cot and smiles. "I'm Molly, and this 'ere's me friend Beryl, come to give me a hand today, morning to you, Mr Connor," raising her voice and prodding Cormack with her foot in a vain bid to rouse him. "Come on now, wakey wakey, you must get yourself up and off to work. We'll take over from here." He doesn't stir, so she hollers loudly in his ear, "Get you up Mr Connor!"

Moaning and groaning, he rises slowly, like some scruffy hibernating Neanderthal, crawling out from under the crumpled mound of blankets and old coats, staggering upright, using the wall to steady himself, trying to blink away bleary-eyed double vision, squinting at the intrusive bright daylight, whilst struggling to focus on the blurred female shapes. "Yeah… yeah… OK… to be sure, ma'am… just let me get me self sorted and I'll be outta yer hair ladies, so I will." Stumbling around, kicking over an overflowing ashtray and several empty beer bottles, before stooping to pick up his tobacco tin, lighter and a half bottle of Navy rum. "Where's me fuckin' socks gone missus?" He grumbles, scrabbling and searching around the floor.

"Would you like me to put the kettle on… before you go?" Beryl offers pointedly.

"Yeah, sure and bejasus, that'd be grand ma'am," Cormack smiles up at her, "cup a char, go down famously wud that, so it wud, tuh be sure."

The women look at each other in a knowing way. Molly raises an imaginary glass to her lips several times in quick succession. Beryl nods in resigned affirmation, world-weary wise as to the base traits of men. She goes to make the brew, returning shortly, and offers Cormack a mug of tea. He nods surly in acceptance and draws the half bottle of rum from his torn jacket pocket, and with trembling hand adds a shot of the cheap spirit as an early morning livener.

"Ahh…thaass fuckin' bedder," he says, eyes watering, savouring the rejuvenating elixir, gulping down the laced tea, before grabbing his things and leaving the caravan without another word.

The carers set about feeding, washing and dressing Calum. "Best we get you outside for some fresh air, my lad," Molly throws open the caravan windows with a snort of disgust, "soon as we've cleaned up this shit hole," pinching her nostrils shut with finger and thumb, "stinks like a bleedin' brewery in 'ere."

"Bloody disgrace so it is," Beryl agrees, "no place for a young child to be brought up." She nods towards the door, "I'm just going for a fag, Molls."

Molly suddenly breaks into song as she works, "Que sera, sera, whatever will be, will be."

Calum cringes, recognising straight off, 'She's no Doris Day, this one', annoyed that the peace of his beloved forest is being compromised. He feels Molly is showing total disrespect for Mother Nature, the magical spell well and truly broken by her tuneless renditions. "Hey you!" He shouts above the din, "Can you not keep the noise down please, and allow Gaia's blessing of tranquillity to prevail."

Molly drops the glass she is washing to go smashing to the floor. "Beryl Beryl, did... did you hear that? The boy... he... he spoke... real grown up at me, big words an' all. That's not normal, not at his age. He's such a strange one. Something's definitely not right with him," pointing to her head, "you mark my words."

Beryl looks in, giggling. "You sure you're not imagining things Molls? You've not been on the sauce too, have you lady?"

"No! Of course not, I swear, as God is me judge, the boy just told me to shut up."

Beryl bursts out laughing. Calum cringes, shaking in panic, fight or flight syndrome kicking in, wishing he had kept quiet, fretting that if they think he's odd in any way, the carers may try to have him locked away... 'like my mother.' Cursing his stupidity, he vows never to speak out again in their presence.

"Sorry, Molls," Beryl goes outside for another cigarette, still laughing as she lights up, "but the kid's not old enough for a proper conversation... not losing your marbles on me, are you old gal?"

"No, no, honestly Beryl, it was just so odd, he did not sound, or speak, like a child of two... more... more like a real adult, if truth be told."

"Well, maybe he's just one of them rare kids who's more advanced for his age? Shouldn't let it get to you, Molls."

"OK! OK, don't believe me then, but there's something very unusual about that boy, I tell you, I just knows it."

CHAPTER FIVE

Calum's enforced captivity continues; that's how he sees it, as incarceration. Becoming increasingly bored, so impatient to embark on the adventures the Great Spirit had promised, yearning to be set free... but Gaia does not answer his call.

Ingrid returns every few weeks or so, on chaperoned visits from the mental institution. He is always pleased to see his mother, but her deterioration is obvious. She rarely speaks now, barely acknowledging his existence, just sitting, staring at the floor, rocking back and forth, often mumbling incoherently. Cormack always ensures he has 'a prior engagement' and is never around when she comes home. A stern looking woman in a dark blue uniform sits in close proximity for the duration of each visit. On one such occasion Ingrid brings Calum a rare present, a cuddly toy lion she calls 'Lenny.'

The carers continue to cook and clean, providing the bare necessities for his survival. The drab and dreary caravan is more often than not miserably cold, with condensation and damp ever-present, and to make things worse, a family of noisy mice have made themselves at home in the cavity between the hardboard interior walls and thin aluminium exterior, disturbing his sleep by squealing and scratching throughout the night. Calum craves meaningful interaction on another level. Having been granted a brief taster from the Great Spirit, he wants more...

As the weeks drag by, a melancholic longing gradually envelopes him, bringing desperate loneliness, until one day, when consumed by

17

utter despair, he hears Gaia's voice. "Look out and above child, out and above."

He peers up at the small window, just as a flock of white doves fly by, assuming that these must be the messengers the Great Spirit had spoken of previously. A swirling magenta mist gradually fills one corner of the room, the dense haze slowly transforming, shape-shifting into the tall ghostly figure of a strikingly attractive woman. She stands before him with her lithe, deeply-tanned muscular arms crossed. Her shiny black hair is adorned with feathers and she is dressed in turquoise embroidered tan buckskin, with sun-bleached white seashell necklaces and small animal bones hanging around her neck. Calum remembers that Gaia had said a Native American was to be his spiritual guide, but he is startled nonetheless to see the apparition in real time. He recognises the birds as they swoop back into view, as the ten white doves from his previous dream. They seem to be conveying the portents of imminent change. The woman introduces herself, speaking softly, "I am Audrey Shenandoah, of the Onandaga tribe. Being born as human to this Earth is a very sacred trust. We have a moral responsibility because of the special gift we have, which is beyond the fine gifts of the plant life, the fish, the woodlands, the birds, and all the other living things on Earth... we are able to take care of them."

Gratefully accepting of this core cosmic truth code, Calum sighs contentedly and drifts into deep sleep.

CHAPTER
SIX

Calum awakes to a hive of activity.

Cormack is busy packing boxes, singing as he works. "I've been a wild rover for many a year, and I've spent all me money on whisky and beer, and it's nay no never, nay no never no more, I'll be a wild rover, no never no more."

Ingrid is back today, chaperone-free, apparently rejuvenated and unusually vital, as she busies herself cleaning and tidying. "It's a beautiful spring morn my son," she smiles, "we're leaving the forest today."

"Yes lad," his father confirms, "off 'n away to Bristol, to the West Country, bejasus, so we are."

For the first time in his life, Calum sees his parents animated and in good spirits together. Cormack dances and jigs in the cramped confines of the caravan, with Ingrid chuckling at his antics and clapping her hands in time to the Glenn Miller band playing out from the battered Bush radio in the corner.

The first rays of early morning spring sunshine caress Calum, and he feels love, not from his parents, but from a glowing realisation of déjà vu, knowing that the Great Spirit of Nature is nearby. Squinting up at bright sunlight, his restricted vision creating a kaleidoscopic rainbow of colours, then hearing gentle vocal intonations, soft chanting, he wonders, 'Am I imagining this? Are the voices real? Maybe it's an incoming message from Mother Nature? Yes, that's it, a telepathic transference, a sublime blessing delivered on a higher frequency of cosmic energy.' Oblivious to all other interference in this moment, he leaves his body, floating up and away in astral travel above the room, looking down on his parents' joyful celebration, as if watching some second-rate B-movie as a precursor to the main event. Painted words are forming within his mind's-eye rainbow.

LOVE… PEACE… COMPASSION… KINDNESS… KARMA…

Each word absorbed and retained, indelibly linked now to the core of his soul.

These words, he knows, are precious grace from Nature, even before the Great Spirit explains, "Not only are the meaning of these words crucial in determining the fate of mankind, they harbour the propensity to evoke a major catalyst for change and will be funda-mental in your quest for spiritual development. The seed is planted within you now, Calum. All will become clear in time. If you heed the meaning of these words, and hold them dear, I shall always remain close."

The cosmic connection is broken abruptly as Ingrid whisks him from his cot. "Come now son, time to go." She carries him outside, setting him down on the ground before locking the caravan door. He takes a last lingering look beyond the clearing. The glaring penetra-tion of bright sunlight is softened somewhat by fluttering forest foliage, diluting this piercing sharp radiance into dappled shade beneath the deciduous canopy of trees. A whispering breeze sets rustling branches to sway as if entranced, enticing dancing sunbeams, infusing the glistening droplets of dew clinging to fresh lime green leaves. Shim-mering, as if each and every tree is vibrantly festooned with thousands of sparkling iridescent jewels.

Turning away reluctantly from this vision of natural splendour, observing his parents' frenetic haste as they gather up their remaining belongings, he's at a loss to why anyone would be in such a hurry to leave this beautiful place?

"Hey, lookee here woman," Cormack shouts suddenly, "See who's a comin' down the track."

The harsh clattering of a tired diesel engine can be heard way up the trail before a battered black lorry comes to a grinding halt alongside the caravan. Three dark, swarthy men jump down from the dented, rusty Ford flatbed. They've come from an encampment on the other side of the forest. Cormack goes to greet them, accepting their enthusiastic handshakes.

The taller man slaps his back. "How goes it friend, heard tell you wus jellin' on, so we thought we'd just come by to say so long afore yuh go."

Cormack smiles, "Well well now! Ain't this somethin', Billy, Clem, Walter, sure is good to see youse boys."

"Likewise friend, likewise... Is it OK to let the Juk out fer a run?" Billy jerks a thumb at the truck cab, where a brindle lurcher dog is sat quiet and still like a stone statue. "Needs tuh stretch his legs a bit."

"Sure, let him out."

Soon as Billy opens the door, the dog leaps out and runs full pelt, speedily circling the clearing again and again as if on rails.

Cormack is impressed. "Fer fucks sake, wud yuh look at that dog run, he's like a fuckin' greyhound, bejasus, so he is."

Clem laughs. "That's cos he is a greyhound... well, fifty per cent."

Cormack bristles, "Yeah... fuckin' knew that son... tuh be sure."

Billy beams proudly. "He's the fastest Juckal in these parts, nothin' to touch him, and a good huntin' dog too." After a few minutes he whistles shrilly and the lurcher runs to his side. "That'll do him fer now, boys." Walter opens the truck door and the dog leaps in obediently.

Cormack turns to Ingrid, ordering, "Get the lads a jar, will yuh woman, what'll ye have boys, a drop of the hard stuff take yer fancy?"

Walter bows and tips his trilby hat to Ingrid. "A livna sure wouldn't go amiss thank yuh kindly ma'am."

She nods, lifts Calum from the ground, and goes to the caravan, returning minutes later to hand the men a large tumbler of whisky apiece. Cormack gestures expansively across the clearing, to where a large black cast iron cooking pot, strongly resembling a witch's cauldron, is suspended precariously on a tripod of rusty metal poles bound together crudely with twisted barbed wire.

"Was just about to put the shackle pot on lads."

The shackle pot contents are a putrefying mixture of five-day-old meat and vegetables. Only the furnace-like temperature achieved by each daily reheating prevents the food from becoming potential poison for any unsuspecting diner.

He grins at the men, "Can I tempt ye to a bit of scran then fellas?"

"Surely can, friend, and we've brought along some cushti canni 'n shoshi for the pot." Walter lifts a brace of pheasant and two dead rabbits from the back of the truck. The limp creatures tied by the neck with orange bailing twine. "Here, for the family." Macho proud, he passes the offering to Cormack, who hangs them like condemned felons over the open caravan door. Blood trickles from the hanging bundle of fresh kill, drip... drop... drip... drop... dripping, like a macabre ticking clock of doom, each droplet marking a spent second of dashed life-force... slowly draining from the lifeless corpses... the mournful echoing... drip... drop... tick... tock... of sudden, violent death.

"Cheers fellas, good of yuh all t' be sure." Cormack strides across the clearing, striking a Vesta match on his steel boot heel before setting light to the prepared fire. The kindling roars away, spitting and crackling ablaze, with yellow and green flames puffing out wispy grey smoke to rise up and go swirling away lazily into the atmosphere.

As Ingrid refills the men's glasses, Cormack calls over, "We've got some choice leg a mutton in the shackle pot boys, but with present company stayin' on fer grub we'll be needin' even more meat, and I knows just the place to find it."

He creeps stealthily towards the caravan... closer and closer... before suddenly leaping inside, and snatching the cuddly toy lion from his dozing child's grasp. Emerging victorious, he cackles and grins like a crazed maniac as he holds Lenny aloft.

"Here ya go me boyos, let's cook this little fucker in the pot, ha ha ha, hee hee," laughing gleefully, he jumps out of the caravan and slams the door behind him.

Calum is shocked into silence, until grim realisation dawns, and he screams loudly.

Clem is feeling uncomfortable at the child's distress. "Aw come on now Paddy, let the chavvy 'ave his toy back."

Cormack pays no heed and throws the lion on top of the log pile, dancing around the blazing fire with a wide grin on his face. He reaches into the cooking pot, retrieving a greasy grey hind leg of mutton from the bubbling brew. Mumbling excitably, incoherently, he runs back to the caravan and snatches open the door. "Here yuh be lad," he sneers at his sobbing son, "here's yer Lenny the fuckin' lion, or what's left of the little bastard." Grinning as he holds up the sheep leg, the steaming limb dripping hot rancid gravy onto the floor, mixing with the congealing pool of blood from the recently slain creatures swinging on the door. Calum screams, his horror compounded by the lifeless gaze of the dead pheasants and rabbits. Ingrid looks on, expressionless, while Cormack turns to his audience with an expectant smile, expecting joyful solidarity, but all three men – although hardened by life on the road, and aficionados of a no-mercy quick-kill policy regarding animals for food – are feeling increasing edgy at the child's distress.

"Hey, come on now, let's call it a day with the lion craic," pleads Walter. "You've had yer fun friend, now give the toy back to the kid."

Cormack suddenly stops dancing, not used to taking orders. He turns sharply, glaring menacingly, before his attention is drawn to the jagged wound on Walter's face. The violent slash of skin, sliced from ear to chin, exposing baby-pink flesh, is strangely at odds with the traveller's dark rugged complexion; a chilling reminder of a recent bar room brawl, etching a disturbing profile. This, and the fact that three to one seems poor odds at this moment, engenders in Cormack instinctive reticence towards any further provocative action.

Holding up his hands, he pleads, "OK now fellas... look... let's just lighten up now, didn't mean nothin', only 'avin' a bit of fun with the kid y'know," sulkily retrieving Lenny from the woodpile, before shouting to Ingrid, "Here woman," and throwing the toy angrily towards her. "Give the brat his fuckin' pet back, if it'll stop the little bugger wailin' an' whinin', then be sure to top up the men here with the good stuff."

She glares at him with unconcealed loathing before handing the toy lion back to her distraught child. Grasping gratefully, cuddling his comfort friend close and tight, Calum cries with relief. But overwhelming grief suddenly shudders through him for the creatures hanging on the doorframe. All of a sudden Cormack snatches the dead animals away. He sits on the doorstep, and, drawing a knife from his belt, deftly skins the rabbit, chops off its head, wraps it in the pelt and throws it under the caravan. Walter sits cross-legged on the ground and begins frantically to pluck the feathers from the pheasant. "Let's get these critters in the pot, Cormack, I'm gettin' mighty 'ungry my friend."

Open-mouthed and shaking, Calum is horrified, seeing this desecration through the half-open door. Walter picks up the small wood axe from the log pile and chops through the pheasant's neck, before casually tossing its head into the fire, to go sizzling and popping as it is swiftly consumed by flames.

A rush of cortisol-induced stress floods Calum's senses, overcome by desperate despair and a sudden desire to flee, but he's trapped here amongst the carnage. Realising there's no escape, he slumps back, trembling uncontrollably, trying to fathom this callous disregard for innocent life. Despite the terrifying reality he's determined to tough it out. No longer will he show sadness or tears, knowing some cruel humans like to see fear, distress and weakness in their prey, before abusing and murdering them. That's what makes the kill more pleasurable for some, depraved desire feeding the blood lust.

The Great Spirit's voice comes softly reassuring to him on a sudden breeze. "Fear not my creatures' demise. The pheasant, and the rabbit too, may have come to the end of their earthly existence, but their souls are being reintegrated into the Beautiful Garden even as we speak. There are planets, many light years away, where all enlightened creatures are herbivores and eat only vegetation, and where everything else is synthetically produced. No animal by-product is ever used. Those humans and animals of the past who lived wilderness lives here on Earth relied on Nature's creatures to provide food and fur for sustenance and warmth. This was also the way of the Native American brave. All would offer ceremonial gratitude, paying homage to Wakan Tanka, and also the deceased creature, for providing these essential provisions. So I understand the primitive evolution of Man. Nature is instrumental in providing a contradictory example on planet Earth, whereby the largest and most powerful creatures such as the elephant, rhinoceros, hippopotamus and gorilla, are all herbivores. Carnivores no longer exist on any other planet upon which life dwells. Earth is now the most primitive planet inhabited by life in the seven universes. I must leave you now child, but always remember... the certain way to always find the Great Spirit is through a forest wilderness."

Calum feels fortified by this truth, the connection easing the trauma somewhat of the fearful situation before him. This information gives him new-found resolve, but recent events reaffirm his resigned acceptance as to the heartless ways of man.

The men party on, gorging themselves on all available food and drink as they sit cross-legged around the campfire, smoking, singing and revisiting tall tales of bygone times. Calum falls asleep, dreaming of travelling the Sacred Path and onward throughout the seven universes.

He is woken several hours later as Walter sounds a prolonged farewell blast of the horn as the lorry leaves the clearing. As soon as they are out of sight, Cormack is spurred into action. "Come on woman," he shouts, "now them sneaky bastards is gone we'll be up and on our way, let's hitch up the Varda."

Between them, they manoeuvre the caravan ball hitch on to the drawbar of the 1941 ex-army 4x4 Humber. Cormack strides to the front of the burly machine, taking a deep breath before swinging the heavy starting handle, then jumps clear, cursing as the dog-leg iron bar kicks back on the swing with such power as to break a man's wrist. He swings again; this time the motor catches the spark, the engine rumbling groggily as if grumbling at being woken from its torpor, before suddenly exploding into life as Cormack prods the accelerator, teasing the twelve reluctant cylinders into a burbling synchronised harmony, the engine pulsating, black blood oil circulating, lubricating the hardened metallic arteries in preparation for the long journey ahead.

Calum is ready to leave. Although feeling a deep affinity with the forest, he is not sad to go. His enforced internment here has tainted the beauty, but he knows in his heart and soul that he will spiritually connect once again with this primeval force in the future, no longer captive, but as a free spirit. Ingrid lifts him from the cot and climbs into the Humber's passenger seat. Cormack engages four-wheel drive, concentrating the brute force of the powerful vehicle, tasking the rugged machine to slowly propel the family along the deeply rutted track leading out of the woods. A great flock of birds suddenly darkens the sky, flying in perfect formation alongside and above the vehicle, as if providing a claustrophobic farewell escort.

Cormack points anxiously, "See them fuckin' birds woman, a bad omen to be sure, them vermin is tryin' to drive us from the forest."

Ingrid, silent, stares vacantly ahead. Calum knows the flying escort is a murmering of starlings, a fantastic spectacle, Mother Nature's messengers, meaning no harm. He feels sure that they are just conveying their blessing for his imminent journey. Cormack guns the throttle in panic. The flock continues to multiply at such a rate that the sky is becoming ominously overcast. The truck lurches along violently, throwing up clouds of dust and stones, as the wheels demand more traction in response to Cormack's anxious acceleration. Calum is thrown from Ingrid's arms into the footwell of the Humber as it careers along the fossilised ruts of the ancient stone track. He curls up, holding tight to her ankles until, a few minutes later, the ride becomes calmer, and clear blue sky is visible again. The great flock of birds has settled into the trees.

"It's OK now folks," Cormack rejoices in shaky relief as they pull out on to the highway. "We're back on the open road again, outta that godforsaken place at last. Them woods be cursed I tell yuh, lucky to get out alive so we is, I ain't ever coming back 'ere, no sirree."

Calum smiles to himself. 'No father, you may never come back, but one day I shall return to this holy place.'

CHAPTER
SEVEN

Bristol, England. Spring 1960.

Three years have passed since Calum was taken from the forest. Now five years of age, he has grown into a healthy, robust child, inheriting blue eyes and blonde hair from his mother. He has felt the reassurance of the Great Spirit's presence in the background of his life throughout these formative years. Even though there has been no communication since leaving the woodland, he holds dear the memory of their profound connection, remaining patient, secure in the knowledge that his universal mentor is always close by.

The family is now living in an old rented houseboat near Bristol docks. Their temporary home is an aged vessel that will never again set sail on the open seas. Decay, and the passage of time, has scuppered her. Previously a slave ship, then a pleasure boat, but long gone are the days of her being a plaything of the rich and famous on the ocean wave, she is now little more than a rotting hulk. The last trace of her past is the discoloured brass name-plate on the barnacle-encrusted hull:

DESTINY

The interior of the old ship is surprisingly well-preserved, suffering only minimal woodworm damage to the thick oak floorboards running full cabin length, and retaining the patina and sheen of many years of enforced polishing by captured slaves. A condemning epitaph of a time not so long ago, when human slavery was legal throughout the British Empire.

The long, pew-like seating is cushioned with soft green leather, deeply lined, cracked and split, with generous amounts of old grey horsehair protruding from the well-worn hide. Calum finds this an ideal height to stand on, enabling him to peer out to sea from a choice of six portholes. Spending most of his internment entranced by the toing and froing of an eclectic mix of sea-going vessels, he would gaze longingly out towards the Bristol Channel, beyond the busy hubbub of daily maritime activity, wondering at the power and mystery of the deep ocean. Captivated by the sea, but also yearning to be once again ensconced in his beloved forest wilderness.

Cormack is still working for the Forestry Commission, felling the many trees perceived as dangerous, or regarded as little more than a nuisance and hindrance by the government. Calum feels great sorrow for the trees – these sentient beings – whose only crime is to stand innocently in the path of mankind's materialistic progress.

His mother's mental health has declined significantly during the intervening years. She is regularly detained under the Mental Health Act, and only permitted to return home occasionally on supervised visits. Ingrid, it seems, no longer has any coherent recognition of Calum, Cormack, or their home. Her personality has changed, she appears vacant and detached most of the time, paler and thinner than before, although still retaining her classic Scandinavian features of chiselled cheekbones, pale blue eyes and long blonde hair.

The year 1959 had seen an act passed in England that was allegedly aimed at a more compassionate understanding of mental health patients. There were to be 'units of care,' rather than what many saw as prisons of abuse. The main focus of treatment for patients previously had involved altering the chemical balance of the brain. Some saw it as scientists and doctors playing God.

This much-heralded new remedy centered on allowing patients out into the community. 'Care in the Community' became the new buzzword, a catchy soundbyte that sounded good and promised much. In reality, though, this new initiative proved no different from the previous malaise, in that there was still precious little 'care' forthcoming. The health workers, those on the frontline, knew that 'Care in the Community' was used as an excuse by the British government to cut costs and free up beds by clearing out disabled and vulnerable people from hospital. Ejected with few belongings, or any help to adjust, they were expected to fend for themselves. Callously left alone in small flats in slum tenement blocks, and then, more often than not, they were persecuted, as all outsiders were, by the localised post-war British 'community spirit.'

During one of her rare visits, Calum notices Ingrid staring out to sea through one of the ship's portholes. Her silent serene countenance, and the apparent lack of recognition, leads him to believe her mind and soul now dwell in another realm. A place so far removed from planet Earth's reality as to be beyond most people's comprehension. Instinctively he realises that the Great Spirit of Nature is somehow involved with Ingrid's transition to this strange nether-world. This knowledge is of great comfort to him, as he does not fully under-stand what has happened to his mother, but knowing that Gaia is involved alleviates and demystifies to some extent the breakdown of Ingrid's mental faculties. 'Maybe one just doesn't need the same full-on self-awareness out there in the cosmos as one does on planet Earth,' he reasons, 'as there are not so many reasons to be fearful and constantly on your guard in outer space.'

The carers are still involved in Calum's day-to-day life, due to what they term as his mother's 'condition.' He has come to accept them for what they are; competent, mostly, in their way, doing just enough to justify their wages. 'And why not?' He allows, 'After all, it's only a job to them.'

Cormack would occasionally make some grand gesture of parental care whilst in the presence of the carers, such as bringing home a comic or pilfered toy, whereupon the ladies would gush and coo, "Ooh, look at what your Daddy has brought you, who's a lucky boy then?" Calum is not fooled by the insincerity delivered deadpan by the fawning females and his inebriated father. Cormack's constant lusting and questing of wine, women and song, rendering any natural parental interaction – or affection – all but nonexistent. This suits Calum. He would wish it no other way.

It is decided that he is to receive private tuition on the houseboat, due to Cormack often threatening to, "Up sticks and hit the road, soon as the wife is well again." He frequently advises the welfare service, "then the boy will be in school full time, so he will, when we settles fer good in the one permanent dwellin'."

This tall tale was told to anyone in the local authority who could be bothered to investigate Calum's welfare. Cormack had no intention of settling down, though. It was all just so much bluster and bluff on his part, another lie, to help preserve the status quo.

Calum found the learning process tough-going, especially as he knew, being a child of Nature, that the human wisdom was seriously flawed. The teaching is administered on a one-to-one basis by Mr Simms, a welfare service-nominated tutor, who tries his best to teach him the rudimentary schooling of English, maths and history. But Calum retains little of the droning diatribe of old-school hand-me-down knowledge, finding the teaching repetitive and boring in comparison to the magical, profound, exciting lessons provided by the Great Spirit of Nature.

One day, as he stares absentmindedly out to sea, bored senseless as usual by Mr Simms' dull monotonous eulogy, Gaia's voice comes to him, crystal clear: "The teacher may open the classroom door, but only the pupil can enter."

CHAPTER
EIGHT

Time passes painfully slowly for Calum… Summer arrives… at last. He feels desperately trapped on the houseboat, holding dear any notion of escape. This sustains him during the dull, grey days, when he is bereft of any meaningful contact, and longing for Gaia's reassuring love.

He continues to learn from the Divine Entity, by way of incoming visions and messages while asleep. A recurring visualisation is of the Native American brave and the white doves. In his latest dream, the doves still fly in formation, but now number only nine. The lifeless body of the tenth bird is held aloft in the open palm of the brave, whose stern expression betrays no emotion as he offers up the deceased creature skywards before speaking plaintively… "I am Chief Seattle of the Suquamish/Duamish tribe. When the buffalo are all slaughtered, the wild horses all tamed, the secret corners of the forest heavy with the scent of many men, and the view of the ripe hills blotted by talking wires, where is the thicket? Gone, where is the eagle? Gone…"

Calum is woken early in the morning by a smiling Ingrid gently shaking him. She seems different today, eyes bright and clear. Gone is the vacant expression that often haunts her beautiful face. She helps him down gently from the narrow bunk bed.

Judith, the carer, comes through from the kitchen with porridge. She is short and overweight, with a rosy complexion to her large, round face, which is framed by collar-length mousy brown hair. There is always a strong odour of stale cigarettes about her. Judith takes many, 'fag breaks' in-between, as she puts it proudly, "doin' the carin'." She fusses about Calum. "Must wrap you up warm son, might be chilly on the beach today." His heart races. 'Beach? Am I to be taken out?' He does not get out often, only occasionally with the carers to the grocery shop, or sometimes with Cormack, when he needs to go for his drink or cigarettes; not from the goodness of his heart, but just to use Calum as decoy in the shop, to enable him to sometimes snatch a bottle or two of booze without paying.

They set off, with Ingrid going ahead. She pauses, waiting on the narrow rickety foot-bridge for Judith to lift Calum over. Taking his hand, Ingrid leads the way as they walk cautiously across the gently swaying, slippery bridge, holding tight to the slimy green rope handrail. Halfway across, she turns to Judith and smiles. "You must call me Ingrid. Please don't stand on ceremony with us, Judith, and Mr Connor is to be Cormack to you."

Judith looks unsure but returns the smile. "Of course, Mrs... um... Ingrid."

Calum looks down at the gently lapping sea as it splashes against the harbour walls, pondering the mysterious world hidden beneath the scudding scummy green tide.

Judith drags him away unceremoniously from his contemplation and leads them away from the docks. Even at this early hour the sun is hot and bright. They come to a bus stop and stand waiting for the next ride into town. Calum squirms, fidgety with boredom, until he sees a small tabby cat sitting on the steps of the butcher's shop across the road. His eyes light up as he is drawn to the creature, feeling an urge to stroke it. He suddenly breaks free from Ingrid's light grip on his reins, and dashes headlong across the busy street. Oblivious to the busy traffic and Judith's shrill shrieks of warning, he almost makes it across unscathed, but just as his left foot touches down on the opposite curb his right shoe is clipped by the wheel of a black MG Magnette saloon. The car slews sideways, locked in a screeching brake-enforced skid. Calum is thrown to the ground, landing heavily alongside the cat, who is purring loudly. Slow-motion shock switches to fast-forward reality as Judith starts wailing. He becomes acutely aware of an all-pervading smell of death emanating from the nearby butcher's shop. His squashed shoe lies in the gutter, and a chattering crowd begins to gather. He reaches out to stroke the cat.

"Hello, my boy. That was a close shave. It's only us cats who are supposed to have nine lives, you know."

Calum catches his breath, peering quizzically into the feline amber eyes, thinking he recognises the soft vocal tone, daring to hope... "Is... is... that you, Great Spirit?"

"Yes child, the one and only."

"Wow! Are you inside the cat?"

"Well, yes, I suppose you could say that... but as you well know by now, my spirit is connected to all flora and fauna, and also to all humans who adhere to the hidden laws of Nature."

From out of nowhere, a tall thin man appears, looming over them. "Don't move a muscle, lad. I am a doctor." Kneeling down, he begins an external examination. "Any pain anywhere, boy?"

"No, I feel just fine."

After a cursory examination, the doctor gets to his feet. "Well... no bones broken that I can see, so fortunately for you, my boy, it would seem no lasting harm has been done."

Calum smiles. "Strange, Doctor, that you were on hand right at this preordained moment."

Taken aback by Calum's sophisticated vocabulary, the doctor is dumbstruck for an instant, before quickly recovering his composure. "I'll have you know, I was driving the car that almost did for you my lad."

Calum chuckles. "Even stranger, positively spooky in fact, this syncronicity; you couldn't make it up, Doc."

The doctor takes a step back, a look of disbelief on his face, surprised and thrown off balance by this curious child.

Judith comes running over to them, crying and sobbing. "Is he injured? Will he need to go to hospital?" She looks imploringly to the milling crowd and screams, "Won't someone call a doctor?"

The doctor grips her shoulder. "Now calm down, madam. I am a doctor. The boy will be alright, I'm sure. He seems an independent little so and so." He strokes his chin, assessing the patient, "hmm... extremely unusual... most odd to find a youngster so advanced for his age." He turns to Judith. "But please, I beg of you, take more care with the lad on these busy roads. I have seen enough needless death and destruction these past war years, don't you know?"

Ingrid is still on the other side of the road, looking the other way, randomly greeting passers-by, seemingly unaware of the accident that has just occurred.

Judith tugs at the doctor's arm. "Please, can you wait with the boy, sir, whilst I go get his mother?"

Glancing at his watch and shaking his head irritably, he sighs, "Very well madam, but please be quick about it, I have urgent house calls to attend to."

Judith crosses the busy main street, hurrying to Ingrid, shaking her by the arms, "Your lad was nearly a goner there, Mrs Connor! Why for Heaven's sake didn't you keep a tight hold on his reins?"

"What do you mean, reins? Let go of me woman," she twists free. "Reins, what reins?" What on Earth are you babbling on about... Do I know you?"

Judith rolls her eyes, looks to the heavens, and sighs. She links arms with Ingrid and leads her across the street. Ingrid pushes past the doctor and leans down to ruffle her son's hair. "He's fine, don't know what all the fuss is about, he just wanted to cuddle the little pussycat, didn't you son?"

Judith groans in exasperation, angry for trusting this deranged woman with the child's safety, knowing that as his carer she should have been holding the reins. She shudders inwardly, thinking of the disaster that may have been, but equally concerned that this lapse could have cost her her job.

The fun is over for the rubberneckers. The crowd slowly disperses, dwindling away, with much murmuring and muttering about Calum's near demise and subsequent miraculous escape.

The cat stands and stretches, yoga-like. "Let this be another lesson to you, child. You can rely on no one but yourself. This is abundantly clear, by the lack of awareness shown by those humans entrusted with your care. Be aware from this day forth, that you, and you alone, must be responsible for your own physical wellbeing and self-preservation on the earth plane. Never, ever, trust human beings... do you understand the importance of this advice?"

Calum nods, gazing deep into the universe through the cat's mesmerising amber eyes, "Yes, Mother, I will be sure to look after myself. I can do a much better job than those humans anyway, but why have you been away so long? I've missed you so much."

"Be assured, I am always with you on the Sacred Path, Calum, whether in a physical incarnation or ethereally, it matters not which form I take. I must reiterate though, that you are responsible for your own wellbeing in the physical sense."

"Understood, but I assume you will be around to help and advise?"

"Yes, I shall be close by, if you remain on the Sacred Path. I may visit you as a creature, or perchance as a raindrop, maybe a plant, a dream, or perhaps as a cosmic thought carried on a cool breeze... Or one of my assigned emissaries may connect with you, for instance St Susan of Grimston, patron Saint of Nursing and Bees, St Francis of Assisi, patron Saint of all Animals, Nature and Wildlife... or maybe St Gertrude of Nivelle, patron Saint of Cats."

"Hmm...? Now don't get me wrong, that's all very well, and sounds so wonderfully spiritual, I'm sure... and with a stellar cast to boot... but how will I know when, or where, you... Gaia... the right honourable Great Spirit, will be with me?"

"Should you ever doubt of my presence child, because you do not see me, remember the unseen force of the tree blown over by the storm, or the caress of a cool breeze on your face." With that, the cat bounds away.

Calum smiles, reassured, secure in the knowledge that Mother Nature had not deserted him after all.

CHAPTER
NINE

Four weeks later, and Calum is unexpectedly taken out again. Judith holds on tight to his reins this time, with Ingrid following meekly as they head off on another warm summer day, going for a picnic at a local beauty spot, high above the Bristol cliffs. On arrival the women unfurl a tartan blanket onto the neat sheep-shorn grass. So engrossed are they with the preparation of their picnic, they pay little heed to Calum running around unsupervised.

He runs faster and faster, feeling pure exhilaration, as free as the cross winds swirling about him, the strong breeze reminding him of his spiritual mother. He sprints towards the cliff edge, oblivious of the deadly void beyond, until the wild wind screams, "Stop! Stop!"

Pulling up suddenly with a short skid on the damp grass, Calum teeters over the sheer hundred-metre drop, neither frightened nor worried as he watches wind-tossed seagulls expertly dodging splashing spume and froth, thrown up by the crashing surf, breaking high above massive waves pounding the monstrous dark rocks below.

"Heed the words of the Zen Master, my child," the Great Spirit warns, "if you gaze long into the abyss… then the abyss gazes into you."

Calum smiles, he has been waiting patiently for Gaia to make contact again. Feral instinct tears his gaze away from this weird soporific pull of beckoning danger. He runs back to the unsuspecting adults, who lay soaking up the sun, blissfully unaware of his close escape. Days like this are rare, though… and Calum is finding life on the houseboat intolerable. Each paltry reprieve only initiates a desperate craving for further freedom.

His wish is unexpectedly granted a few days later, when Cormack, housebound due to another debilitating hangover, is being urged by a despairing Judith to go out for some fresh air, her harsh tone indicative of the loathing and contempt she feels, despising him for his selfish boorish attitude.

Cormack is suffering from delirium tremors today, sweating profusely and shaking uncontrollably. The DTs are payback time; the unavoidable occupational hazard of his long-term alcohol addiction. The only 'cure' for this debilitating malaise, though short-lived, was the legendary 'hair of the dog,' which meant imbibing even more booze so as to hasten a return to one's previous inebriation. Cormack sees Calum as his chance to escape for another session, and being in such close proximity to the hostile carer is grating on his fragile temperament.

"Get the kid dressed then, woman, then I'll take 'im out and about fer a bit."

"Well now then," Judith fakes a swoon, "At last! I thought I'd never live to see the day, some time for the boy from his father." Hands on hips and glaring, she chastises with unconcealed sarcasm; "Good for you, Mr Connor, oh my, what a nice kind daddy you are."

Cormack scowls at her, dark eyes glowering with hate, cursing under his breath, "Thought you'd never see the day hey, is that right missus? Well, you may not live to see out this day yet, you fat fuckin' cow."

Judith crosses her arms and looks pointedly at him. "Did you say something, Mr Connor?"

"Said fuck all," he mutters, grabbing his boots with his back to her. Judith helps dress Calum in preparation for the outing and orders curtly, "Be sure to be back in time for tea Mr Connor, there's a stew on the go. The lad needs regular nourishment, you know."

Cormack mumbles more obscenities as he lifts Calum under his arm like a bag of coal, carrying him out over the gangplank and onto the rope bridge, hurrying away like a shifty child snatcher to the dockyard car park, heading for a beaten-up dark green Austin Seven. He opens the back door and orders, "Get in kid." Calum climbs in. Cormack fetches a starting handle from the boot.

After several wild swinging attempts, he manages to start the engine. The tired old car shakes and rattles, and is eventually cajoled into some semblance of running order by a delicate mixture of choke and throttle, before Cormack drives away, bouncing over deep rain-filled potholes as they head down a narrow street hemmed in by rubbish-strewn slum tenements.

ST PAULS... the area announced by a black and white cast-iron sign set high up on a weather-beaten brick facing. A short distance further on and they arrive in the car park of St Patrick's Tavern. 'A busy pub', thinks Calum, 'going by the loud chatter and raucous banter coming from the bar.'

"Stay put there, kid," Cormack orders, "and I'll fetch you out some lemonade and crisps, no young'uns allowed inside this kitchema."

The pub is enclosed by an old crumbling stone wall topped off with rusting black iron railings. Cold rain drizzles from the dark sky, empathetically contributing to the depressingly dour scenario.

Late afternoon drags on into mid evening... Calum sits and fidgets, waiting, cold, bored, hungry and thirsty. Cormack eventually reappears, staggering out from the pub with a bottle of lemonade and a packet of crisps. He throws open the car door. "Ere yuh go lad," he slurs, "this'll keep yuh goin' fer a while." Calum shivers at the sudden blast of cold air. "When can we go back to the house boat? It's cold and damp in here."

"Won't be long now, just a little more business to attend to and then we'll be on our way, I promise thee." Cormack weaves his way slowly and erratically back towards the tempting delights of the grimy old drinking den, stopping briefly to relieve himself against the pub wall.

Calum rips open the Smiths crisp packet and wolfs down the contents. So hungry, he nearly swallows the tiny bag of salt grains wrapped in blue paper. He gulps down the fizzy drink. A faint buzzing sound attracts his attention, gradually growing louder... and louder... enabling him to pinpoint the exact location of a trapped house fly caught in a shimmering intricately spun silver web. The fly struggles frantically in a vain bid to extricate itself. The urgent vibrations transmit to a dozing black spider ensconced under a damp flap of peeling rubber windscreen surround. The master of the web dashes across the silky strands, speedily weaving strong adhesive threads, before silencing the fly by entombing it, mummified within a cocoon. The spider finishes the grisly task and turns to face Calum.

"Greetings, so we meet again, my child."

Calum smiles, "Hello Mother. I've been waiting for you to appear. I felt your presence here tonight."

"I am never far away from my children."

Although excited to be reunited, Calum is somewhat perturbed by the fate of the fly. "It's good to see you, but I must say I am more than a little surprised, what have you done to that insect... is it dead?"

"Yes, correct, the creature's demise is final."

"Hmm... that doesn't seem much like a caring compassionate act from the Great Spirit of Nature... if you don't mind me saying?"

"No, not at all, I'm all for free speech, and granted, yes, while it may seem confusing, and somewhat of a contradiction in terms, it is just one of many facets of the phenomenon of Nature constantly ongoing in the cosmic cycle of the seven universes."

"How can that be right, though? It's hardly the Sacred Path philosophy you always advocate."

In one slick movement the spider folds it rear legs under its haunches and sits back... "Well now, here's the thing. The death of the fly is a form of natural selection that is necessary to maintain a universal eco-balance. Insects are a most vital mainstay of this continuum. Without them your planet would be unable to support human life, or indeed, the animal kingdom." The spider pauses, stretching out its long spindly front legs, one by one, before rubbing each of the four limbs frantically together. "Take our deceased friend here, for example. Without this form of population control, not only would mankind's existence be severely threatened, but so, too, would the continuation of many other life forms throughout the universe. This natural selection is a prerequisite of Nature conservation."

"Hmm... I think I understand... but what useful purpose is served by the fly living here, amongst us, in the first instance then?"

"Most perceptive Calum, allow me to explain further. The fly, alongside the rat and mosquito, are but cosmic examples of the Yin and Yang of the solar system. These creatures host the negative properties of being carriers and distributors of deadly disease. They have the propensity to cause death and destruction indiscriminately."

"Then why are they here amongst us? What is their point?"

"I was just coming to their positive aspect... They exist on planet Earth as a karmic warning to mankind. They visit in the guise of prophetic messengers, providing portents of the gravest consequences that will befall humans, should they continue to destroy, desecrate and commit their depraved crimes against Nature. The wanton destruction of sacred flora and fauna is contributing significantly to the hastening of mankind's downfall. Should man continue in this vein, in the end, the only creatures populating this planet will be the fly, rat and mosquito, who, ironically, hold information in their DNA that enhances the possibility of creating medicines and vaccines with which to preserve human life. This primitive planet Earth spins in the galaxy of the Aurora universe and is the last bastion of plague and pestilence. All other planets are now disease-free. The ubiquitous fly and mosquito also provide other creatures, such as me, with sustenance."

Calum snorts, "Oh yeah, the gift that keeps on giving... the good old fly, ain't it just, but no, I don't think that's fair because—"

The spider jumps to its feet and curtly cuts him short. "Life isn't fair, never was, never will be. There are too many unexpected twists and turns and emotional complexities to deal with if one is human. So save your sentimentality, for these aforementioned creatures are but karmic creations. They are their own self-fulfilling prophecy, without feelings of love, care or compassion, devoid of consciousness, absent of soul, and projecting only negative properties; in short, just an accurate reflection of most humans, but more of this later. I must rest now, take care, my boy."

"Whoaa! Hold up… just one more thing, Great Spirit, before you go." The spider turns back and lets out a long weary sigh, "Yeeesss?"

"Who eats the rat?"

"No one, but no one, ever eats the rat… not even another rat." The spider chuckles as it scurries away to its cold gloomy lair.

Calum leans back against the cold, ripped, brown leather car seat, reflecting on the dire warning issued forth, feeling the cosmic truth, at one with the universe again in this moment, at ease with the enormity. It feels a natural progression, indeed, had Gaia not told him some time ago that he is now a true child of Nature.

The oppressive gloom of dense darkness is penetrated only by the flickering blue flame of a Victorian gas lamp from the police station across the road. Festivities are now in full swing inside the bar, with out-of-tune renditions of 'Danny Boy' and 'Summer Time' flowing forth, accompanied, just occasionally, by the merest hint of musical melody, this harsh vocal assault resonating seamlessly with Bristol city's incessant noise pollution.

Calum looks on dreamily, as the mizzle of smog-induced acid rain forms snaking rivulets of polluted water to meander abstractly across the misty windscreen. The faint glow of a hesitant full moon, cowering coyly behind a huge black rain cloud, is slowly enticed by the supernatural elementals to join with Mother Nature in creating haphazard blurred images of a glittering star-studded universe. Calum feels himself being slowly but surely engulfed by this paranormal melancholic atmosphere…

An hour or so later, Cormack comes out of the pub, swaying unsteadily, forlornly attempting to keep time with the music playing inside. Buttoning his old army greatcoat he looks up warily at the threatening tumble of black clouds. Taking a last deep draw on his cigarette, he flicks the glowing butt up into the night, the dying embers sizzling briefly like frantic fireflies fleeing from the rain, before the soggy smoke lands in the gutter at his feet. Staggering over to the car he wrenches open the door. Calum wrinkles up his nose at the stale reek of cigarettes and booze.

"OK son, let's be on our way now. Did yuh get the drink and crisps I sent out?"

"Yeah? You brought them out yourself... several hours ago," Calum replies wearily.

Cormack stares blankly, trying to recall, his damaged mental rewind facilitators blocked by the merciless disconnect of alcohol-induced short-term memory loss... "Uhhh... yeah... thass what I meant... OK then, let's be off home now, and get some hot scran down us."

He starts the car, letting the engine warm awhile, in a vain attempt to disperse some of the dense condensation bred by the continuous rain, speeding up the process by wiping the back of his coat sleeve furiously across the windscreen, before turning to Calum. "So lad, what 'ave yuh bin up to then?"

"Waiting..." Calum moans, "a long, long time, for you... oh... and talking with my friend the spider."

Cormack sniggers, "Is that so kid? Talkin' to a fuckin' spider hey? Well, I've heard it all now, bejasus, to be sure. Haaahaha, I hope youse, and the insect, will both be very happy together, yuh silly little bugger."

Calum glares at him, and snarls with contempt, "A spider's no insect! It's got eight legs, insect's got six."

Cormack turns sharply and replies angrily, "OK, yuh clever cunt! Where's the fuckin' thing now then?" Holding out his open palm, demanding, "Gimme the bastard, then how's about I tears off two of its legs, hey? Be a fuckin' insect then... won't it?"

Calum flinches, taken aback by the cruel venom spat his way. It wasn't so much the c-word that made him wince, after all, he knew that was only four innocuous letters from the alphabet, and as such held no significant power, the letters just forming a word, when spoken or written by humans. No, it was the way Cormack expressed his feelings, by way of venomous attack, the harsh cruel intent conveyed in the connotation that hit home. The nuance – the way he said it – is what offends Calum, 'as effectively painful as an unexpected punch to the heart.' He knows he should not be surprised by this ubiquitous human trait, the malicious vindictive victimisation of the weak and vulnerable. He's well aware of Cormack's premeditated intention to cause distress, but even so... to a child! His own child? Calum in this moment becomes hardened, conditioned, allowing this was a cruel given of his father, but also conscious of not getting too hung up about it, not showing he's wounded, or Cormack has won, achieved his objective. 'After all,' he reflects, 'are humans not past masters at causing anguish and suffering to those who cannot defend themselves?' Nature, he knew, was not like this. Although some sensitive souls found the natural world to be cruel, there was never any pre-planned malevolent intent. There was no previous thought-out strategy with Nature, nor any ulterior motive or agenda to harm for kicks.

Laughing loud and revving hard, Cormack steers the old Austin jerkily out onto the road. Crunching the gears constantly, stalling the engine several times, he manages, more by luck than any driving skill, to eventually get back to the docks in one piece. Staggering from the car, he shouts to Calum. "Come on then son, let's be 'avin yer, gotta get ourselves in out of this godfersakin' rain." Cormack walks on ahead, pulling the collar of his coat above his ears against the worsening weather. Calum lags behind, his vision obscured by the biting cold downpour and dim darkness, with only the muted flickering of a lone Tilly lamp from one of the neighbouring boats offering any illumination. Arriving at the rope bridge first, Cormack bursts into sudden song. "I'm singin' in the rain, what a wond'erful feelin', jus' singin,' jus' singin,' in the rain, dee de dee dee, dee dee de dee," before lurching drunkenly across the slippery walkway and just managing to stagger the last few steps to the safety of the ship's deck.

Calum is halfway across when he slips on a wet plank, loses his footing, and plunges sideways into the murky depths of the harbour.

Sinking slowly, down into the emerald green mass, he does not struggle, holding his breath naturally – instinctively – feeling composed and serene as sleek dark fish swim all about him, the more inquisitive darting up close, checking out this brazen intruder in their domain. Calum remains strangely calm, knowing he should be struggling and fighting for his life, but instead transfixed by billowing blankets of heavy green weed swaying hypnotically in time to the current's ebb and flow. Suddenly his sedate descent is curtailed by a big strong hand gripping his arm. The rescuer propels them both swiftly to the surface. They break water, coming up gasping for air and floundering. The policeman lifts Calum above his head, and into his colleague's arms.

"Here, Cyril, take the kid to safety, then help me the hell out of here."

"OK, Sarge, will do." Wrapping Calum in his jacket, he rushes him to the houseboat and bangs hard on the door.

Judith appears, rubbing her eyes, before throwing up her hands and crying out, "Lawks a mercy! What has happened to the child... I took a nap... thought he was indoors?"

"Don't worry about that now!" Cyril shouts, sounding close to panic, "just take him inside, woman." He runs back in a desperate attempt to save his seargent, and is relieved to find him still treading water. Cyril grasps the outstretched arms, and with a superhuman effort manages to haul his soaking superior on to the gangplank, where he lays flat out, panting and spluttering.

"Are you OK Sarge? Speak to me! Sarge, please."

"Y... y... yeah... I'll be alright," he groans, coughing up ingested salty sea water, before gradually sitting up, his breath coming laboured in wheezing gasps. He gets shakily to his knees, panting, slowly recovering from his exertions.

Cyril, in his early forties and slight of build, shakes his head in disbelief, wondering how on Earth he has managed to lift his fifteen-stone sergeant from the water.

"Cyril, you saved my bacon there friend, and no mistake... how's the kid?"

He sits down, suddenly overcome with fatigue. "Seems OK, Sarge, he's inside, recuperating with his ma at present."

As their heavy breathing slowly returns to normal, the policemen's gaze is drawn to the pure white light of the moon, enveloping them, as they sit, bonding together in subconscious camaraderie, silently reflecting on the ever-present danger of their chosen profession.

CHAPTER TEN

Calum sleeps soundly in his bunk. Cormack, snoring loudly in a drunken stupor, is sprawled in an armchair. A loud rap tap tap on the door brings Judith bustling from the kitchen, asking, "Who is it?"

"Police... open up."

She slides the big black bolt through the rusty door latch. The sodden lawmen stand to attention and introduce themselves.

"Sergeant Willis, ma'am."

"Constable Jones."

"Come in officers, please, come in," Judith ushers them through, "before you catch your death."

"How is the boy, Mrs.. ?"

"Roberts, Sergeant... Mrs Roberts. He appears to be fine, sir. I dried him off, gave him a warming drink, then put him down to his bed. He dropped off straight away."

She gestures towards the soundly sleeping Cormack. "No thanks to his sad, drunken excuse for a father though... can I get you some hot tea, gentlemen?"

"That would be most welcome, Mrs Roberts," Cyril replies, "milk in both, two sugars and one without, if you please."

Judith smiles and heads for the kitchen. Sarge follows her. "Would you like us to call a doctor for... err... what is the boy's name, Mrs Roberts?"

"No, that shouldn't be necessary. I think he'll be fine... oh, I'm sorry officer, I should have said, the lad's name is Calum. Calum

Connor, and that's his father, Cormack Connor." Grimacing in revulsion, she points the finger of fire and damnation, turning up her nose and recoiling as if a black plague carrier were in their midst. "Just look at the useless article, lying there, drunk as a skunk, yet again. This isn't the first incident, you know, oh no. Him and the mother, they shouldn't be allowed to have children, in my opinion. Him always boozed up, and the mother as scatty as a nine-bob note. I'm at the end of my tether with it all, why, once they even–"

"Whoa, calm down now, Mrs Roberts," Sarge interjects, placing his hand on her shoulder and looking her straight in the eyes, "are you not the boy's mother?"

Judith trembles under the policeman's steely scrutiny, before recovering her composure. "Oh no, sir, no. I'm his carer, from the welfare service. The mother, Mrs Connor, is at present locked away in a loony bin, best place for her if you ask me... Why, Sergeant, you are looking very pale, and have the shakes about you, are you feeling alright, sir?"

He shakes his head, murmering, "No, not good, not good at all," before sinking to his knees.

Cyril jumps up. "Now look here, Mrs Roberts, I'm going to get my Sarge back to the station, get him checked over by a doctor. He's saturated, and exhausted. Is there any possibility you can stay here tonight to look after the boy?"

"Why of course, constable. The child will be safe with me. I've qualifications y'know," Judith declares proudly, "and besides, I've no one to go rushing home to... not since Mr Roberts passed," her voice takes on a melancholic drone, "it were the consumption y'know... lingered dreadfully, did my Stan... he was never the same man, and he–"

"Many thanks to you, ma'am," Cyril cuts her short. "We'll make enquiries into this matter and be back with you in the morning. It was most fortunate for the lad that we were passing when we were. In the meantime, when Mr Connor awakes, be sure to advise him to remain here until we return tomorrow. We shall need to interview him."

"Yes officer, I'll be sure to let him know your wishes. Judging by the state of him he'll be sleeping off a hangover well into tomorrow."

Cyril nods curtly, "Then goodnight to you, madam." He helps the unsteady sergeant to his feet, lowering his head with the gentle pressure of a flat palm so as to safely exit the low doorway.

Calum wakes early next day to the sound of Cormack snoring loudly. Judith comes bustling through from the kitchen. "Here lad, you must be thirsty." She hands him a baby's bottle of warm sweet tea. "How are you feeling today?"

"Hungry," he replies, gulping greedily from the bottle.

"I've some porridge on the go, won't be too long now." She goes back to the kitchen.

Judith returns some minutes later with his breakfast to spoon-feed him. After eating his fill, he lies back sleepily on his pillow. The faint hum of an aeroplane gradually becomes louder. Flying over the docks, the hypnotic drone reaching its peak as the twin-engine aircraft soars high above the houseboat. A word, in capital letters, forms in Calum's mind. "GOD," he says aloud, wondering why this manifestation feels so strangely resonant. But whatever the meaning, the word GOD appears to fit in perfect context in this moment. Struggling now to focus sleepy eyes on the porthole as bright sunlight streams in, he sighs contentedly, "Mmm," recognising the Great Spirit's warm and soothing caress. Whispering, "Thank you, God," his eyes closing, drifting, sleep lulling… a beautiful female voice murmurs seductively soft, filling his soul with love; 'Nature is God… God is Nature…'

Calum is woken some hours later by Judith quarrelling with Cormack. "Now see here, Mr Connor, the policeman specifically said you were to wait here for their arrival, they—"

"Yuh gotta be kiddin' me!' Why should I wait for them pox-ridden gavvers?" Cormack snarls, "Them bastards is rotten to the core, fuckin' corrupt, every man jack of 'em, and you'se tellin' me, you crazy stupid woman, that I should wait 'ere for 'em to capture and lock me up."

He punches a fist hard into his palm, voice rising in fury, "I'll 'ave them bastards good 'n proper if they comes for me, make no mistake." The dire threats, spat from the cruel, sneering mouth, spraying forth spittle-laced contempt, mutating into moist droplets of hate, blending visibly with the sunbeams streaking through the cabin. "I'll break every bone in their puny bodies, so I will, so help me God."

Judith stubbornly holds her ground, bravely interrupting his vicious, verbal onslaught. "If it weren't for them policemen, Mr Connor, your son would not be alive now... they saved his life y'know? Just look at you, you disgusting excuse for a man," she sneers, taunting him, "drunk again, and not a jot do you care for the child. You should be ashamed of yourself. I hope they lock you up and throw away the key."

Cormack moves ominously towards her. "Is that so? Well, let me tell you something, you fat meddlin' bitch. Neither you, nor any gavvers, will be seein' me inside, and that's a fuckin' promise. I'll kill them coppers, and you too, afore that day comes to pass, bejasus, so I will, you mark my words, woman," he raises his left hand threateningly.

"No you don't! Leave her alone," shouts Calum.

Cormack stops in his tracks, dark eyes radiating primitive menace, relaxing his bunched fist, turning slowly, looking quizzically at his son. Surprised and taken aback by the audacity of a child boldly holding his intimidating stare. Averting his gaze, Cormack laughs nervously, "Well, so be it lad, you've chosen yer bed. Now you and the fat one, yuh can both lie in it, cuz you won't be seein' me ever agin', yuh pair a fuckin' ejits, and that's me sworn oath, God strike me down, bejasus, so it is." He grabs his coat and is away, slamming the heavy oak door so hard behind him that the violent vibration reverberates throughout the cabin for several long seconds afterwards.

Judith slumps down in a chair and shakily lights a cigarette, taking several deep draws in quick succession, trying to regain her composure. Staring into space, occasionally releasing a stifled sob as she chain smokes, welcoming the calming effect of the nicotine, whilst unwittingly reversing her life-force with each drag on the burning tobacco stick.

Calum, although used to his father's selfish unpredictability and volatile outbursts of anger, feels sorry for shaken up Judith, and thinking ahead, is apprehensive of what the future may hold for him now Cormack has left. But overriding this lonely uncertainty is his wish that his father keeps to his word and never returns.

Hearing a faint fluttering behind him, he turns, to find a Red Admiral butterfly on the curtain, basking in the warmth of the sun. Calum smiles, realising the Great Spirit has returned.

"Greetings once more, my child, I bring news of a major adjustment that is now imminent in your life. Neither Judith, nor your parents, will be accompanying you on this journey. But understand, one may often feel lonelier in the company of humans than when one is alone. Now, concentrate on the circles on my wings."

Entranced, Calum gazes at the beautiful coloured discs slowly rotating and undulating in tandem, forming a natural interwoven dynamic of the spiritual and the physical, suddenly feeling giddy and disorientated as Gaia's soft intonations fill the room.

"At the end of the longest journey comes the deepest slumber, at the end of the fiercest storm blows the gentlest breeze, at the end of life is the most beautiful beginning."

The butterfly flutters at the porthole. Calum reaches as high as he can, but he is not tall enough to open the small circular window.

Judith comes to help. "My my, you are a kind lad, trying to free that poor creature." She lifts him up to open the porthole, presenting the butterfly with the opportunity for escape.

The butterfly pauses on the window ledge. "Farewell, Calum. I must leave you now, but remember, my spiritual essence can always be found in every aspect of Nature; my genes are present in the DNA of every creature, insect and plant, integrated within all life forms that you may encounter on your journey of the Sacred Path… remember, kindred souls will always reconnect."

Calum whispers, "Goodbye, Mother."

She takes flight, and wind-assisted, flies swiftly across the sea and beyond. Calum's gaze follows longingly, until the insect becomes the merest speck on the horizon.

Judith leans across to close the window. "Who were you talking to, son?"

"God."

Frowning, concerned for his sanity, she concludes, 'Surely this is certain proof of the child's fragile mental state.' "Poor lad," she mutters to herself as she lights another cigarette. "I blame the parents, me."

The policemen return mid-morning. Calum overhears them talking to Judith at the door. "We've made our enquiries, Mrs Roberts, and it has come to light that Cormack Connor is wanted for a string of criminal offences. He is an army deserter, a thief and all-round deceptive villain who is also required for interview concerning a very serious charge of grievous bodily harm."

"Oh my Lord!" Judith holds her face in her hands, "And to think I've been spending time under the same roof as that scoundrel. He's gone, officer. I couldn't stop him. I feared for my life at one point as–"

The policemen rush past her and begin searching. "Do you have any idea of his whereabouts today, Mrs Roberts," demands Sergeant Willis, annoyance evident in his tone.

"I can only think he may be in one of his regular haunts, sir, the local pubs," Judith sobs. "I'm so sorry officer, really I am."

The policeman rests a hand on her shoulder, and his tone softens. "Calm down, madam. There is no way you could have stopped him. He is a dangerous reprobate. No harm will come to you now. Mr Connor will be apprehended soon enough, mark my words, then locked away as he deserves."

Her face brightens at his comfort. "But what's to become of the boy, sir?" Cyril removes his helmet and scratches his head. "That's not for me to speculate ma'am. His best interests will be decided by the child welfare authorities. We'd best take the lad now."

Judith looks shocked. "So… so soon, officer?"

"For his safety, you understand," he reassures. "You must leave also, Mrs Roberts, in case this felon Connor should return. He's one dangerous individual, you mark my words."

"Of course, yes, forgive me," Judith is spurred into action by the warning. "I'll pack the boy's things."

CHAPTER

ELEVEN

Cormack is arrested three weeks later, subsequently tried and found guilty by a court of law, and sentenced to fifteen years' imprisonment.

Meanwhile, Ingrid's mental state has deteriorated further and she has been detained indefinitely under the Mental Health Act. Calum, in effect, now an orphan, is taken in to the care of the City of Bristol Child Welfare Service, where he is detained under lock and key and supervised in his own room for three weeks, before being sent to a council-run children's home called, 'The Albany.'

On his first day Calum is led by two female court welfare officers to the front door of the oppressive grey stone building. Holding Lenny his cuddly toy lion tight, he's shaking nervously, apprehensive, and looking around for any chance of escape, thinking that the Albany looks more like a prison than a sanctuary.

These children's institutions were set up by the Labour government in 1948 and proclaimed with great fanfare as vastly improved replacements of the English workhouse. The long, cold, stark dormitory of 'The Albany' has one hundred metal-framed beds covered with thin hard mattresses. Frightened, lonely and bewildered children are locked into ever-present sadness, crying and sobbing plaintively, day and night. Just innocent youngsters, mostly, with some split up from siblings due to poverty, others unfortunate orphans or kids snatched from parents deemed unfit to look after them.

It seems more like a detention centre for young offenders, although most of these inmates are incarcerated here due to circumstance and bad luck, and through no fault of their own. Calum feels for these poor souls, praying that the Great Spirit and karma would somehow look out for them. But his first concern is his own survival. Knowing he must be strong-willed, his instinctive feral priority must always be to look out for number one.

Practice and procedures are almost non-existent at the Albany. It is primitive care at best. Calum sees firsthand that a child's emotional wellbeing is not remotely considered here. The stodgy food is of poor quality and basic. Breakfast is always the same; watery porridge with salt and no sugar. Dinner is either greasy stew or gristly gruel, with sugar-laden synthetic jam sandwiches for tea. Those purporting to care for the children seem like soulless automatons, devoid of any kindness or compassion. Fortunately, he sees no evidence of beating or sexual exploitation here, although some of the kids have told him such abuse is widespread in other children's 'homes' around England.

He survives the ordeal of the Albany by remaining quiet and withdrawn, covering his ears with a pillow to minimise the constant forlorn wailing at night, keeping himself to himself, daydreaming of the forest, fantasising of freedom...

Until, three long months later, he is allocated to live with foster parents, Mr and Mrs Brown.

The female liaison officer dealing with his re-homing informs Calum that the Browns' only son had been killed in the war, and tells him sternly, "you are not to mention this, ever, as the loss is still very raw."

Janet Brown is in her early fifties, slim and wiry, with deep worry lines creasing her face. The greying hair scraped severely into a tight bun only makes her appear older. Despite a ready smile and friendly nature, Janet's eyes seem to betray a constant sadness. Jim Brown is a retired civil servant, overweight and paunchy, with receding grey hair, and a stooped body stance due to many years of slovenly inactivity. A sallow, liver-spotted complexion is the highlight of his flabby face. He wears the air of a man constantly fatigued by life.

The welfare representative tells Calum that the Browns have been fostering for ten years, adding that they are a kindly couple who always do their best for any child placed in their care. They live with four dogs in a period mid-terrace three-bedroom house, in the small Hampshire village of Brockenhurst. Their home is kept fastidiously tidy due to Janet's almost obsessional preoccupation with housework. The third bedroom door is always kept locked. When Calum asks why, Jim states forcibly, "It's not to be opened, you're never to go in there, do you hear me lad?"

CHAPTER
TWELVE

Spring, 1962. Several months later... Calum has just turned eight years of age.

As far as the child welfare authorities are concerned he appears to have settled well into living with the foster parents. This is far from the truth, though. His heart remains loyal only to his spiritual mother, Gaia. There are some concerns within the welfare service regarding the unusual speed of his adjustment, and his apparently casual acceptance of the sudden separation from his parents. The swift transition to his new surroundings pleases Janet Brown, though. She is asked to keep a close eye on developments, as the appointed child welfare officer thinks the boy is perhaps traumatised and suffering from delayed shock.

But Calum is just acting. In reality, he feels lonely and disorientated living with these strangers, although he keeps these feelings to himself, reasoning, 'Best I pretend to be happy and well adjusted here, in case I'm taken back to the care home.' Instinctively biding his time, knowing from the Great Spirit's teaching that unconditional love and guidance would be provided in his time of need. From where this divine spiritual entity originates, or indeed resides, he knows not, but he feels the power of Nature constantly linked to his soul.

Calum is becoming progressively more detached and wary of human beings. After all, in his preceding formative years, has he not experienced at close quarters, the predilection of mankind towards cruelty and insincerity? These early warnings, and Mother Nature's guidance, triggers an instinctive sixth sense that forewarns him to be ever alert and on his guard where humans are concerned. This feral instinct enables a form of cosmic thermal imaging, whereby he sees colours at the onset of powerful emotion. Love and compassion are pre-empted by contrasting hues of pink, danger alert is preceded by muted shades of grey, and the colour black prewarns of dark evil energy.

The intuitive germination and cultivation of this seed of self-preservation is a high priority in his life now. Knowing the Spirit Mother will guide and love him if he remains true to the hidden laws of Nature, he is also acutely aware that this spiritual interaction cannot guarantee his physical survival on the earth plane.

CHAPTER
THIRTEEN

Calum senses a deep morbid apathy hanging heavy about the Brown household. They seem to treat fostering as a job, for money, just like the warders at the children's home. He soon comes to the conclusion that Jim and Janet are not naturally proactive in offering any emotional tenderness, but he prefers it this way, as it keeps things uncomplicated. Their cold impersonal caring methods suit him just fine, as he feels no affection towards them. Living with these fosterers is just a means to an end as far as Calum is concerned, and he accepts, 'At least there are more options available here than when I was cooped up in the caravan and houseboat, or locked away in the horrible care home.'

There are other children living nearby, but Calum is never tempted to make friends or play with them. He passes the time of day, occasionally, but under duress, and only if they approach him first. He keeps his distance from other kids, seeing their games and activities as infantile and inconsequential. His childhood has been short, as is the way with Nature's offspring. They do not have long to acclimatise to the real world before being cast adrift to fend for themselves. Wild creatures would not survive long by playing games. So it is with Calum, due to the Great Spirit's early intervention in his life he has no time for childish frivolity. Other children keep their distance, too, sensing correctly that this 'strange child' is different.

Calum likes the small village of Brockenhurst. Cut in two by a main railway line, it is a slow-paced, sleepy little place. For him, the best part of living here is the close proximity of the New Forest National Park, which, tantalisingly, he can see glimpses of from his bedroom. Jim Brown enjoys his pipe and whiskey every day. When Janet is out he takes his bottle and spends hours alone in the large garden shed, which is always kept double locked. Occasionally, he would take Calum along when walking the dogs – Bess, the family labrador, a three-legged whippet called Tripod, and a pair of Cairn terriers, both summoned as, "Here boy," by Jim, as he cannot tell them apart. Invariably, they would walk the well-worn footpath around the village green. Although, for Calum this short excursion is a welcome reprieve from the boredom of 1960s English household domesticity, the brief stroll leaves him yearning to leave the well-trodden way. Escape into the depths of the mysterious forest, so close by; a return to his spiritual home becomes the alluring goal.

One day he asks if they can walk the dogs in the woodland for a change. Jim seems shocked and upset by the request. "No! No, most definitely not, boy!"

"But why not, Mr Brown?" Flustered, Jim replies, "Because... because... the dogs may be bitten by adders... or the many other snakes in the forest."

Calum is irritated by what he feels is a lame excuse. He takes this to be a further denial of his destiny and swears to himself he will explore further, at the very first opportunity.

He does not have long to wait. One week later, on a Friday morning over breakfast, Jim informs him that he and Janet are, "due in town to meet with our solicitors, to attend to some important business."

"All will be explained to you on our return," Janet adds, seeming unusually animated. 'Almost excited,' Calum notes, suspicious. 'She never gets excited, that one... over anything.' "In the meantime you can go out to play on the green, or you can bide indoors. There are sandwiches in the larder for your lunch," she smiles, wagging a finger at him, "with no butter, before you ask."

"Thanks, Mrs Brown." He hates butter, the very mention of the word causing him to retch involuntarily, especially when recalling how the greasy rancid dairy blocks in the children's home were often a resting place for large black flies, only brushed off and swatted away just prior to the butter being spread on the inmates' sandwiches.

"Will you be alright here alone, son?" Janet asks.

"Oh, yes," he states, a little too enthusiastically. "I was often left alone by my parents."

Janet's smile instantly transforms into a stern expression. "That's as may be Calum Connor, but you did not have any choice then," a tremble of emotion catching in her voice. "Things are different these days. You are... you are cared for in this house."

He shakes his head in scornful pity, thinking, 'Careful now Mrs B, don't go getting too emotional, you almost said the love word there. Pah! Cared for, you don't know the meaning of the word, you humans.' Although despising her timid reticence, he keeps his cool, agreeing mock-respectfully, "Yes, I know that. I am so, so fortunate, thank you ever so, Mr and Mrs Brown." Willing to grovel and agree to anything, so he can satisfy his longing to abscond to the New Forest, anxious now for them to be on their way, eager and excited at the prospect of what adventures this glorious day may bring forth.

Calum cringes as Janet hugs him on their way out. As soon as the car engine starts he rushes to the kitchen. He has often wondered about a bunch of large black keys hanging from the top shelf of the larder. Standing on a stool, he lifts them from the brass hook, and then runs upstairs, eager to try them in the door of the forbidden room. Grinning, excited, he tries them one by one. First key... nothing doing, second key... the same, the third... "Bingo!" he shouts. The door is stiff, creaking loudly as he enters the cold musty space. He goes to the window to open the curtains. Bright light immediately floods the room, as if the sun is keen to cleanse this dank, dark place.

Calum is drawn to a large faded photograph of two young boys. The black and white portrait takes pride of place on the mantelpiece. He guesses the children to be about eight years of age, both have dark hair. 'Identical twins,' he realises, on closer scrutiny. Two small dusty teddy bears repose either side of the time-worn sepia image. Another photograph of the twins, grown now into young men, set in an oval silver frame, rests on the shelf below. One is wearing an army uniform, the other civilian clothes. Suddenly he feels icy cold, and a shiver courses through him as a dazzling white sheet of light shoots back and forth from wall to wall and across the ceiling. Black! Black, black is the emotion flooding his soul... sudden darkness... Black evil, panic overtakes him, 'must get out, out, now!' He runs from the room, stopping on the landing, cursing, realising he has not closed the curtains. Returning fearfully, he draws them to before dashing out again. He locks the door and bounds downstairs. Still shaking, Calum returns the keys to the larder. After the fright upstairs he doesn't relish being alone in the house now. He takes several meditative deep breaths, inhaling the positive and exhaling the darkness... surveying the bigger picture from the sanctuary of the cave in the back of his mind... accepting, 'besides, it's a lovely spring day with full-on early morning sunshine, a clear blue sky, with just the hint of a cool breeze. All of which bodes well for an excursion into the woodland wonderland of the New Forest.'

Bess comes running with tail wagging. Calum smiles and kneels down to ruffle her fur. "Sorry old girl, but you can't come today. I'm going into the forest. Mr Brown wouldn't like it if I took you there." Stroking the dog, he sniggers, "the ridiculous old fool thinks you will be killed by snakes."

"Highly unlikely, but that's fine. Welcome to my world, go and explore, enjoy your day."

Calum recoils in startled surprise, falling back on his heels and landing flat out on the floor. "Oh, Gaia!" he gasps, heart pounding, "You made me jump, I didn't expect you to be in the dog."

"You should not be surprised by now at the many manifestations my appearance may take." Calum smiles in acceptance of that given. "No, no, of course not, Mother... but it still feels strange sometimes."

"Yes, I know it must, but hopefully, if our connection shall remain true, this interaction will eventually become second nature to you.

Now, before you go, listen carefully to these words from my child, the Buddha."

Calum nods obediently, sitting cross-legged, giving his full attention.

"Sit... rest... work... alone with yourself, never weary on the edge of the forest... live joyfully without desire."

He ponders this, absorbing the words of wisdom. "Thank you, Great Spirit."

Bess pads back to her bed. Calum leaves the house, walking quickly across the green, repeating over and over the Buddha's mantra, 'Never weary on the edge of the forest, alone with yourself,' feeling and holding that great truth at his core. He comes to the footpath that leads into the woodland. Excited, he strides on. The path widens after a while into a deeply rutted track densely overhung by blackthorn, hawthorn and hazel branches, these native hedgerow trees fashioning a natural living arch, interwoven with wild clematis and thorny dog rose, this rambling double act tangling abstractly into springy spindle tree branches. The spindle looks unremarkable now, but will be gloriously transformed when autumn infuses rich red and orange colouring to the leaves, and later presenting resplendently again when hung heavy with bright red berries in winter.

This tumbling overgrown mass of green foliage creates coveted dappled shade, encouraging foxglove and fern to grow abundantly throughout the forest floor, their root systems cosseted by soft, damp, citrus-green moss. The ericaceous soil colonised in spring by pure white snowdrop, yellow primrose and vibrant bluebell flowers, with prolific ivy spreading almost unnoticed under these naturalised perennials. The ubiquitous tight-knit dark green invader occupying every available space, with its hyperactive growth overwhelming and unintentionally strangling any less hardy species of plant life, rampant in its own random suffocating way, but improbably influential in knitting the rest of the forest together. Calum stands enraptured as honey bees and hover flies buzz contentedly in and out of the white ivy flowers as if entranced, whilst large fat yellow hornets zoom loudly all around him. Big coffee-coloured wood ants scurry to and fro around his feet, lured in by their addiction to the sticky sap at the base of the straight and true scots pine and douglas fir conifer trees.

Calum is in his element here in the New Forest, at peace now within this alternative world, his natural habitat. He sighs and breathes deeply... even the air feels different here, so clean and refreshingly cool on his face. Walking on, rabbits, sensing Calum's approach, instinctively run for cover, as do any grazing deer alerted to the danger of his human scent.

After a while the forest opens up into a wide expanse of low growing mauve heather, densely under planting huge old oak, beech, ash, sycamore and elm trees. These aged forest patriarchs interspersed with clingy young offspring, the self-seeded saplings growing close under the parent's protective canopy.

A profusion of elegant silver birch trees stand to attention nearby, as if in subservient compliance of their monarch, king of the forest, the mighty oak. The bark of most trees is encrusted with bright orange and lime green lichens. These slow-growing fungal organisms flag up the fact that this area of the forest is pollution-free.

A number of trees, although dead, remain standing, as if frozen in death. Others lie where they have fallen, the deceased timber providing a home to many forms of fungi, which vary greatly in colour and texture, some glossy red, others a striking orange, creamy white and several shades of brown. There are many varieties of toadstools and mushrooms, some edible, others deadly poisonous. All live and grow on this decaying wood, which also provides precious sanctuary and shelter for a multitude of small creatures and insects.

"A blessed gift from the Great Spirit – seems nothing useful is wasted by Mother Nature," Calum acknowledges aloud in wondrous appreciation. Wandering on, he happens upon a beautiful glade, where wild ponies and cattle graze, peacefully content. Rhododendron shrubs lay claim to any unoccupied space. Their gnarled and twisted stems have smooth green leaves and deep, pink-tinged purple flowers, which never seem to bloom as vibrantly away from the forest shade.

A fast-flowing river powers a wide snaking torrent of water through this close shorn clearing. Calum stands in awe of the magnificent splendour before him, enjoying a fabulous sense of freedom, the like not felt since he ran the breeze atop the high cliffs of Bristol. Suddenly feeling woozy, overcome by this overdose of natural beauty, he sits on a fallen tree trunk and sighs contentedly. Feeling hungry, he greedily tucks in to the cheese sandwiches, leaving the crusts of bread as a surprise snack for any fortunate creatures that may happen along.

From out of nowhere a phosphorescent green dragonfly appears before him, wings vibrating frantically, urging Calum, "Come, come to the water, where the cycle of my soul occurs; life's departure and rebirth. I speak to you of metamorphosis. Look deep into the stream, concentrate, and you may see the reflective imagery of your own life."

He follows the dragonfly, mesmerised by the shimmering silver gossamer-like wings as it flies ahead. The dragonfly pauses to hover above a large fish laid out on a massive prehistoric slab of stone in the centre of the river. Ruddy foaming water flows forcefully around the circumference of this gigantic flat rock, the persistent liquid caress and constant smooth erosion of multiple millennia imperceptibly sculpting the rough-hewn surface.

The dragonfly lingers briefly above the supine fish, before darting away at tremendous speed. Perplexed by this strange scenario, Calum slides carefully down the wet muddy bank, wading cautiously across the river, heading to where the fish lies motionless. The strong current is almost shoulder height before he hauls himself up on to the grey surface of the warm stone. Glistening sunbeams create a kaleidoscopic sheen of colour to play on the sleek mottled skin of the aptly named rainbow trout. Calum lies back on the rock, yawning... weary now from his exertions, believing the creature to be dead, his eyes close as the warm sun lulls him to doze... dozing into deep slumber...

He's suddenly awoken by the stranded fish writhing and flapping beside him in a vain attempt to reach water. He gently helps the struggling trout back into the river, where it quivers underwater as if in the throes of resurrection, seemingly resuscitated by the rejuvenating elixir of the Great Spirit-infused Holy Water. After several minutes of recuperation, the fish swims away slowly, in perfect rhythm with the river flow. Calum stands, gazing, locked into this blessed vision, meticulously absorbing every last detail of this panoramic view of paradise. Captivated by the widescreen magnificence of this parallel world… until dwindling daylight prompts him to make his way home, running back, arriving breathless, just before the Browns' return.

"Have you had a good day, son?" Janet asks as she enters the house.

He looks up at her from the sofa, "Oh, you know, so-so Mrs Brown, just stayed around here and played some with Bess in the garden."

"Good boy, I'll make a pot of tea and then we shall all eat. We have important news, but it can wait until morning. We're really tired now. It's been a long day." Janet still seems uncharacteristically upbeat, and strangely wired, putting Calum on red alert. 'Something's not right here, normally the Browns never get the least excitable, remaining mostly unmoved by pretty much anything and everything going on around them, as if living out their days is a preordained chore, with planet Earth existence and material gain the aim at all costs. Goals of greed, human avarice work that must be accomplished before death, so they can sleep the long sleep without fear of missing out on their due.' He spends a restless night wondering what the Browns' important news could be, sensing instinctively that it is not to be good tidings.

Next morning at breakfast, Janet calmly announces that they will soon be leaving Brockenhurst. "We are moving some thirty miles away, to Weyhill, a small village in Hampshire. We have relatives there and have been thinking of relocating for some time."

Calum gasps, rocked by this bombshell, feeling that his whole world has suddenly collapsed… and just as he has got used to living here, on the cusp of discovering the magical secrets of the New Forest. He is seething, sure that the fosterers have conspired to deny him his destiny. 'They have no regard for my feelings! Their own wellbeing, that's all that matters to them.' Seeds of revenge are now firmly planted in his mind. Scowling darkly, he asks, "Will I be coming with you?"

Janet chuckles. "Why, of course son, we wouldn't leave you behind, now would we?"

"I wish you would," he growls at her, "I like living here, near the forest."

"We are bound by law to take you, boy," Jim Brown sneers, "otherwise I, for one, would be sorely tempted to leave your sorry ass behind."

"Aww, pay no heed Calum," Janet puts an arm around his shoulder and glances sharply at her husband. "Jim is only joking... aren't you dear?"

"Am I?" He snorts, before snatching up his newspaper and storming into the lounge.

Calum shrugs her off and goes to his bedroom.

CHAPTER
FOURTEEN

Two weeks pass before Janet informs Calum that they have been summoned once more to the solicitor, "To tie up a few loose ends regarding moving house." This unexpected news provides him with the opportunity to venture once more into his beloved New Forest. As soon as the Browns leave for their appointment he runs across the common and is soon back in his natural paradise again.

Piercing sunlight is squeezing through any accessible gap in the burgeoning tree canopy today, illuminating the forest floor with darting golden rays, casting long shadows of light and shade on the cold green moss and ivy, creating a natural contrast with the warming orange tones of random lichens. The bright yellow flowers of prickly gorse shrubs, sunshine highlighted, cohabit and colour coordinate perfectly with the vibrant green foliage of spiky young holly trees. Grey squirrels, scrambling up trees, catch his attention, bounding acrobatically along branches, seemingly leaping across the whole forest, should they wish, without ever touching terra firma.

Deviating from the man-made route today, Calum leaves the well-worn tourist trail, roaming amongst a swathe of wild windswept heather, bordered by hedges of sloe and elder, walking a soft spongy path of decomposing leaves and dead bracken. This mulched detritus a red herring, seemingly strewn haphazardly, but a calculating design by Nature, serving to protect any infant plant growth from the cold severity of winter's icy grip.

The Great Spirit's voice comes to him here, "This forest floor a holy sanctuary, where spirits tread lightly, unobserved."

Calum smiles to himself, 'Yes, Mother, this ancient forest is indeed the place where one could always find solace and truth.' Walking on, he follows an old winding rutted track, this well-trodden way leading deep into the forest. Rounding a bend, he catches his breath, coming face to face with an elderly woman carrying two large baskets. He is amazed to see scores of cats following her.

"Good morning," she smiles warmly in welcome.

The cats home in on Calum, some purring loudly, others leaning and folding softly against his legs, an exquisite feeling this, as he accepts their healing bonding.

"Does your mummy know you are out alone in the forest?" The woman asks.

"Yes," he smirks smugly, "Mother Nature always knows exactly where I am."

Nodding her head, the woman agrees, "She surely does child, she surely does. My name is Eleanor. Folk in Brockenhurst call me the Cat Woman. I live not far from here."

"Pleased to meet you, I'm Calum, and live in the village," he frowns, "for the moment at least. I thought maybe you were St Gertrude... the Patron Saint of cats?" She chuckles coyly, "No son, no. But we are connected... the great lady is my mentor and guide."

"I see... what's in your baskets, Eleanor?"

"I am collecting various woodland flora; flowers, berries, moss, mushrooms, nuts, lichens, tree bark. Fruits of the forest, one could say." Intrigued, he asks, "And what do you do with these forest fruits?"

"I make medicine for any cats that are unwell. Would you care to help?"

"Yes please!"

She leads on, patiently pointing out what is edible and what is poisonous. Some grazing rabbits up ahead all run for cover, except for one, which doesn't move. Calum feels excited that the creature seems to be waiting for him, assuming, 'It must be Gaia!' Walking up close, he realises all is not well. The rabbit is ill, its eyes coated with a running, grey mucous film, the body emaciated and covered with sores.

Eleanor joins him, placing a firm hand on his arm and warning, "Don't touch the creature! It has myxomatosis." He feels sick. "What the hell is that?"

She shakes her head, "A terrible, cruel disease, invented by man in an attempt to control Nature. This poor creature is doomed to die a slow death, wandering like this for weeks, in some cases even months."

"That's so disgusting! How can one living being do this to another? Especially as man thinks himself so superior to other animals."

"This is what some humans are capable of, I'm afraid, son. Many kill for bloodlust or greed. One need only study their history and see the vile atrocities they have committed against their own kind to realise that Nature's welfare will be of little consequence to them. That is why I retreated from their depraved world... many, many years ago."

"Is there no way to end this poor animal's misery, Eleanor?"

"I know I should, Calum... it would be the compassionate thing to do, but I cannot kill... I do not have it in me." He shakes his head. "Nor I, Eleanor," and then looks up to her in sudden hope, "but maybe a natural predator will soon end its suffering, as it is such easy prey now." She shakes her head, and tears fall on her scarf. "No, I am afraid that won't happen, now that the poor rabbit has the full-blown symptoms."

"How about a rat? They will kill and eat anything, the Great Spirit told me... except for—"

"Another rat."

Calum glances sharply at her, briefly surprised by the interjection, before realising, 'Of course... she knows.'

"But... the rat is a carrier of disease itself, is it not Eleanor?"

"Yes, I know, and a horrid creature it is too, but it carries nothing so obnoxious, so wicked, as the like of what this rabbit has been subjected to. Even something as dreadful as the rat will distance itself from human evil. Are you aware that the humans have invented similar chemical concoctions in the form of germ and biological warfare, so as to inflict slow death and suffering on their fellow man?"

Calum shakes his head, "I've heard enough Eleanor. Like you, I'm going to distance myself from mankind. I despise some humans... no, most... I'm sorry, but I really do."

"Not all are callous and cruel. Some have Mother Nature's genes, you know. Come now, we must leave this poor creature and carry on foraging, the sick and hungry cats are relying on us."

"We can't leave the rabbit... not like this." Looking around desperately he shouts out, "Come on, Great Spirit of Nature, if you're so great, then show yourself! Come forth and put this poor being out of its misery."

Eleanor taps him lightly on the shoulder. "One must not order the Great Spirit, child. Besides, there are thousands of rabbits wandering around in this condition. The divine Mother could not deal with them all... not without setting off a karmic armageddon."

"Well! So what? So be it, if that's what it takes." Calum screams at the top of his voice. "Come on then, Gaia, do your worst! Wipe the scourge of humans. Cleanse this disgusting planet!"

Eleanor walks on, with Calum following reluctantly, still ranting, until he hears a mew... meeew... meeew. Shielding his eyes from the glare, he looks up. The high-pitched mewing is coming from above, in the sky. 'Sounds like a... but no... surely not... a... a cat, up there, how could it be? That's just plain crazy... isn't it?'

The mewing has changed to a high-pitched screeching as suddenly a large buzzard drops from the sky. With a whoosh of coasting wings and juddering thump of contact the outstretched claws snatch up the rabbit, and in one fluid movement the powerful bird flies up and away, high over the tree-tops before dropping the rabbit into a large pond set back from the track. "Wow! Did you see that, Eleanor?"

She turns to him and smiles grimly. "The Great Spirit works in mysterious ways, child, and will always do what she can... but one must never try to force Nature to do one's bidding. It doesn't work like that, the great Mother cannot be dictated to."

"I'm sorry, I was just so upset about–"

"No apology needed, Calum, Gaia understands human frailty. She is firm but fair."

They spend the next two hours wandering along the many tracks and trails of the forest. Calum suddenly points ahead, "Who's that?" A slim ethereal female figure, dressed from head to toe in a flowing turquoise dress, is walking towards them. Eleanor puts her fingers to her lips, "Shhh now son, don't spook her. Stay quiet and still, until she passes." The woman stops and kneels down, holding her palms flat, just above the ground. "What's she doing Eleanor? " Calum whispers. "Healing, it's her vocation, for she is St Susan of Grimston, Patron Saint of Bees and Nurses... Saint Susan is very humble though, and feels no need of title. She prefers to be known as Susie Sprite... or the Bee Lady. Her spiritual mission is to save and rescue injured and poorly bees from harm. She's even been known to resuscitate and resurrect them." "Ahh... yes," Calum recalls, "Gaia told me of her before, she is an emissary of Nature, I believe?"

"Yes, that is correct, child. The Great Spirit's envoys are chosen only after great deliberation." Calum is overwhelmed by the magnitude of this sychronicity. "I am in awe, truly in awe, I did not expect to connect with two Saints, so soon, let alone on the same day, and to meet your good self is such an honour and a pleasure, Eleanor. How cool is this, I feel so privileged today."

Eleanor beams, and blushes, "Why, thank you, kind sir. You are indeed connected with St Gertrude through me, but such praise is not warranted on my behalf. I am no saint, just a humble servant of Mother Nature."

The Bee Lady comes close by, nodding and smiling as she passes. "Wow! Eleanor, she's so light on her feet, and so radiant, as if she's gliding above the ground, like a ghost. And her smile, is so... so beautiful – full of kindness and compassion – I've never seen a smile like that. It makes me feel... loved... so loved... I've never felt love like that ever before."

"Yes, she loves us all. There is an aura of angelic love about her. You are correct, Calum. Susie Sprite is now in angelic spirit form.

She was a nurse with her own ward. A ward sister, a damn fine nurse, you know. So well respected and regarded by patients and colleagues alike, she always thought of others before herself. Even when she was dying, she still went to work in her beloved hospital. She was like a cross between Florence Nightingale and Mother Teresa. Susie was a one-off though, on a different level even than those two great ladies, as she also incorporated the natural world in her vocational healing."

"What happened to her then, Eleanor? She looks too young and vibrant to die."

"A cruel twist of fate, my boy, the poor soul was ravaged by cancer and gone within three months of diagnosis."

"No! That can't be right, after all she did for others, where's the justice in that?"

"No justice, no logic. She was the kindest woman one could ever wish to meet. As close as you will find to an angel living among us here on Earth."

"I don't get it though, Eleanor, why couldn't Gaia save her? After all, even now, she is still working for the greater good of Nature."

"Mother Nature cannot save us from our own susceptibility to human diseases and ailments. But what the Great Spirit can do is teach us to integrate the fruits of Nature in medical healing and so create medicine to cure all manner of ills. If man would only invest his time and money into that scenario, rather than wasting all his energy on building ever-more destructive weapons for waging constant war, then this world would be a much better place.

"Gaia will welcome all compassionate souls, such as Susie Sprite, to the Beautiful Garden, to live on after their earthly demise. Sacred souls such as hers will never die."

"Hmmm, I'm still not sure I get that, it seems unfair and wrong to me for such a delightful soul to be stricken down so cruelly."

"Yes, I know it's hard to fathom in this moment, but in time, you will understand, if you stay true to the Sacred Path."

The Bee Lady is now well into the distance, when she turns, smiles, and waves back to them. "Wow! Did you see that Eleanor, she waved to us."

"Yes Calum, she wants to reassure you, she is accepting of Nature's hidden laws and content in her work."

"It's such a sad tale, Eleanor, but she did look so peaceful and serene, so happy and at one with herself."

"Yes, the Bee Lady is at peace, and she's such a joyous soul... why, sometimes I see her laughing and singing as she skips and dances along the forest floor."

He feels so immersed in this special moment... acknowledging from his heart, 'what a blessing to have connected with Susie Sprite'... but all too soon daylight is fading, fast. Eleanor stops and looks to the sky. "You and I must be going home now, Calum."

"Oh, really, why?" He's disappointed, "I thought we needed to forage some more?"

"We must make do for now, a human should always be sure to leave the forest before dark."

"But we are not like other humans, are we Eleanor?"

"That is true, thank goodness... but even so, I do not presume to be under any privileged protection programme, so I never venture out alone in the forest after dusk."

"OK, so where do you live?"

"Not far from here. Would you care to visit sometime?"

"Oh, yes please."

"Come again then, if you can."

Calum waves a cheery goodbye, but he is sad to be leaving. "I'll be back tomorrow, same place and time. Will you come to meet me?"

Eleanor waves back and smiles at his keenness. "Yes, of course, child, I shall be here at noon." She walks away into the rapidly descending burnt orange glow of dusk, the cats following her devotedly. Their feline steps so light, like graceful apparitions, as the shrill wild cry of a tawny owl precipitates Nature's magical melding of day into night. Calum skips home happily, thinking excitedly of tomorrow.

CHAPTER
FIFTEEN

Calum is up early the next morning, pondering his first meeting with the enigmatic Cat Woman, and wondering if he will see the beautiful Bee Lady again, agitated in anticipation, longing for a swift reunion. Wondering how best to make his escape, he knows it's imperative to get away soon. Dashing to the bathroom, he brushes his teeth and takes a quick wash, before dressing quickly, and creeping quietly along the landing, peering covertly through the banister rails, before sneaking his way stealthily downstairs. The Browns are in the lounge, engrossed, studying reams of official-looking documents spread over the kitchen table.

The last step creaks loudly. Calum pauses, cursing, 'Fuck,' under his breath.

Janet turns. "Oh hello son, sorry, but we are busy dealing with the solicitor's forms and other paperwork this morning, won't you help yourself to breakfast?"

"Yes, thank you." He hurriedly eats some cereal, before asking hesitantly, "I was wondering, Mrs Brown... um... as you are so busy today... could I... uh, um... go and play on the common?"

Janet glances at her husband, "What do you think, Jim?"

"Say what?" He snaps, sorely irritated by the interruption, "I'm trying to concentrate here, woman. Yes, yes, if you say so," he waves dismissively, without looking up from the table, as if swatting away some annoying fly, "go on then, be off with you boy."

Janet comes over. "You can go play son, excuse Jim today, he's a little preoccupied at present. We could be moving very soon," she giggles happily, "it's all so exciting, don't you think?"

Calum scowls, 'Exciting?' He cannot imagine anything worse than moving away from his beloved New Forest, especially now that he has met the Cat Woman and Bee Lady.

"Off you go then, run along now." Janet sighs, disappointed by his lack of enthusiasm. "Be sure to be back by lunchtime, though."

He wastes no time in taking advantage of his good fortune and is gone before they can change their minds, running across the dew-damp green, and arriving early at the designated meeting place, but Eleanor is nowhere to be seen. He frets, 'What could have happened?' worried for her, striding on, imagining all kinds of nightmare scenarios as he follows the same route she had taken the previous evening.

A male fox slinks across the mossy track some way ahead, picking up on his human scent, before turning to glare at Calum with a look of nonchalant disdain, utilising Nature's innate radar, calculating safe distance between creature and danger. This instinctive snap decision, the dog fox's crucial judgement call, a vital factor between safety and harmful human association.

A little further on Calum comes upon a mound of banked up earth with round entrance holes – ancient chalk burrows that are home to many reclusive badger families. He continues along the track, following a steep incline which levels out into a sharp left-hand curve, walking half a mile further on, he enters an open clearing where a dark-green Morris grocer's van is parked. Eleanor is busy filling her baskets with provisions passed down by the driver.

Calum whispers, "Thank you, Great Spirit," relieved she is OK, but at the same time annoyed with himself for worrying unnecessarily, cursing his weak submission to the nagging negative energy of anxiety. His attention is drawn to a small enclosure where five dilapidated old caravans form one large L-shaped dwelling. This rough and ready encampment is fenced off from the forest by tall bark-clad pine posts and rusting wire. He is amazed to see scores of cats milling about inside the caged area.

"My my, you must be keen, lad," Eleanor smiles, glancing at her battered wristwatch. "We have not been out yet."

Although still a little irked by her lack of awareness at his concern for her safety, he decides on diplomacy, but cannot resist chiding, "Oh, sorry, am I early?" whilst tapping his wrist pointedly.

Looking briefly bemused, chuckling, she replies,"Oh… you mean my watch… oh no, take no notice, wearing it is just force of habit. It doesn't work, not for many years. I am no longer governed by man-made time restraints." Eleanor pays the driver, "Bye bye Bob, see you next week." She waves as he drives away. "Come, come Calum, let me show you round our home, I'll introduce you to the rest of the family."

She lifts the rusty latch on a rickety sun-bleached larch gate and gently ushers him to enter. The crowd of cats immediately converges upon them; tabbies, tortoiseshells, black-and-whites, brindle and greys, all sorts, small and large, young and old. Calum is suddenly overwhelmed by cats.

A number of these unfortunate creatures have suffered the loss of an eye, ear, or, in one extreme case, even a leg. Others appear to be in various stages of ailment recovery, with many wearing hedgerow berry and pine-tree sap poultices for the mange. Some cats have been strapped with sloe gin alcohol swabs to encourage the extrication of tenacious ticks, or to relieve the pain and possible infection of wounds and bites. There are those that have fur and skin torn away, a legacy from fighting off predators, or as a result of territorial skirmishes amongst themselves.

Calum receives a mixed welcome, with some cats mewing plaintively, others hissing and spitting unconcealed venom at this stranger who dares enter their domain. Others approach benignly, offering love and affection. He smoothes the soft fur of a large ginger tom, and immediately receives the loud purring warmth of unconditional love in response.

Eleanor opens the door of the largest caravan. "Please come inside, son."

Calum is surprised to see row upon row of wooden shelves, crammed full, floor to ceiling, with neatly stacked old glass sweet jars, all containing various liquid concoctions. Several families of kittens lay resting, sleepy and content, in large wicker baskets. She taps one of the jars. "These are my medicinal remedies."

He's intrigued. "How do you make the medicine, Eleanor?"

"Well..." she hesitates, momentarily unsure whether to tell, but graciously relents, "I use only plant-based natural ingredients, which are found in abundance throughout the forest, some of which you kindly helped to collect yesterday."

"Please Eleanor, can you show me how? Can I make the medicine too?"

She looks at him thoughtfully... "Perhaps I could teach you... we shall see. The formula is bestowed by Mother Nature and passed on to me by the divine spirit of St Gertrude of Nivelle. If it's meant to be, I am sure our blessed Gaia will intervene when she deems it appropriate. But please be under no illusion, should you be chosen, child, it will take a great deal of discipline and dedication on your part."

Trembling with excitement, he blurts out, "Second nature to me, dedication, piece of cake! Look, if I were to visit, say... every day... of every week, how long would it take for me to learn this magic?"

Smiling at his naivety, she gently tries to diffuse his eagerness. "We must be realistic, let's just bide our time a while and see what transpires."

"But I—"

"No buts now," Eleanor says firmly. "Besides, the Great Spirit may have other plans for you. There is much work to be done on the earth plane, you know."

"Tell me about it!" Calum snorts, "I am well aware of the mess the humans have made. But I can—"

"That's my last word on the subject." She gestures to a chair in the corner. "Now please sit down. There is something important I must pass on to you."

He slumps down grumpily on an old tatty cat-clawed armchair. She takes down a book from the shelf, brushing off dusty cobwebs from herself and the tome before sitting down. "Do you read, Calum?"

"No, not really, never felt the need. I get all my facts straight from Gaia."

"Oh! Do you mean like I do, by way of emotion, feelings, symbols, intuition?"

"Yes… sort of, Eleanor, but also from direct feral confirmation through the hidden laws of Nature. From what I can understand, the Great Spirit has blessed me with cosmic clarity enhanced reality receptors."

"I see… sounds rather grand. But yes, that makes sense, as you seem so erudite for your age." She holds up the frayed book. "The extract I am about to read was written by an American, Henry Miller… not everyone's cup of tea, he's rather an acquired taste in many respects – sex-mad, some would say – and there may well be some truth to that, many males seem to be a slave to sexual desire. But he is also regarded by many as perhaps the finest American writer of his generation. He was not afraid to admit his most influential work came from somewhere other than his own mind… a higher force, if you like."

Calum smiles knowingly, "You mean the Great Spirit, don't you, Eleanor?"

"I will leave you to interpret, how you will, this paragraph from his book. But what I can say, with the utmost certainty, is that, despite his inherent human weaknesses and perceived failings, the excerpt I am about to read is a universal truth that was channelled through Henry Miller… for all humans to digest." Settling back in the armchair, she reads aloud, "And I quote… 'I realised the world would only begin to get something of value from me the moment I stopped being a serious member of society and became… myself. […] From the little reading that I had done I had observed that the people that were most in life, who were moulding life, who were life itself, ate little, slept little, owned little or nothing. They had no illusions about duty, or the perpetuation of their kith and kin, or the preservation of the state. They were interested in truth and in truth alone.'

She closes the book and stares at Calum.

He understands. "It's Nature incarnate, Eleanor... the Great Spirit connected with Henry Miller."

"Yes, it's irrefutable corroboration, I would say." She puts a finger to her lips. Suddenly feeling tired, he closes his eyes. Some time later Calum is awoken by Eleanor gently tapping his shoulder. He has no clue as to how long he has slept, and – still half asleep – rubs his eyes until clear vision slowly returns.

She puts on her coat and urges, "Come now, Calum, we must feed everyone before we go foraging again." Handing him a wooden scoop, she lifts the lid from a large cooking pot. Leaning forwards, inhaling the fresh scent of warm bran, berries, and the various other fruits of the forest bubbling and simmering gently, he turns to her and asks, "So, there's no meat in here, Eleanor?"

"That is correct son, no meat, poultry, fish or any other animal by-products."

"I thought not, the food smells"... Calum leans in further, ingesting the pure aroma, "so... so–"

She smiles, "So clean, fresh, innocent? Yes, because it is unsullied by cruelty, suffering and death."

"Yes, I see, and the cats don't seem to mind eating fruit and berries?"

"No, not at all, I also add ground nuts, oats and bran to the mixture, to bulk it out with protein and fibre. I eat the same, it is also my diet, Calum. It's the way forward for all enlightened souls. When changing to a vegan diet one immediately experiences a great energy shift of enlightenment. Like a veil being lifted. You immediately gain a supernatural insight into the universe. Although taste-wise it can take a month or so for one's palette to become fully adjusted... Would you like to try some?"

He hesitates. "Uhhh... yes, please."

She half-fills a clean white bowl and hands him a spoon. He tries it tentatively... until it suddenly explodes with flavour as he chews. "Wow! It's... it's like... zingy on my tongue."

Eleanor clasps her hands to her heart. "Hee hee, my my, I have never heard it described in that way before, but yes... I suppose it is zingy."

"Yes, Eleanor, the food is tingling with purity, a flavour... like Nature's nectar."

"That it is, son, that it is, truly vegan nectar from the Gods. Why do you think the cats love it so?"

He looks up at her, knowing the answer, "Because this food is blessed by Gaia."

"Yes, Calum, the rest of the universe has evolved to be cruelty-free. No inhabitant of any other planet in the universe eats murdered life forms... only human beings do so."

"How do you know that, Eleanor? Have you been to other planets?"

"No, not as yet child. But as a vegan myself I know and feel it to be true. There is a karma attached to humans killing and eating animals. It is a form of cannibalism, and the cruel, horrific methods employed by those responsible for the poor animal's extermination is a grotesque abomination. Mankind has no need, in a nutritional sense, to eat other living beings. It is a fabricated pretence, enabling some to achieve their bloodlust desire to abuse something weaker and meeker than themselves that cannot defend itself. Humans have evolved beyond the need to act cruelly towards one another, and the innocent animal kingdom. Until this lesson is learnt and put into devoted practice, man will never attain the highest form of enlightenment that is available and will continue to be immersed in war and conflict. This is their karma."

Calum shakes his head and growls, "I hate those humans."

"Some would say hate is too strong a word, but I understand your anger, son."

"What happens when the cats are recovered, Eleanor, do they resume hunting and forget the vegan diet when they leave you?"

"Hee hee hee," finding this highly amusing, she gestures to several edgy and impatient cats tugging on her skirt, "do they look like they are going anywhere soon? Come, let's all eat." Eleanor fills the bowls quickly, to avoid being scratched and bitten. The cats fight like crazy over the food, tumbling all over each other in a mad scramble to feed. Calum is impressed by her swift dexterity in avoiding being injured during the animals' ferocious eagerness. There is obviously no lack of enthusiasm, even though meat is off the menu.

"Are there many vegans on planet Earth, Eleanor?" asks Calum. "They are in the distinct minority at present son, but there is a young girl who lives not far from here, her name is Apple Amber, and most unusually she has been vegan since before birth. I feel this girl will go on to be a great ambassador for the vegan cause, and a saviour for her beloved animals."

"Mmm, she sounds lovely, I hope I can meet this Apple Amber one day, Eleanor."

"Yes, I hope so too, Calum, I feel you may have a strong connection and a great deal of synchronicity between you, because of your mutual core compassion for the natural world."

When the cats are all fed, Eleanor picks up a galvanised tin bucket, locks the gate, and leads the way out to the clearing. Grabbing a handful of oats from the pail, she throws the food to the ground. All of a sudden a gang of wild horses come galloping out from the undergrowth, snorting and whinnying, rushing headlong towards their feeder, skidding to a halt, right before her, throwing up clouds of swirling dust as they scrap for the food, nipping and bustling each other, snorting and raking the ground with scything hooves in their frenzied urgency. Calum cowers behind Eleanor, shocked and frightened by the ferocity of the stampede. She tries to comfort him. "Fear not, child, they are just hungry creatures, no harm is meant." Not wholly reassured by her confidence, nor convinced of the rowdy ponies' benevolence, he backs away slowly.

Chuckling at their antics, Eleanor throws the wild-eyed animals the last of the oats. "They come here every day to be fed and expect it now. Come, Calum, they won't bother us any more." Leaving the clearing, they walk on together, united, bonding as compassionate companions with a common goal.

A large expanse of deer-grazed land looms up ahead, where a massive old oak tree stands tall and true. Eleanor stops suddenly and grips his hand tightly. Startled, Calum asks, "What is it, what do you see?"

"This mighty tree holds a tragic secret, my boy, a sad forlorn tale."

He looks at her anxiously. "Why? What's happened here?"

She gazes up into the branches, pausing... composing herself. "It was many years ago now... I shall always recall the awful sight though, as if it were yesterday. I came into this glade, as I do every day, and there he was, right before me... a young man... hanging... up there, from that great arching bough, hanging dead... he was dead."

Calum shivers. "Who Eleanor, who was it?"

"A young man from the village, name of John Brown... a twin, a conscientious objector to the Great War. His brother Jack was in the army and was killed in active service."

Calum feels faint as he comes to a chilling realisation, 'So... that's the meaning of the foster parents' locked room.'

"But Eleanor, why, why would he hang himself?"

"It was said that he suffered merciless verbal abuse from the locals, and even his own father, because of his pacifist beliefs. Things came to a head when he could no longer tolerate the cruel insults. He decided to get his own back so informed the police of the petty theft and poaching of a local family. The story goes that one of the policemen, unsympathetic to young John's anti-war stance, passed the name of the informant to the thieves. John Brown was attacked one dark night and beaten badly. From then on he was harassed and hunted down, threatened on a daily basis. The poor lad took it hard and never fully recovered mentally... or so they say. It must have become unbearable... so I assume he decided to end it all."

Calum understands now, feeling terribly sad for John Brown, and sensing the Great Spirit's presence strongly. "This is now a sacred place, Eleanor."

She turns to him, tears in her eyes. "Yes son, you are right. It most certainly is hallowed ground. Sometimes this violent and hostile life on planet Earth becomes too much for some of the innocents. So the weak and meek, they send out a cry for help, a melancholic prayer to the universe."

He feels it now, the immediacy of this overwhelming sadness. The young man's suicide was such a plea, a longing for everlasting peace and compassionate coexistence on Earth. The denial of this altruistic goal led to a deep yearning to be at one with Gaia, and surely brought about Johns Brown's earthly demise.

The overpowering forest force is so palpable that Calum can feel the psychic crackling of latent energy, a melancholic atmospheric radiation so all-pervading, so smothering, he knows it could only be tolerated in small doses. Realising the truth of this moment, appreciating that if you were human and not of Mother Nature's spirit world, you would be wise to beware the devastating supernatural power of the forest. 'Visit without lingering,' he feels, is key, 'as the energy here is too strong for mere humans to withstand. One should never under any circumstances outstay your welcome in the forest, or the consequences could be dire.'

"I understand now, Eleanor... Gaia has spoken." She suddenly appears frailer and looks older than before. Calum senses a deep sadness about her. "Will you ever leave this place, Eleanor?"

She shakes her head, attempting to regain her composure before speaking. "No child, I cannot leave."

Her resolve is steadfast. "My future is preordained. It is my destiny to remain here and work for the greater good of Nature." The unwavering gaze leaves no doubt as to her devotion. "I will not desert these poor creatures, never, ever, just as the Bee Lady will never give up on her beloved bees."

"Yes, I know, I understand... goodbye then, Eleanor."

"Farewell, my boy. May the great Mother's blessed love always be with you," she says, taking his hands in hers. "I feel the healing power for the flora and fauna within you. It is a precious ability, use your gift well, Calum."

He's stunned, "Really, you do, you sense that in me? Why, yes, of course Eleanor, I will always work for the greater good of Nature, by intent and action, I promise you."

Both have tears welling up as Calum walks away, without a backwards glance, somehow knowing he will never see the cat woman again.

CHAPTER
SIXTEEN

The next morning at breakfast, Janet announces that they will be moving house in a few days. "I know its short notice son, but that's the way it is I'm afraid. Our cousins need to exchange as soon as possible. Jim felt it best to wait to tell you when we knew for sure."

Calum is stunned speechless, and then furious at what he perceives as the Browns' calculated deception, raging inside, 'How could they do this to me? It's a crime against Nature to deprive someone of their destiny.'

The smell of frying bacon filters through from the kitchen... the obnoxious odour of yet another dead animal cooking, assaulting his senses, causing such nausea-inducing revulsion that he concentrates on breathing only through his mouth.

Janet trills cheerily, "Sit down at the table, Calum, bacon and eggs on the way."

"No way! I'm not into eating murdered life forms."

"Oooh... my dear boy, I wish you wouldn't talk like that, it makes me feel really uncomfortable."

He scowls at her, "Sorry, I'm sure Mrs Brown, but yes, the truth often is... uncomfortable."

"But come on now, son, it's not like they are pets, is it? Not like cats... or our dogs, for instance."

"Yeah! It's just like that, the animals can see, hear, walk, run, they can think, play, show love and affection... so yeah, it's just like eating your pets... or your children."

Janet shudders inside as she considers this. "Well... I suppose when you put it like that, it's probably best not to think about it."

"That's exactly what most people do, try not to think about it, or they just don't give a damn. Only a small minority are vegetarian... even less of vegan persuasion. But whatever... that's your way. So long as you understand, I ain't never gonna be no cannibal."

Jim throws down his paper. "You will eat what you are given, boy, and be bloody thankful."

"No, I won't... not any more."

Janet comes through hurriedly, anxious to diffuse the situation. "It's alright Jim, Calum can eat what he likes... he never eats meat anyway," she smiles kindly towards him. "Do you son? I often find it hidden underneath his leftover veg."

Calum is caught unawares by her canny knowledge. "Uhh... yeah... well, thank you for understanding, Mrs Brown. It's just a personal thing. I know it's not for everyone... each of us are at differing stages in our evolutionary spiritual development, and look, I'm not judging anyone, but—"

"Pah! What utter bloody rot," Jim interrupts, "where did you dream up all this vegetarian clap trap?"

Calum realises he's probably said too much, surprising himself with the gushing forth of spiritual zeal, but knows he's fighting a losing battle here, so keeps it short. "Someone told me."

"Ha ha ha, you'd better watch out who you associate with boy, or else the men in white coats will soon be coming for you, ha ha ha."

Janet puts an arm around Calum's shoulder. "Aww, don't tease so, Jim. Sit down lad, I'll bring you some cereal and toast." Heading for the kitchen, she pauses and turns back, smiling, to ask, "You will still eat my special cottage pie though, won't you, son? After all, it has only lean beef mince in it, so it's not really meat as such... is it?"

Smiling ruefully, shaking his head and sighing in exasperation, Calum explains, "Still murdered cow, like your bacon is murdered pig, Mrs B, however you dress it up." He thinks back to the refreshing aroma of Eleanor's forest forage mix yesterday, and says, "Cereal will do me nicely, thanks."

He spends the next three days housebound, sullenly silent whilst reluctantly helping with the hurried packing. The day before they are due to move Jim announces that they are all going out for a drive. Calum sits in the back of the old black Riley saloon, while Jim calls all four dogs to jump in. Janet has the little Cairn terriers in front, sitting at her feet, while Bess and Tripod climb in with Calum, who's taken aback by this unusual act of kindness, as Jim never has the dogs in the car, and it's unheard of for him to take the family out for a drive.

It is a cloudy, windswept morning as they set off. After about half an hour of travelling the narrow roads in silence, they pull into a forest enclosure, signposted:

WILVERLEY PLAIN

Janet is snuffling and whimpering into her hankerchief, making Calum edgy, as he senses something's not right here.

Beyond the car park is a gravel track that opens out into a large wide clearing of grazed-to-the quick scrubland, dotted here and there with a scattering of windswept gorse and heather shrubs. This public right-of-way enclosure borders the New Forest and is a popular dog-walking area. Not a house or dwelling can be seen for miles. Wild ponies mingle here with roaming cattle, and there are hundreds of grazing rabbits dotted around. Jim lets the dogs out. Janet remains seated with her head down. She seems to be stifling sobs. Calum moves to get out.

"No, you stay put boy," Jim orders, "just the dogs."

The dogs jump out and sniff about the ground in eager exploration. Jim gets back in the car, starts the engine and drives off. Janet is crying now, a disturbing mix of high-pitched wailing and shrieking. Turning to look out the rear window, Calum sees the dogs chasing after the car, realising now, with a sinking feeling, that Jim has dumped them. He shouts "What the hell are you doing, Mr Brown?! You can't leave them here without food or water!"

"Quiet, boy, someone will care for them. It's not my problem now. We can't take animals to our new property, so it's better than having them put down at the vet's, isn't it?" Calum slumps back in the seat, staggered by this callous deed, hating Jim with a passion, while Janet wails on. "Shut up, woman! Stop your goddamn snivelling, for Christ's sake," Jim yells at her. "It's for the best, and you know it."

The removal men arrive early on Wednesday. Their lorry is fully loaded by late morning. Calum is seething, gutted there will be no chance of a farewell visit to the New Forest. Janet turns back to bid a last goodbye to the house. With tears welling, she lingers mournfully, pressing her palm to the wooden front door. Jim calls to her, "Time to leave now, dear."

Cradling his Lenny the lion tightly, Calum climbs into the backseat of the car. He can still smell the dogs and see their black and grey hairs stuck to the carpet.

The journey takes nearly two hours before Jim spots the sign proclaiming:

MEADOW BANK

He pulls into the drive ahead of the removal van and continues down a driveway bordered on each side by overgrown native hedgerow. To the left stands a brick-built bungalow in a half-acre plot. The garden is overgrown with weed-infested meadow grass, interspersed here and there with a few straggly old shrubs and neglected fruit trees.

Bizarrely, a rusting 1930s Mercedes convertible sports car is parked up on a mound of earth. To the right is a large horse paddock. The rear of the place is buffered by a sloping railway embankment, colonised by a profusion of spindly saplings of ash and sycamore trees, with a vigourous undergrowth of choking nettle, ground elder and strangling bindweed. This tangled vegetation almost covers the grey stone chippings scattered down the sharp incline of the railway bank.

Jim and Janet seem dispirited, dejected even, as they exit the car, their lack of positive reaction evident as they wander aimlessly about. "Come on, then, Calum," Janet calls with forced gusto, "let's go take a look."

He curses under his breath but joins them, reluctantly. Feeling miserable, picking up on the low-key atmosphere, he has no great inclination to explore what he sees as just a run-down old dump.

Sat in the far corner of the plot is a shabby-looking mobile home. He ambles over to take a look. It appears by all the old junk piled inside that it had been used latterly only as a storage area. Jim comes across to look at it." That will make a fine study for me, once I've cleared it out."

Janet points towards the bungalow. "Shall we go inside then, folks?"

She leads the way and pushes open the stiff wooden front door. The dwelling has a soulless air and smells damp and musty. Small windows let in very little natural light. A narrow hallway leads directly into a dark and gloomy windowless kitchen area. There are two bedrooms and a tiny bathroom. At the front of the bungalow is a lounge with a small open fireplace.

The removal men come to the door carrying boxes. "Come on in, gents." Jim shows them through. "Just put the stuff down anywhere for now, we'll sort it out later."

Calum follows Janet into the dreary kitchen and through the rear door. Out back is a brick-built toilet block standing at the end of a short path. She tugs at the handle of the rotten wooden door. It creaks open reluctantly. They cautiously peer inside. A single shadeless lightbulb hangs from an old lead-cased electric cable. Ancient dusty cobwebs droop like rotting grey candyfloss from the damp ceiling. Decades-old yellowing newspaper, torn into neat squares of primitive toilet paper, litter the bare earth floor. Taking pride of place on the white 'DOULTON' cistern lid, proudly displayed as if only to be used on special occasions, is one half-used roll of 'Izal Medicated' toilet issue.

Sensing Calum's reticence to enthuse positively about these primitive sanitary arrangements, Janet exaggerates the positive. "Nothing a good dousing of disinfectant and a lick of white emulsion won't put right, my lad."

Suddenly feeling a rumbling vibration beneath his feet he imagines, 'Earthquake! Now that's more like it,' welcoming Nature's entertaining intervention, 'even a natural disaster is eminently preferable to the mind-numbing boredom of traipsing around with this pair of goons.' He hopes that Janet, Jim and the boring bog will be swiftly swallowed up in some deep dark crater. A shrill ear-piercing "whooooo, whooooo" whistling is followed closely by a loud gasp of escaping steam. Puzzled, he runs to the front of the bungalow, just catching sight of a black behemoth of a steam locomotive, belching out great billowing clouds of white vapour from its dual chimneys as it rumbles by on the trembling elevated tracks, gamely tugging a long line of rusty freight carriages behind.

The engine driver and stoker wave grimy blue-peaked caps in greeting at Calum, their excited faces streaked black with coal dust and sweat. High on adrenaline, these men living the dream of these last glorious days of steam as they power on into history. It is a thrilling moment, numbing the anguish somewhat of Calum's abrupt departure from the New Forest, and imbuing him with newfound enthusiasm to explore the local area.

He begins to adjust and adapt to his new surroundings during the following weeks. One bright sunny day he scrambles up the steep embankment, walking alongside the old railway track, until he comes to a chunky steel bridge. The supporting red-brick pillars are chalk-scrawled randomly with fickle adolescent graffiti: 'Dave luvs Lyn,' 'Kim 4 Pete,' 'Phil's a queer boy,' 'Pam's got the pox,' 'Mary takes it up the bum', being the highlights amongst many other enlightening juvenile observations.

Looking down from the bridge, Calum is captivated by a tall blonde girl in a short black miniskirt and thigh-high PVC boots walking on the road below. Feeling edgy and excited, he is suddenly overcome by a new sensation, sexual desire. Ogling her, he lets out a long low whistle as she strides off towards the nearby council housing estate of Fairways, nestled in the small village of Weyhill, some four miles west of the old market town of Andover. Calum gazes longingly as the girl crests the hill, until this hazy sexy mirage fades from view. He continues to amble along the track, pleasantly preoccupied with a lingering vision of the leggy young blonde. A hundred yards further on he comes across the dour, grey concrete warehouse of:

LENHAM STORAGE

A local commercial distribution company that receives hundreds of tons of pre-bagged fertiliser, delivered to the adjacent railway sidings twice weekly. This agricultural cargo is the only freight hauled these days by the last steam locomotive still in use on this single-track line.

A scattered colony of straggly buddleia shrubs (known as 'Belsen Buddleia' by the nearby factory workers because they somehow survive here without any apparent nourishment, miraculously clinging to life despite constant malnutrition) grows tenaciously from any crack or crevice in the concrete floors and walls of the warehouse. Hundreds of fragile butterflies congregate upon the plants' silver-grey foliage, basking in apparent ecstasy on the heavily-scented mauve and lilac flowers. Calum bows reverently to the insects' magnificence, before walking on towards the ramshackle remains of Weyhill Railway Station. It is clear from the few remaining exterior adornments that this must once have been a handsome black-and-white wooden building. But now its dilapidated shell is just another decaying relic from a bygone age, when commuter travel was a staple of this main line to London. This station, like many others, was in regular use until the infamous Beeching railway cuts in the early 1960s. Over 2,000 stations were closed on Mr Beeching's orders and most of the track ripped up. The line at Weyhill only survived because it was used on occasion by the MOD (Ministry Of Defence) based in Ludgershall town, some four miles away.

Calum saunters across the wide sun-bleached wood worm riddled promenade, startling several dozing yellow sand lizards to dart away at the first vibration of his footfall. Cautiously, he negotiates the prickly wild dog rose bramble and twining tendrils of poison-ous deadly nightshade scrambling and sprawling across the boarding platform. Opening the wide pine door of the waiting room frightens a large grey rat to rush by him, the surprised creature emitting an angry, high-pitched squeal at the unexpected human intrusion.

Holes in the roof and broken windows have allowed in many years of rain, ice and snow, the inclement weather causing widespread deterioration of this once impressive Victorian edifice. A sycamore tree, growing up through decaying oak floorboards, has forced its branches through the roof in a determined quest for sunlight and succour. The interior walls are still decorated with damp peeling hardboard signs, advertising Woodbine and Senior Service cigarettes, and one jagged rusty blue-and-white tinplate plaque, bearing the legend, 'Ales By Strong's of Romsey,' hangs precariously lopsided by its last remaining lead nail. Faded train tickets lay scattered about the floor, nostalgic withered remnants of brief encounters, departures and arrivals, journeys to and fro, sad farewells and joyous reunions, illicit meetings and romantic liaisons; day-to-day experiences of people from all walks of life. The emotive events, as with the participants, now relegated to forgotten obscurity of the past.

Calum leaves this time-warped room to stand gazing out beyond the station. The sleek blue-grey iron railway tracks appear to be bending and quivering in the hot midday sun. This shimmering heatwave illusion summons an image of melancholic majestic power as the tracks carve a sweeping swathe for many miles ahead, inspiring Calum with a strange daydream longing. He frowns, grimly determined, lost in reverie, anticipating the mysteries and adventures of his own future travels, before snapping out of it, and turning back, he heads for home. His lone footsteps scrunch into the sharp grey granite chippings. All of a sudden, he's overwhelmed by maudlin sadness, as he traipses along, feeling like an alien orphan, bereft and alone, shipwrecked here on planet Earth.

CHAPTER
SEVENTEEN

Calum is woken during the night by loud angry voices, he runs to the lounge to see what all the fuss is about. Jim, obviously drunk, is standing in the centre of the room, ranting and raving. Broken ornaments litter the floor. A tearful Janet tries to hustle Calum back to his bedroom, but Jim is having none of it, shouting, "Leave the boy be, woman! Sit down, sit down, the pair of you."

"But it's three in the morning," Janet whines, "he needs his sleep."

Jim laughs loudly, "Haha, sleep! You can forget about sleep. It's about time you two showed me the respect I deserve. Me, a kind and gentle man, a man who provides food and shelter for you both. Am I not the best, the greatest? I tell you, I am the greatest provider..."

The drunken diatribe continues for several hours, until Jim falls asleep in his armchair, snoring loudly, with yet another empty whisky bottle at his side.

Calum is angry and sad for Janet, knowing how she so loved her little china figurines. "The cruel bastard, he's smashed up all your treasures, Mrs Brown, then kept us here while he praises himself like Cassius fucking Clay." Janet gasps, before scolding, "Calum Connor! How dare you use that kind of language here, in a house of God, what would the Lord think?"

"Well, I don't know about the Lord, but I know what I think. Come on Mrs B, wise up, why don't you? Don't turn this back on me, Jim's a wrong 'un, isn't he? With all due respect, you're deluded if you think any differently. I hate him for this... and for what he did to the dogs." He pauses, breathing hard, surprising himself with this release of pent-up anger. Janet bursts into tears. "He doesn't mean it, son. It's just the drink talking. Jim's a good man, really he is, when sober. He will have forgotten it tomorrow."

"So that makes it alright, does it? I won't forget it, never ever." Cursing as he heads for his room, turning back at the door. "Goodnight Mrs Brown, I must try and get some sleep, in what little is left of this dire night." Lingering in the hallway, he looks back to see Janet on her hands and knees, her body wracked by stifled sobs as she sweeps up the broken remnants of her life's memories with dustpan and brush. Calum is so furious he can't go back to sleep, tossing and turning the rest of the night, fuming at the injustice.

A few hours later, at breakfast, Janet presents him with more bad news. "The time has come to start your education, son. The summer holidays are nearly over and you must soon begin attending the local primary school. You are nine now and have missed a fair bit of schooling. But you are a bright lad and will soon catch up, I'm sure."

He looks at her with distaste, shaking his head in disbelief that she has conveniently chosen to ignore Jim's behaviour of last night. He dreads the claustrophobic confines of school, knowing little of importance can be learned from humans. "Really, must I Mrs Brown? I know all I need, I can assure you."

She chuckles, "Yes, you must, son. It is the law of the land, I'm afraid. Besides, you will enjoy meeting new friends."

"Friends!" He snorts. "Kids? Give me a break." Janet's stern look and the folded arms only reiterate her determined stance. He sighs resignedly, "OK, so when do I start?"

"One week from today. We need to get you a uniform beforehand, though." He groans with exasperation, cursing inwardly, 'Oh no! Not a fucking uniform as well, get me well and truly institutionalised, why don't you.'

CHAPTER
EIGHTEEN

One week later, on a sunny Monday morning, Janet introduces Calum to his first experience of England's education system; Thruxton Primary School. She leads him into the imposing Victorian brick building to join twenty-five other pupils sitting cross-legged on the green-and-black tiled floor. The headmistress, Mrs Pearman, stands stiffly to attention before her young congregation, flanked on two sides by her assistants, Mr Rogers and Miss Jolly.

"Goodbye son!" Janet calls to him. "Be sure to be a good boy now." Calum scowls and murmurs under his breath, "Second word is off!" He feels let down and deserted, waving her away dismissively. She smiles, feeling a warm glow, assuming he's waving her a fond farewell.

The headmistress instructs the assembled children. "We shall now pray. Repeat after me, the Lord's Prayer: 'Our father, who art in heaven, hallowed be thy name. Thy kingdom come...'". The children follow her lead, their naive young voices praising the Christian god. But not Calum. He dedicates his worship to Gaia, resisting the head-mistress's chosen deity, instead chanting softly, "The Great Spirit of Nature is my God," over and over. He recalls the day on the house-boat in Bristol, when the word god first came to his soul and he received Gaia's holy blessing. Now, as in that precious moment, he feels serenity and reaffirmation, knowing that Nature is all-powerful. The Great Spirit's energy suddenly comes through, sublimely trans-mitted on an instant truth vibration, "Whatever may be taught in this school of humans, always remember that it is only with the heart that one can see rightly. What is essential is invisible to the eye." Calum logs, processes and smiles.

Praying over, it's time for lessons to begin. The pupils are led to their respective classrooms. Feeling ill at ease with the teaching and refusing to take in any of the outdated hand-me-down knowledge, Calum switches off from the repetitive drone of Mr Rogers' voice, keeping his mantra going, murmuring to himself, "The Great Spirit of Nature is all, Gaia is my God," whilst fidgeting, rocking back and forth, trying to loosen the chair legs. He uses the metal tip of a fountain pen to inscribe his initials deep into the lid of the wooden desk. Sensing a presence, he looks up to see a ghostly human form shrouded in magenta mist appearing before him.

"I am Wounded Buffalo, a Native American brave. I visit you in my spirit form. I also went to the white man's schools. I learned to read from schoolbooks, newspapers and the Bible. But in time I found that these were not enough. Civilised people depend too much on man-made printed pages. I turn to the Great Spirit's book, which is the whole of creation. You can read a big part of that book if you study Nature. You know, if you take all your books, lay them out under the sun and let the snow and rain and insects work on them for a while, there will be nothing left. But the Great Spirit has provided you and me with an opportunity to study in Nature's University; the forests, the rivers, the mountains and the animals which include us."

Calum sighs in acceptance of this wisdom as the apparition fades away. He recalls Cat Woman Eleanor's philosophy, agreeing that all one needs is Nature, creation and truth. Natural sunlight suddenly floods in through the stained-glass windows of the former chapel, inspiring fantasy thoughts of flight and freedom. His wish is suddenly granted by the loud clanging of a brass hand bell.

"Playtime!" The teacher shouts over an urgent hubbub of scraping chairs and desks, as the children scramble to be first out of their enforced confinement. "Right you are, all pupils," Mr Rogers shouts over the din. "Single file, please!"

Calum hangs back, following as they pour out onto the playground. The freed interns are at once loud and boisterous, slotting easily into their territorial groups, everyone seemingly overjoyed to escape from the imposed discipline of the classroom. He wanders alone around the perimeter of the school, exploring amongst tangled blackthorn and gnarled old holly trees, finding a stark grey concrete moss- and ivy-covered Second World War air raid shelter hidden beneath the overgrown shrubbery, seemingly preserved by Nature as a precautionary shrine to the folly of war. The school boundary is fenced off with barbed wire, as if to deter pupil escape.

A massive horse chestnut tree takes pride of place at the centre of the adjacent village green. He wonders, 'How old is this magnificent tree?' Calum's train of thought is suddenly derailed by a group of noisy children pointing and chattering excitably. He makes for the centre of attention, where one child is crouching low, like a big fat bullfrog, in the centre of the playground. The obese boy is swiping away with a rusty old hammer. Unable to see clearly because of the cheering crowd, Calum, using jabbing elbows, and shoving violently, squeezes through to the front of the jabbering throng, where a small mouse zig-zags this way and that in frantic fear, running for its life, as the boy repeatedly attempts to deal the terrified creature a mortal hammer blow. Calum spots an opening, and, seizing the opportunity, he leaps instinctively between hunter and prey, catching the young mouse adeptly by the tail. The thwarted executioner lets out a delayed roar of surprised indignation, but Calum is already dodging the lumbering tormentor and evading the grasping hands of the frustrated crowd. Running full pelt to the fence, and with a quick flick of his wrist, he flings the pardoned mouse into the long grass of the village green. The frustrated kids shout and scream, enraged by this betrayal, even at their young age seemingly incensed by the denial of bloodlust. The hammer-wielding bully reaches Calum first, raising a pudgy fist and landing a stinging punch to his nose. Blood spurts over his new uniform. He grins at the bully and his disciples, showing no fear, staring them down. He does not let on he's hurt, his pain coming secondary to the exhilarating rush of realisation that he has been instrumental in saving one of Mother Nature's creatures.

The young hunters retreat, huddling in a circle, observing Calum warily. They mutter from behind their hands, pointing at him as they begin to shuffle away. The bell suddenly rings loudly, summoning them all back for lessons. The bully slinks off, looking down, scuffing his shoes nervously. He is unable to meet Calum's unwavering gaze, taking a sly glance back as he goes into class, shaken by this new kid's audacity.

"Thank you, my child," Gaia's voice carries on the cool breeze. Calum smiles, and bows to his almighty, "You are most welcome, Mother dearest..."

Over the next few months, Calum is ostracised by the majority of pupils at school. They are now extremely wary, but their hostile rejection means nothing to him; he has nothing in common with them. Seeing most of them as just preconditioned young abusers, dead inside little ghouls, cast in the mould, with sins of the father karma activated accordingly. But throughout the following weeks he does grudgingly accept some boys into his circle, bonding easily with classmates Leigh and Rod, who both live in Thruxton Village. He instinctively identifies them as innocent souls – harmless, with no dark side, devoid of violent tendencies and harbouring no cruel intent, as yet untainted by the material world.

Winter comes harsh and sudden in 1962, the worst England has endured for some two hundred years, or so say the meteorologists. Those same experts who failed to predict it occurring in the first instance. The big freeze is great fun, initially. The making of snowmen and snowball fights, and Calum goes sledging with Rod, with both nearly meeting a grisly end as they jump clear at high speed, just before their wooden sleds smash to pieces into the wrought-iron fencing at the foot of steep Kimpton Hill.

More snow falls quickly that weekend, continuing unabated for days, engulfing them all in misery. This means no school, which is a bonus, but it also means an enforced absence from his new pals. Even worse, though, is the drudgery of being trapped indoors with his faux parents. The humdrum monotony of life cooped up with the Browns drives him stir-crazy. He awakes each boring day to the nauseating soporific smell of the two 'Esso Blue' paraffin heaters, continuously burning and pumping out toxic fumes. The three of them huddle under coarse grey blankets in the lounge, with just the merest comfort of an old two-bar electric fire with its orange glow. It hums away in the background, throwing out just minimal heat, serving only to cruelly entice and then toast the occasional kamikaze moth. Rampant black fungal mould is rife, with the bubbling secretions seeping from the walls and ceiling, as if the dingy dreary place is undergoing some form of punitive exorcism, liberating festering spores to float into the warm atmosphere like a cosmic curse. This kismet directive, combined with the smell of dissected dead animals cooking at every mealtime, makes life unbearable for Calum. Gruesome mutilated body parts are lying around the kitchen like a mini slaughterhouse. An abhorrent assortment of chicken legs and wings, pork and lamb chops, offal, black blood pudding, liver, kidneys, tongue, anaemic octopus-like tripe innards and bloodied bones seem to be everywhere. Calum observes with disgust Jim and Janet's carnivorous consumption of karma: three times daily, for breakfast, lunch and dinner. He feels so glad that in the autumn he had had the foresight to squirrel away an assortment of nuts and dried forest fruit, hiding it in an old biscuit tin at the bottom of his bedroom wardrobe, before the weather got so bad. That was it though for protein, just nuts. The only other food available is cereal, bread and Janet's soggy overcooked vegetables.

Deep snow-drifts piling up outside, up to fourteen feet high in some places, make the surrounding roads and paths blocked and impassable. Calum is desperate to escape, to get away from the condensed carnage in the bungalow. So, after a few days of this suffocating confinement, as a last resort, he attempts walking across the tops of frozen hedgerows. This is really hard-going, and he covers only a short distance before giving up, exhausted and wracked with chill. Slowly retracing his steps, he curses Gaia for not aiding his escape.

There has been no further connection, not since his first day at school. Calum falls into a deep black depression…

The bleak winter days continue until the snow begins to thaw in March. Clearing quickly now, the big freeze has lasted nearly four months.

CHAPTER
NINETEEN

One year later, Calum, now ten, is told Thruxton Primary School is soon to close, the old building deemed unsuitable for modernisation. This closure is influenced by the new buzzword from the corridors of power, 'health and safety.' The pupils are to continue their education just half a mile away, at a new school being built in a field just above the village of Kimpton.

Calum is neither inspired nor motivated by this news. He detests school, any school, and is well aware he is just treading water in the humans' dismal hall of learning, enduring their brainwashing teaching methods under extreme duress. He's just biding his time though, waiting for the right opportunity to flee, praying that the Great Spirit will soon engineer the wherewithal for him to escape from the dreaded Brown household, and away from boring schooldays for ever.

The conventional form of teaching is totally foreign to him, so the location of the school is unimportant. The teachers had picked up on his reticence early on. Even after punishment by slipper and cane to backside and bare legs, Calum makes no effort to conform. Refusing to absorb and learn their soiled social history prevents him from suffering the indoctrination of immoral and unethical teaching. He is determined not to fall foul of man's repeated bad habits. The tutors have mostly given up on him, seeing him as a traitor and a bad influence on the other pupils. They want only devoted protégés to mould into their own egocentric image. Otherwise, what's the point? Only utter control and dominance over a pupil could massage some teachers' narcissism sufficiently, and thus promote their self-deluded illusion of mastery. Calum made sure he always fell well short of their expected criteria. His connection with and teaching from Gaia ensured that he was always one step ahead of the human game. Knowing the authentic cosmic truth codes of Nature as he does, he sees no need to remember anything else, no point in cramming one's mind full of inconsequential nonsense, no reason to lie, as there is only universal truth in the natural world. The retention of useless egocentric psycho-babble is thus eliminated. 'Live for the moment, obey the hidden laws of Nature, and in so doing free your mind and soul,' is his interpretation of spiritual enlightenment.

CHAPTER TWENTY

The newly built school is a pleasant surprise. The building is modern and spacious. Best of all, though, as far as Calum is concerned, the headmaster is a kindly soul, so there is to be no corporal punishment here. The playground occupies an elevated position with good views over the surrounding fields, which are used as gallops by renowned local race-horse trainer Toby Balding.

This sea change however, is just a brief respite. He soon reverts to being bored and disillusioned at school. Even though the teachers and staff here are mostly benign and benevolent he still finds it impossible to adapt to their unrelenting dogma, especially after experiencing Gaia's magical teaching.

Calum and his schoolmates meet at the local sportsfield each evening after school, playing football until dusk and beyond. This interaction with other children is a welcome distraction from the increasingly heavy vibe of spiritual obligation, and brings some much-needed light relief. He accepts these are the breaks for being a half-breed, part human, part feral, a spiritual duty – it's just how it is. Although consenting to this caveat, he finds it such hard-going at times, but then again, so fulfilling, to be involved so closely with Nature. It's a dilemma, especially as now he is older he also craves his hedonistic pleasure, and feels, 'One can only absorb so much purity. I am, after all, also a human.' Although instilled with, and acclimatised to, the Great Spirit of Nature's enlightening truth codes, he realises, 'I am not, and never will be, fully feral.' What he really wants is the best of both worlds, often wondering hopefully, 'Is that possible?'

Little has changed at home for Calum. Janet Brown still attends to his general daily welfare, but as with the carers previously, the fosterers provide only the essentials for his everyday survival. It is a ubiquitous human trait, he accepts, this lack of basic awareness and caring for one's own kind, reasoning, 'No matter, I'm just going with the flow anyway, ready to leave at the earliest opportunity.'

One day after school, Calum is invited to his schoolmate Leigh's house for his tea. His parents are a friendly, easy-going couple who live in a former servant's house in the grounds of the old Thruxton Manor house. They do their best to make Calum feel at ease, but despite the warm welcome he feels uncomfortable with the formal rigidity and expected etiquette required for social dining. Leigh's mother brings through a platter of fish paste and cucumber sandwiches as the boys recline on the large plush sofa. Calum is revolted to be served mashed up dead fish! And, horror of horrors, the bread has been liberally coated with his nausea-inducing nemesis... butter! He nibbles cautiously at the protruding crust, the only part of the sandwich untouched by dead creature or dairy product.

Leigh's mother, noticing his reluctance, urges him, "Come come, eat up now. You are a growing lad and need your nourishment." As she returns to the kitchen, Leigh asks, "Don't you like it?"

"M'mm, yes, lovely," he lies.

"Come carry the tea tray please, son," Leigh's mother calls.

"Coming, mother."

With Leigh gone, and his father absorbed in smoking his pipe and reading the newspaper, Calum seizes his opportunity and hurriedly stuffs the sandwiches deep down the back of the sofa, just before Leigh's mother returns with tea and cake. She takes away his empty plate. "My my, Calum, you were hungry after all. You've eaten the lot, good lad," she says, ruffling his hair affectionately, smiling, whilst lavishly buttering a fruit scone. "Now for your reward."

Calum, grimacing, anticipating where this is leading, interjects swiftly, "Oh no, not for me, thank you ma'am," refusing politely, tapping his stomach for effect. "I'm plumb full now."

"Are you sure?" She asks, holding the dripping delicacy close to his face, the butter slowly melting from the scone in the summer heat. Recoiling, pushing back into the sofa and smiling sickly, he replies adamantly, "Quite sure, thank you…"

Calum remains friends with Leigh, despite the disastrous dining experience, but is not expecting further invitations to high tea any time soon. He cringes with embarrassment when he recalls that dreadful day, wondering how long before the stench of rotting fish and butter would lead to the discovery of the decomposing stashed sandwiches.

CHAPTER
TWENTY-ONE

Calum sleeps well, and the next day is up early and raring to go. Creeping out of the bungalow, he heads for Thruxton Village, taking a short-cut through the old airfield. This former RAF base is a favourite haunt of the local youngsters, who would sneak in through gaps they had made with wire cutters in the ten-foot high fencing. This intended 'security barrier' snaked in a figure of eight around the three-and-a-quarter mile circumference of the Second World War aerodrome. Venturing there alone today, he wanders around, enjoying the solitude, casually exploring, before coming upon an old concrete water tank sunk deep into the ground, surrounded by a makeshift safety barrier of crudely welded scaffolding poles. Leaning against the steel support system, he peers over into the dirty grey water, where bloated corpses of dead rats and mice float on the surface amongst old car tyres, several sodden half-eaten birds, and most bizarrely, the partly-submerged skeleton of a dead apple tree, complete with its root system.

Calum is surprised to see many large great crested newts basking languidly in the sun on rotting planks of wood, while some swim lazily amongst cruising goldfish in the stagnant putrefying mass. Amazed at the amphibians' uncanny resemblance to miniature dinosaurs, he inches along slowly, intrigued, so absorbed in the moment that he fails to notice that the scaffolding drops to a lower level at one section. All of a sudden, he topples forwards as the safety barrier changes height abruptly. Falling hard against the lower rung of the scaffolding, taking the full jarring impact on his chest, arms flailing in mid air, he hangs over the edge, balancing briefly on the brink. Survival instinct pulls him back just in time, gasping, badly shaken, grasping just how close he has come to falling into this deep poisonous pit. Calum cannot swim, had never felt the inclination, ever since the day he had fallen into the sea from the gangplank of the houseboat in Bristol.

Trembling and breathing fast, shock quickly turns to anger, and shaking his fist at the heavens he screams at thin air, "Why did you not warn me of this danger, Great Spirit?!" Rubbing his sore ribs he moans, "You are supposed to be my protector."

A large black newt swims up from the bottom of the pit, clambering onto a floating piece of timber, before replying, "As I have often warned you, Calum, I cannot protect you during your physical life experience. Extreme caution is advised when in the company of humans."

"But I'm not anywhere near any fucking humans! This is all to do with your Nature experience, that's the truth of it it. Right! That's me done with you, Gaia," Calum shouts, temper rising, tears falling. "I will use my free will, use it to never rely on you again. I'll look after myself from now on. I hate you – hate you, and I will never speak to you again."

"So be it. As you wish, my child. It is only right that you do not rely on anyone. Your free-will decisions alone will determine your destiny."

"Don't you dare call me your child! I have no parents, you hear! None... no one... I am alone." The reality of his lonely existence suddenly hits home as he walks away, sobbing forlornly.

CHAPTER
TWENTY-TWO

Three months pass...

There has been no further interaction or contact with the Great Spirit, not since the altercation at the poisoned pond. So Calum stubbornly refuses to acknowledge any previous connection. When involuntarily he thinks of his previous bond with Mother Nature it seems more like a dream sequence. As time goes by he even begins to doubt if the connection between them had ever really been real. Lingering bitterness relegates the once divine ethereal presence to little more than a figment of his imagination. But deep down he misses the bond. Far more than his hurt pride will allow him to admit. Sure, he has his school friends, playing football, and the adolescent adventures. But there are also the lonely sad occasions, when housebound on a cold rainy day, whilst enduring another boring lesson at school, or cooped up of an evening with the foster parents. Disconsolate at being sat with them in their dingy living room, watching Janet click-clack clickety clacking her long needles as she knits old-fashioned shapeless clothes that no one will ever wear, while Jim dozes in a drunken stupor, snoring loudly, pipe hanging from his mouth, dead grey ash and burnt embers dropping onto his dirty grey vest.

Calum also misses Gaia in the early hours, when woken by the Browns' raised voices and cruel spiteful words, Janet's china and glass smashing, doors slamming. In such moments he endures a deep melancholic loneliness, which causes him to concede his stubborn stance – a softening of heart occurs and he calls to his spirit mother, silently, soulfully. Pining for her unconditional love and blessed insight into the wonders of Nature's hidden laws. Craving the cosmic interaction that once elevated his mortal soul to a spiritual paradise, but she does not answer his call.

CHAPTER
TWENTY-THREE

Calum turns eleven and is due to move on from primary school to the Andover Secondary Modern Boys' School. An educational elevation he anticipates with some trepidation. The mixed blessing of acute tonsillitis means his date with destiny is put on hold... but the day he has been dreading finally arrives. Monday, December 7th, 1968. It's a cold frosty morning. Janet wakes him early, preparing him for the big day with a bowl of hot porridge and a mug of warm tea, before ensuring he is wrapped up well against the wintry day. Flinching irritably at her hugs and fussing, and sneering at her good luck wishes, he leaves the bungalow, setting out on the half-mile trek to get the bus. His shoes make brief crunching imprints in the frozen ground before a bitter wind blows in more snow to swiftly cover his tracks. He walks slowly, resignedly, with a heavy heart – cold hands deep in pockets, the hood of his duffle coat toggled tight. Calum feels a deep longing for freedom as he trudges along. Leaving the bungalow for this new school feels like jumping from the frying pan into the fire.

Rounding a bend, just before the bus stop, he's suddenly startled by a loud creaking high up in an aged timber barn to his right. The rotting wooden shutters of a hayloft window struggle against the decaying seal of time, before being thrown open to frame the grizzled profile of a haggard-looking man of the road. He wears a rumpled, dark-brown suede cowboy hat studded with old military badges,. A varied assortment of Second World War campaign medals and many dusty cobwebs liberally festoon his grey ex-military trench coat. Resembling a beaten and battered Punch and Judy character, his weather-beaten face bears testimony to the hard-living existence of a roaming travelling man.

Calum stares open-mouthed as the bedraggled stranger yawns wide and long, before nicotine-stained fingers nimbly hand roll his first cigarette of the day. "Hello there me chavvy, Tinker's the name, cold morn' to be sure." He draws deeply on the cigarette, before blowing warm smoke into his calloused cupped hands.

"Morning sir."

"Be you off to school, son?"

"Yeah, 'fraid so mister, worse luck... do you live in that old barn?"

"Sure do, lad, and many other such places on me travels about the English countryside."

"Isn't it too cold, though?" Calum's feeling sorry for this Tinker man. "Not so bad son, the hay and straw provide warmth enough," he smiles friendly, exposing four tobacco-stained teeth, all that remain of his original dental set, "but the rats and mice can be a mite tiresome at times."

A deep droning diesel engine forewarns the imminent arrival of the smoky old school coach. Calum is intrigued by this strange-looking man, inwardly cursing the untimely interruption. 'This is way more interesting than school, this real-life stuff.'

"Gotta go now, Tinker, looks like my ride's here, you gonna be around tomorrow?"

"Yea chavvy, to be sure I will," he assures, taking a long slug from a cheap bottle of wine, before raising it aloft and saluting, "Slainte!"

"What does Slainte mean, Tinker?"

"Why, cheers of course... cheers! To your good health, my boy."

Calum laughs, "Same as, friend, same as. See you later."

Running the last fifty yards to the pickup point, he arrives just as the coach skids to a halt at the junction with Dauntsey Lane and the A303 main road. The driver Harry works for Bob Razey (AKA 'Crazy Razey' by the schoolkids), he gets out of the driver's seat and pulls the double doors manually inward. He is in his early sixties but looks older. A short, balding, pot-bellied figure with flyaway wispy ginger hair. His twitchy rheumy eyes are framed by battered horn-rimmed spectacles, the broken frames held together by peeling strips of clear sticky tape.

Razey's, of Amport and District, is Bob's own small bus company, based in a yard near Thruxton Village. His four beaten-up old coaches cover school runs for the local rural villages around Andover, and also provide a twice-daily public return run to the town. The quartet of Bedford Duplos, (liveried in maroon and accessorised with wide silver go-faster arrowed stripes) bear many dents and scrapes, due mostly to the boss man's erratic driving and excessive speeding, hence his nickname, 'Crazy Razey.'

"Do me a favour, son," Harry calls to Calum, "before you get on," he points across the road to an old green railway carriage which has been converted into 'Greens Grocers', a makeshift village store set on the wide grass verge and leaning alarmingly, as if about to collapse. "Go over and fetch them two lazy buggers outta the shop, I ain't got all bleedin' day y'know."

Two lads, both a little older than Calum, emerge from the ramshackle shop, dawdling nonchalantly and showing indulgent disregard for the waiting school transport. Scoffing sherbet dabs and penny chews from crumpled white sweet bags, they amble lazily, not a care in the world, contemptuously dismissive of deadlines. A given of the young, this scathing dismissal of time, that dogged stalker of all but the reaper.

Calum crosses the road to greet them. "Hi'ya lads, look, bus driver says he wants you both on board, soon as like."

The tall blonde lad laughs. "Fuck that old fool."

His shorter slightly built pal introduces himself. "Hi matey, I'm Stevie, and this 'ere's me mucker Pete. I lives in Fairways, just down the road. Where'd you live?"

"Name's Calum," he turns and points, "Meadowbank... a bungalow... just up the lane aways."

Stevie offers him a damp fruit salad sweet. Most everything bought from Mrs Green's store had the dampness about it to some degree, condemning all perishable items to a very short shelf life.

"That's my gaff, in there," Pete gestures to a hardboard sign, tied with orange baling twine to a rusting five-bar gate. The scrawled white painted capitals proclaiming:

DAUNTSEY CARAVAN SITE.

Harry leans out of the driver's window. "Come on you lazy buggers, I ain't got time for all these bleedin' pleasantries. We've not got all bloody day you know. Let's get this show on the road, boys."

Pete laughs. "All right, keep yer friggin' hair on mate, what you've got left of it." The boys titter and giggle as they slowly climb aboard the coach, while Harry curses and frets. "Like a fucking old woman," Pete observes scornfully, as they run to the back of the coach, throwing and kicking their torn and battered satchels carelessly before them.

The kids from Dauntsey Lane are always first to be collected, and so get to sit in the coveted elevated rear seats. Harry revs the tired, worn engine, causing the high-mileage old motor to chuck out huge dirty black clouds of carcinogenic diesel smoke. Crunching the long gear stick into first, swiftly changing up through the gears, barely giving the boys time to take their seats, he cajoles the beaten-up bus into a jerky dance along the road.

Harry suffers from a nervous affliction that causes him to convulse involuntarily every few minutes, triggering his body to spasm in a macabre dance like some gruesome deformed marionette. Most of the locals are amazed that he is still allowed to drive a school passenger coach. Romantic rumour had it that Harry's condition was caused by shrapnel wounds inflicted at Monte Cassino during the Second World War. Those of a more cynical nature believed it was more likely due to the combination of his generous daily ingestion of gin and prescribed medication.

The coach continues to rattle along for a few minutes, before stopping at the Fairways council estate to collect more pupils. Hushed whispering and shrill wolf whistling erupts from the lads as they spy the lithe long legs of a pretty blonde girl walking along the aisle. "Cor! Won't you look at Valerie in that mini-skirt," Pete sighs dreamily, putting an arm around Calum's shoulder. "Do y'know, my mate, I sees her every day on this damn bus, but I never gets tired of lookin' at them gorgeous pins."

Valerie moves regally to her seat, haughtily dismissive of the testosterone-enraged teenage voyeurs ogling her every move. Calum catches his breath, recognising her... it's the sexy blonde temptress he'd seen from the railway bridge. A strange yearning for this seem-ingly unobtainable girl still nags at him. She is chaperoned today by a mean-looking lad carrying her bags and books. He's scowling a 'keep away' warning to the pack of young sexual predators waiting to pounce.

"Is that her boyfriend?" Calum asks. Stevie snorts. "Nah, but he tries it on with her nonstop does Jan. The nutter wishes he could get in her knickers. The slimy dope's only her slave though, like some creepy, grovelling minion... pathetic, really."

Calum thinks he detects more than a hint of jealous envy from Stevie so winds him up a bit more. "Can't blame him man, wow! She's something else, that one."

"Don't fucking get him nowhere though!" Stevie's seething teenage angst infects his words with vitriolic hate towards bodyguard Jan. "She's only using the poor sucker."

"Yeah, cos she's saving herself for me," Pete laughs, serenading Stevie with a painful rendition of the Monkees' hit pop song, "Valleri, oh Valleri."

"Yeah, right, as if, you deluded fucking wanker!" Stevie screams, launching himself at Pete. The pair roll around on the floor, lashing out with flailing fists, throwing punches and insults while the coach trundles on, the unrequited lust of these juvenile males transforming them instantly from friends into antagonistic foes.

Pete struggles to his feet, breathing heavily, placing one large foot firmly on Stevie's chest, casually pinning him to the floor, before turning to Calum. "See what I have to put up with, mate?"

He laughs. "What class are you in at school, Pete?"

"Won't be in yours pal, I started last year," he replies, slurping noisily on a yellow cardboard sherbet wrap, before slowly releasing the pressure on the squirming Stevie. "Best be careful on your first day, though. Whatever you do, don't go near the bogs," Stevie warns, brushing himself down and adjusting his clothes, whilst glaring surly in defeat at Pete. "Why... what happens in the bogs?" Calum tries to control the anxious tremble in his voice. "Any new kids, they get it, from the prefects and their cronies, the fourth years."

Instinctive apprehension gushes up from the pit of his stomach. "How do you mean Stevie... get it?"

"It ain't nice pal... ooh no, not nice... not nice at all..." Stevie pauses for effect, relishing this chance to get his own back, Calum's laughing at him over Valerie still fresh and raw. "First they all goes for a crap, or a piss, then they push the newbies' heads down the toilet bowl, and flush 'em for ages, until the poor buggers are nearly drowning in sewage."

"Yeah, and it carries on, that and the bullyin', for the rest of term," Pete adds ominously, "or at least until the poxy prefect gets bored."

Calum shrinks back in his seat, shaken up by these revelations, vowing to do his utmost to get the hell out of this school.

The bus careers on, stopping to pick up more kids from the local villages of Thruxton, East Cholderton, Amport, Monxton and Abbotts Ann, collecting the last pupils from a trio of interlinked villages called the Clatfords. Meanwhile a riotous mix of fear, excitement and fun ensues, with some kids scrapping amongst themselves, while others stand on their seats throwing classroom textbooks and pencil rubbers at each other. During the chaos Pete sneakily hides some homemade vile-smelling test-tube stink bombs in the gaps between the seats. Paper planes made from homework pages are hurled at driver Harry as he steers his old jalopy erratically along the narrow country roads, seemingly unconcerned by the chaotic high jinks. He chuckles acceptingly of his lot, "Hahaha, boys will be boys... boys will be boys."

CHAPTER
TWENTY-FOUR

The coach arrives in Andover, slowing at the top of London Road, before joining a long queue of other buses and coaches, all coming to a halt outside of the Secondary Boys' School gates. Directly opposite, across the road, is the Secondary Girls' School. The older boys jostle and shove, desperate to be first off the bus to cat call and wolf whistle at the female pupils, while the younger kids traipse off in trepidation, entering the school grounds apprehensively with heads bowed, cowering, waiting for the inevitable bullying to start. Their demeanour reminds Calum of the damaged, frightened children in the Bristol care home. 'Cowed, like lambs, innocents to the slaughter.'

To the left side of the drop-off point, a long straight tarmac driveway leads to the old brick-built boys' school. Alongside the large square concrete playground stands a lean-to green corrugated tin-roofed bicycle shed, where several prefects are enjoying a sneaky fag break. Beyond the school grounds is 'Ladies' Walk', a two-and-a-half-mile-long footpath circling the school boundary. A favoured spot, historically, for those humans with suicidal tendencies to hang or throw themselves from the old iron bridge and down on to Micheldever Road below. This grim overpass was erected in 1785. Legend had it that the ghost of a young female horse thief could be seen here on occasion. She, and the stolen horse, had jumped from the bridge in the 1800s after being pursued by angry townsfolk, with both perishing in the fall.

Crowds of chattering boys pour from the long line of school transport, creating a noisy bustling throng as they make their way into school. Calum follows cautiously, staying up close to Pete and Stevie. "Gotta go now buddy," Stevie slaps him on the back. "Let's try 'n meet up at break time, if not, then how about tonight, after school?"

"Yeah, sure thing, guys." Calum feels reassured to have made these new pals, but self-preservation is kicking in, alert and on his guard now, as he attempts to integrate amongst the milling crowd. Cunningly weaving in and out of range, he dodges the attentions of the older kids who seem to be stalking in packs, singling out and separating their younger and weaker victims from the crowded playground, like hunters scenting blood, fixated on the anticipated pleasure of their bloodlust, seemingly driven by an all-consuming desire to cause pain and punishment to anyone younger or weaker than them.

Calum sees two pupils punched violently in the face and kicked hard in the shins, for no apparent reason other than they are new boys, and easy prey. One has his spectacles ripped from his face before one of the prefects stamps them to bits in the grit-covered playground. The terrified boy, sobbing, stumbles blindly amongst his elders. The senior pupils push and pull him, shoving him from one to the other like a ravaged rag doll. Unable to just stand by and watch, Calum runs to help, shouting at the abusers, "Leave him be! He's done nothing to you."

The nearest tormentor, a prefect, hesitates, momentarily surprised by the outright nerve of a lowly sprog's intervention... until a few slow seconds later, the thug's sluggish Neanderthal thought process reacts violently to this impudent affront, and he punches Calum hard in the face.

Although hurting sorely, akin to some years previously with the primary school bully, he refuses to show pain, staring down his attacker, swearing from this day forth he will never allow himself to be intimidated by sadistic predators such as these. A loud shrill whistle breaks the tense stalemate, bringing a temporary halt to the persecution of the first-term pupils. Mr Braun, the deputy headmaster, emerges from a corridor. A tall man, dressed in a dark brown suit, he fiddles nervously with his greying brush of moustache whilst constantly nudging slipping spectacles back up on to the brow of his nose. He runs his fingers through slicked-back Brylcreemed grey hair before holding a loud hailer to his mouth. He stammers self-consciously, "R...ri...ri...right...y...y...you are. All n...nn...new pupils l...l...ll...line up...f..f..f..fall in... single f..ff..ile to the left. All other boys f...fa...fall into line and lead on...to ass...ass...assembly."

The older boys sort themselves into the relevant order, walking in formation to the assembly hall.

"Righto, all new pupils continue in s...s...single file, f...f...follow on, then take your s...s...s...seats at the r...r...rear of the hall."

"S...sss...ssh...shut the fuck up," mimics Calum under his breath.

Most kids obediently follow the deputy head's stuttering orders. Those bolder, like Calum, cheekily imitate his faltering speech impediment. But the majority are already beaten into submissive servitude by this frightening first-term experience, with many appearing as if in mortal fear of their lives. A few hardy characters remain cocky and arrogant, though. Calum remains defiant in the face of this adversity, pledging to treat the enforced tutoring as a challenge, fiercely determined to use every trick in the book to escape from his captors. Whatever it takes, he aims to get out of this hell-hole in one piece.

The boys take their seats in the Great Hall, which also serves as the dining room. A low muted murmuring of dissent echoes throughout the building, just audible above the impatient scuffling and scraping of chairs. The boys are always made to wait longer than is necessary for the arrival of the headmaster and his deputies.

"Good to make them wait, instils patience and discipline, provides moral fibre, fortitude, don't you know," was the oft-repeated mantra of Mr Grantham, the headmaster. A tall thin man, with a long horse-like face and greying ginger hair, which although his own, resembles an ill-fitting toupee. He always seemed to be wearing the same pale grey-green suit with its ingrained worn sheen, and grey tie, colour coordinating seamlessly with his deathly facial pallor.

"Hush now! Hush, I say," the urgent voice of a senior prefect admonishes the chattering pupils, his reverential tone indicating that someone of great importance has entered the room. "All rise now for your headmaster."

The noisy chit-chat dwindles to silence as Mr Grantham climbs the steps to the stage. Following subserviently are the deputy head, Mr Braun, and Mr Coezens, the paunchy South African religious instruction teacher. The assembled boys all stand, with heads slightly bowed, while the headmaster undertakes the solemn formality of sitting for the Lord's and several other assorted prayers, before he and his dutiful assistants take their seats at the long Formica tables always used for morning assembly. After this traditional initiation the pupils are led from the hall by prefects, before making their way to the relevant classrooms to begin lessons.

Calum's allocated form class is designated as 4D – D for dunce – as mockingly branded by those in class A, B or C. He is one of twenty other kids who are deemed academically sub-standard and soon bonds with several other boys, recognising them as kindred spirits who also harbour similar rebellious intentions. These fellow young outlaws are nicknamed Gypsy Cleeve, Big Pete Foyle, Greaser Eddie and Gringo Tee. Although all from different backgrounds, they share the same hatred of secondary school and authority in any form, and so gel seamlessly as one mutinous comrade in arms group. Their form teacher is Mr Ellison. Aged fifty-seven, he is a short, squat man, whose receding greasy dark hair and blazer collar is always liberally speckled with dandruff. He is intolerant of anyone slow to learn, punishing severely those who could not, or would not, catch on swiftly enough for him. One of his favourite methods of punishment was to creep up behind the unsuspecting victim before landing a hefty whack on the back of the head with a heavy atlas. If enraged enough, he had even been known to hit some unfortunate boys about the body with a broken chair leg. Unsurprisingly, Ellison was despised by most of his class. "A right sneaky little bastard," as Cleeve succinctly described him.

Calum suffers Mathematics and English lessons on this first morning. Maths holds no interest for him, although he is aware through the teachings of Gaia that the power of numbers is a very real phenomenon throughout the universe, allowing, 'Now, if they taught numerology here, instead of boring multiplication tables, well, that would be a different story.' He goes through the motions of participating in the humans' foolish behaviour of adding and subtracting numbers but spends most of the lesson wishing away the time, fantasising, vividly daydreaming of a magical forest wilderness, Valerie's long slim legs and exciting football games with his pals. Several of these friends, including Leigh, having passed the qualifying exams, had been accepted at the posh grammar school on the other side of town. After what seems like an eternity, his first tutorial ends. Break time is announced by a loud electric bell. He has retained nothing of the mathematics lesson, finding the whole hour's experience mind-bogglingly tedious and utterly pointless.

Calum makes his way cautiously to the main playground, hanging back, staying on the fringes, keeping himself to himself, until the shrill screaming of two new boys grabs his attention. A pair of prefects are brutally twisting and pinching the youngsters' ears, causing them to squeal and squirm in pain. Eventually the bullies set the terrified pair free to run a gauntlet of fear to the playground steps, dashing for the dubious safety of the school corridors. The prefects chase them down. Both hunters take a set of old pub darts from the inside pockets of their jackets, closing in, flanking their prey, taking aim, and letting fly with the weapons just before the pupils can reach sanctuary. The darts are thrown with great force into the boys' legs and buttocks. Screeching, they writhe on the floor, twisting their bodies back and forth, reaching out with clawing hands, desperately trying to extract the darts. The prefects laugh loudly, kicking both kids hard in the ribs for good measure, before moving on in search of more sport.

Calum keeps well away from the toilet blocks, relieving himself when the need arises behind some tall shrubs at the rear of the old timber-built classrooms. He witnesses first-hand the fate of any first termers foolish enough to venture in to the 'bogs'. These unfortunates are pushed headfirst in to the filthy lavatories and flushed repeatedly, staggering out from the toilet block, emerging wet and bedraggled, covered in urine and faeces, coughing and spluttering, and gasping for breath.

After enduring further futile lessons, the lunch bell rings. Calum joins a long queue for his first secondary school meal, following the other pupils single-file to the white uniformed dinner ladies, who ladle out the 'dish of the day'. This culinary delight consists of a dollop of overcooked white cabbage, a piece of gristly mutton, some lumpy anaemic-looking mashed potato and tepid grey gravy. For pudding there is stodgy semolina, with a teaspoon of cheap watery jam. Calum eats nothing.

Lessons for the remainder of this first day are woodwork, metalwork and biology. The deputy head takes biology and seems to find great pleasure in teaching the class how to experiment on a dead frog. Calum grits his teeth and closes his eyes as Mr Braun slices open the creature, before explaining in great detail the workings of muscles, sinews and ligaments in relation to the frog's movement when alive. Calum cannot see the point of this depravity, and is of the view that it would surely be more informative, and certainly more beneficial for the pupils, and the poor frog, to have observed the animal active and alive.

Mr Braun notices him with head down and eyes shut, and booms, "You, boy!" "Are we keeping you up? Evidently, as you are showing little or no interest in this lesson."

Calum looks up and snarls, "You've got that right, mister! Karma will have you good and proper for what you've just done to one of the Great Spirit's offspring, be warned, the curse is on you now."

Mr Braun hesitates, momentarily taken aback by this blatant insubordination. "Why... you... you insolent brat! How dare you speak to me like that... get out of my classroom this instant." Rushing over, he grabs Calum by the ear and marches him outside. "You can stay out for the rest of this period. Then you will go to the headmaster."

After standing in the chilly corridor for some time, Calum spots the tall gaunt figure of Mr Grantham, some way off, talking to a prefect.

Calum thinks the headmaster resembles a suited and booted version of the grim reaper. He's well aware that if the head comes his way he will most likely be hauled to his office for a painful dose of the birch cane. So he leaves the scene quickly, heading up the stairs that lead to the art room, where he pauses, hearing a loud angry voice on the next level. He creeps on... step by step... until he is able to peer around the corner at the top of the stairway... Calum gasps, shocked to see the religious instructor viciously beating a first year pupil. A box of broken eggs are scattered over the floor. Mr Coezens has hold of the boy by his coat lapels and is banging his head repeatedly against the concrete wall, shouting, "I'll teach you to bring eggs into this school to throw at other pupils."

Suddenly the boy slumps forwards. The teacher stops his attack, letting the boy drop heavily to the floor before looking around furtively, realising he has gone too far. When certain no one is around he lifts the youngster up by his hair and throws him sideways down the steel stairway, before casually jogging back to his classroom.

Calum runs to the semi-conscious victim. He looks in a bad way, moaning and groaning, his eyes – although half-open – have a glazed vacant look. Shaken by this callous act, he bounds back down the stairs, snatches up the red metal fire extinguisher and smashes it into the glass fire alarm, before running back to his place of detention outside the biology classroom. Calum's hoping the loud ring tone will bring someone to the injured boy's aid. Seconds later, pandemonium ensues, with teachers and prefects dashing back and forth, all checking for a non-existent fire. No one pays any heed to Calum in the commotion, and he is caught up in the mass exodus as first the biology class, and then the rest of school, is evacuated. It's three forty-five. The large circular electric 'home time' bell in the corridor sounds a shrill reprieve, ending an eventful first day at Andover Secondary School. His punishment date with the head is briefly forgotten, or at least, for him, fortunately postponed. "Good timing or what!" He says aloud, expelling a long shuddering breath, an overwhelming rush of relief coursing through him, culminating in joyous euphoria at his survival and impending freedom. He likens it to being pardoned unexpectedly from purgatory or being woken from some terrible nightmare to find all is well, and you are tucked up safe and sound in bed.

Calum suddenly feels guilty, so preoccupied with his own escape he'd temporarily forgotten about the poor lad thrown down the stairs. But although extremely concerned for the injured boy, he knows it's every man for himself in this hellish place. Surviving just this first day has taken all his feral nous. He runs fast along the school driveway before bounding breathlessly up the aluminium steps of the coach. Pete and Stevie, already ensconced in the rear seats, beckon him over. Pete's grinning. "You lived to tell the tale today then, mate."

"Oh yeah, no problemo guys," Calum replies, with much false bravado, "those buggers don't frighten me none."

"Good on yer mate," Stevie slaps him on the back, "you comin' out after tea then?"

"Yeah, sure thing, where you wanna meet, guys?"

"See you at the field near the old barn, opposite the bus stop… say half five?"

"You got it."

CHAPTER
TWENTY-FIVE

Calum is greeted warmly by Janet upon his return from school. "How was it then, son? Did you enjoy your first day?" He throws his satchel to the floor, snorting derisorily, "Enjoy it?! You must be joking, Mrs Brown. I hated every single goddamn minute of it." She cringes at the perceived profanity, "Calum! Really." He holds out his hands, looking at her blankly, demanding, "What?" Janet is grim-faced. "You've taken the Lord's name in vain, that's what, son."

"Oh come on! Give me a break Mrs B, it's just a word, nothing personal meant."

"Well, never mind," says Jim, looking up from his newspaper, "I'm sure you'll get used to secondary school in time. We all have to go through it you know. Now, in my day–"

"Sorry to butt in, I'm sure," Calum interrupts, "but this is my day now, mister, not yours, and I can tell you categorically that I'm never going back to that godforsaken place." Janet holds her hands over her ears, groaning at his repeated use of the G word. He looks at her with loathing, despising her indoctrinated idealism, and shouts out, "There is no Lord saviour gonna save us all, get fucking real missus! Here's me been ducking and diving, swerving hellfire at school, just to survive, and all you care about is your make-believe god?" On immediate reflection he almost laughs at the absurdity of his argument. 'Of course she is going to take God's side over mine.'

"Right, that's it lad, I've had enough of your rude insolence," Jim splutters, ash spilling from his pipe as he staggers up from his armchair.

"You are intentionally upsetting Janet. Get to your room this instant. There will be no dinner for you until you apologise for that outburst. After all we've done for you, you ungrateful wretch."

Calum contemplates aiming a karate kick at Jim's big fat gut, but reluctantly he resists the desire and screams, "Done for me?! Thats a fucking laugh, done me in, more like, I surely would be fucked if I were to follow your preconditioned dogma." He storms to his bedroom, festering in anger, feeling utter distaste and contempt towards his foster parents, 'After all, was it not they who had me banished to that dismal hall of learning?' He would never forgive them for that.

Jim is shaking with anger, Janet hurries to comfort him. "Now, now, calm down dear. Don't take on so. You will only set off your ulcer again. Sit yourself down and I'll get you a nice cup of tea."

Calum flops down on his bed, seething with anger and frustration. Janet enters the room a little while later. "Now see here son, Mr Brown has done a lot for you. It's unfair of you to upset him so, and the profanities spewing from your mouth, it's like you are suddenly possessed by the devil." She looks to the heavens and mutters, "Dear Lord, please save this innocent child, he knows not what he is saying."

Calum grits his teeth and stares at the ceiling, not interested in her opinions or her fairytale religion, instead focusing telepathic intent on the cracked swirling plaster above, aiming to bring the whole lot crashing down by mind power alone. He desists from his demonic deliberations, and tries to explain, "You don't get it, do you? I'm the one who's upset, Mrs Brown. I can't stand that school. Kids get seriously hurt there. It's dangerous. That's the bottom line."

She smiles, "Oh come, come, now, I'm sure it's not as bad as all that. We all have to go to some school or other. It's the law of the land. We have no other choice, lad."

He sits up, imploring, "But why can't I learn at home? Like I did before, on the house-boat?" She sits on the edge of the bed and takes his hand. "Hush now, that's not an option, I'm afraid." He pulls away abruptly from her touch as if he's been electrocuted. "But why not?" She sighs. "The cost for one thing, son. Home tutoring is expensive, and besides, the results of your past teaching were not exactly impressive, were they?" Calum takes umbrage at this. "On the contrary, Mrs Brown, the teachings of my real mother, the Great Spirit of Nature, are always impressive. For instance, don't you see how Gaia is always working seamlessly in perfect balance and harmony whilst totally connected with the cosmos, with all her species co-existing in universal truth, without greed or material goals, no coveting of each other's partners or property, all co-existence altruistically achieved and devoid of ego – is that not fucking impressive enough for you, Mrs Brown?!" She gets to her feet and holds onto the doorframe, swaying unsteadily, as if in sudden receipt of great shock. "My dear god, Calum! Your language is atrocious and your cruel tone uncalled for. Whatever's come over you, I don't know what you're going on about. What is all this ridiculous talk of spirits anyway? Its against God's will, it's… it's… depraved.'

He laughs. "You are off your fucking rocker, Mrs B. Nature is pure and unsullied. Look through your blood-tainted history books, England and religion… look at what they did in the crusades, for example. Or how they treated the innocent pagans… Well? It's hardly saintly, is it?"

"I will hear no more of this blasphemy, Calum, you must attend school. That's my last word on the subject. Now please go and apologise to Jim, then come for your tea."

Cursing under his breath, "for fuck's sake", he rises reluctantly from the bed, shoulders slumped in miserable acceptance as he follows Janet to the lounge. So desperate to get out tonight, and suddenly conscious of the possibility of missing out on the proposed meeting with his new pals, he's feeling it may be wise to eat a little humble pie at this moment, bracing himself, as this so goes against the grain, bowing his head slightly in mock subservience, before reluctantly apologising. "I'm very sorry for my outburst earlier, Mr Brown."

Jim glances up sharply above his spectacles. "Harrumph… well… yes… I should jolly well think so. Now sit down at the table and eat your tea before it gets cold. I'll hear no more ridiculous moaning from you about school. Do you hear?"

"Yes, Mr Brown," he replies sullenly, then whispers under his breath, "gimme a fucking sick bucket," as he turns away and imitates two fingers down his throat. He eats quickly, asking hopefully, "Can I go play with my new friends from school, Pete and Stevie... please?" The Browns look at each other. Jim is non-committal, so Janet replies, "Yes, I suppose so... for one hour only tonight though, son."

Calum smacks his fist into his palm, whispering, "result" under his breath, leaving the house quickly before they have a chance to change their minds. The cool breeze feels fresh and invigorating as he runs to the rendezvous point, arriving before his friends, and finding the tinker man leaning over the handlebars of an old-fashioned pushbike, with sparks flying out like a mini meteor shower as he sharpens a big carving knife on the hand-operated grindstone fixed to the front of the bicycle.

He stops when he sees Calum. "Hi'ya there lad, how you doin?"

"Fine, Tinker, just fine," he replies, pointing to the red-hot grindstone. "What's with the firework display?" Tinker laughs. "This is how I earns me livin', chavvy, travellin' round the country sharpenin' allsorts, knives, tools, scissors, all 'n sundry really."

"What's your real name? Never heard of anyone called Tinker before." Taking a break from his work, he deftly rolls a cigarette one-handed, before answering, "No, it ain't me real moniker." Pulling a half-bottle of whisky from his jacket pocket, he takes a long swig. "Me birth name's Thomas Henry Green," adding proudly, "I'm a scouser, me."

"What's a scouser?"

"Liverpudlian... means I hails from Liverpool... the Scottie Road, born and bred. I was a serviceman previous... Royal Navy."

"Do you not have any family then, Tinker?"

He lights his cigarette, drawing deeply, gazing into the distance. Calum thinks he sees tears in his eyes. "Yes lad, I had family, me dear wife Jeannie... and... and... a daughter... Annie... bonny wee lass so she was."

"Where are they now then, Tinker? Why aren't you with them?" He takes a long slug of whisky before continuing. "I had just turned twenny-five... and was at sea, Navy, when I received the news... the awful, awful news... that...that... me wife... and little girl... just turned three... just a wee babby... bless her cotton socks... both killed outright... by a runaway lorry... in Liverpool city centre." Calum feels terrible. "Oh my god! Tinker! I'm so sorry... I wouldn't have asked if I had—"

"No, my chavvy, it's about time I told someone." He waves away the apology. "It don't do a man no good, to keep this bottled up inside, festerin' away like I has all these live long years... After the funerals, I took heavily to drink, in an attempt... I s'pose, lookin' back now with hindsight... to numb the terrible grief I felt. I left Liverpool depressed and stony broke, vowing never to return. I rode out of the city, on me old butcher's treader," he points to his bicycle, "I fitted that sharpening stone on her, and ever since then I've travelled the length 'n breadth of the country, callin' on all manner of folk – the housewife, the gardener, even them high-falutin' Lords and Ladies – just earnin' me livin' by sharpenin' their utensils 'n suchlike."

"How do you get by without any possessions though Tinker?"

"All I owns, just the basics, are strapped to me bike, behind the saddle there, in that leather tool bag, a man of the road don't need many trinkets and belongins. Travel light, sleep at night, that's me motto, son. See that rolled up bivouac, fixed underneath the bike frame, that's me summertime home, me tent fer when I camps in the fields. When it turns cold, I kips in the barns," he turns, gesturing grandly to his latest des res, "like this 'un."

"What do you do for food Tinker?"

He points a finger, "Dik that old fryin' pan, 'angin' from the 'andlebars, well, I makes me self a little fire, and then bobs yer uncle, I cooks all me scran in that pan, me fried potatoes, bacon, sausages, eggs, everythin'."

Calum likes this Tinker man and thinks of warning him about the karma involved with eating meat, but keeps his counsel as he spots his schoolmates walking towards him in the distance, four more than he was expecting. "My pals have arrived, best I go meet them, maybe see you again, Tinker?"

"Yeah, go and 'ave some fun lad, while yer still a young'un. I'm off to the pub fer a pint, me, afore I gets me 'ead down." He cycles away as the boys saunter up.

Pete introduces everyone. "Lads, this 'ere reprobate is Calum, our new mucker. Calum, meet Keith." A tall black boy steps forwards and shakes hands. "And this is the one and only Mickey." This thin, scruffy young man glares daggers at everyone and doesn't offer his hand. A contemptuous fixed sneer highlights the absence of his upper front teeth, the rest of his swiftly decaying dental set remaining only on borrowed time. Mickey's long angular face is pockmarked by severe weeping acne. Greasy lank black hair hangs matted to his shoulders. He's only nineteen, but looking burnt-out older, with dull dark eyes and a sunken hollow of a chest.

Mickey's sharp angular features remind Calum of the Beano comic's Victorian villain, Janus Stark. There is a strong smell of oil and petrol about him. His Popeye-like muscular forearms and large hands seem in peculiar contrast to the rest of his puny body. This queer physical disparity is caused by the repetetive working out of his hands, wrists and forearms, in the repair and renovation of anything mechanical, whatever he could lay his hands on. Mickey was especially fond of restoring old motorbikes, scooters, mopeds and pushbikes, into some semblance of working order.

A tall, slim boy, with long blonde hair, raises his hand. "Hi, I'm Paul."

"And last, but not least, is our old mate Rod," Pete continues, "who I believe you've already had the pleasure of meeting."

"Mmm... not sure pleasure is the right word," Calum chuckles as Rod glances over, a hurt expression on his face. "Haha, only having a laugh friend, but no... yeah... me and Rod go way back."

Mickey presses a finger to one nostril and snorts out a stream of snot from the other, before addressing the group. "OK... OK... that's enough fuckin' meet and greet. Now, look 'ere youse lot, I reckons all of us 'ere tonite oughta form us a gang." He pauses, looking at each boy solemnly. "Like a secrit suciety... a bond that kin never be broken."

"Yeah, we could call ourselves the Weyhill Wanderers," Stevie offers enthusiastically. "Like it mate, yeah, likin' that idea already," Mickey approves, producing a pack of Players Number Ten cigarettes to celebrate the momentous occasion. He lights one with a beaten-up stainless-steel petrol lighter. The green flame briefly engulfs his hand and singes his shirt sleeve, before he snaps the lid shut.

"Giss us a puff then, mucker," pleads Pete.

"OK, but don't draw all the fuckin' life outta it, geezer," Mickey orders menacingly, taking a long drag, then passing it to Pete, before lighting another smoke, handing this one to Keith and warning, "Don't go hoggin' it, mind, pass that fucker round."

Keith and Rod take turns to draw down on the smouldering cigarette, before reluctantly offering the glowing butt to Calum, who, seeing little semblance of tobacco remaining declines emphatically. "You're having a laugh, ain't you, fellas?"

"I fuckin' knew it!" Mickey scowls in disgust as he snatches the butt from Rod, examining the mutilated remains with all the diligent zeal of a forensic scientist. "Jeez! Wud yuh adam and eve it... the wankers 'ave only gone and dragged out all the fuckin' goodness," groaning in exasperation. "Means I'll 'ave to spark up another bugger now." He directs a withering look at the guilty pair. "You bastards will eat me outta house 'n fuckin' home, given half a chance." Mickey lights up again, before suddenly poking Calum in the chest with a long bony finger... "Beatles or Stones?" Caught off guard, he hesitates. "Um... uhh... Stones... yeah... Rolling Stones, for sure."

Mickey slaps him on the back. "Right answer, Geezer, don't want any Fab Four-lovin' sissies in this gang, 'ere yar kid," rewarding Calum with the freshly lit cigarette. Feeling a little scared, but also excited, he takes a tentative draw on his first ever filter tip. The taste of the burning tobacco feels strong and acrid. Calum does not inhale deeply, but even so, this new sensation makes him giddy and light-headed. Mickey gestures impatiently for the return of the cigarette. "Gimme back the fag, c'mon, gimme 'ere kid, that ain't smokin', dint yer parents teach yer nothin', yer puffin' on it like a right fuckin' Jessie." He shows how it's done, drawing so long and hard half of the cigarette immediately burns to ash.

The boys spend the next hour excitedly making plans for their new gang. It is to be a secret sect, they all agree, with initiation tests. The leader and lieutenants chosen on the strength of the level of daring and audacious deeds accomplished. These soldiers of fortune all concur that the main priority is to make some quick and easy money, so as to provide them with the staple diet of a young up-and-coming outlaw gang... cigarettes, sweets, chocolate bars and soft drinks... in that order.

"I knows the local scrap metal merchant, guy called Darky, he's got a yard down in Ragged Appleshaw village," Mickey informs. "I've sold him shit before." Pete is interested. "What kind of shit exactly?"

"Whaddya think? Scrap metal, yuh fuckin' drongo. He'll buy all sorts will Darky, copper wire and pipe, aluminium, brass, even rusty old iron. You name it he'll take it, and no questions asked."

"Where can we find this scrap metal?" Calum wants to know.

Mickey spits on the ground and sniggers, "Wherever it's to be found bud... it don't fall from the fuckin' trees though, you lot is gonna have to graft for it, I kin tell yuh that much. I'll leave it to youse boys' imagination as to where y'all finds the gear."

Paul speaks up. "Do we need any implements to extract these precious metals, Mickey?"

"Say what? Talk fuckin' English mush! Whass imp... imple... imple fuckin what?"

"Implements, sorry Mickey, y'know, tools like."

Mickey sighs as comprehension dawns. "Yeah, course yuh will, ya dozy lookin' cunt. Tools of the trade yuh'll be needin' is a hacksaw,

fer cutting yer piping, a pair of pliers, and a sharp knife for shreddin'
the 'lectric wire."

"Wow! When can we start?" Rod, being habitually lazy, is excited
at the prospect of some easy money.

"No time like the present, lads." Mickey walks away, pointing
ahead Messiah-like. "C'mon, I knows of a place not too far from
here, where we just might pick us up a bit a spare gear."

"Where's that to then?" Stevie enquires.

"Jest down the road aways, at the old Appleshaw dump."

The gang members look at each other... undecided on whether to
follow. Mickey lights another cigarette, inducing a hacking coughing
fit, before spluttering, "Who's up fer it then?"

"Yeah, why not," Calum enthuses, "count me in, let's go." The
others whoop and holler agreement as they all swagger off along
Dauntsey Lane towards the local landmark, Whitey House. This
unremarkable 17th-century thatched dwelling is notable only for
posters promoting the visiting circus and fairground plastered on its
white-washed windowless walls.

The gang cross the main road as one and run the long steep lane
down into Appleshaw village. Mickey, wheezing and struggling to
keep up, points to a field on their right. "Hold up guys... this...
this is it... the... the..." He places a hand on his chest, gasping for
breath, "the land of plenty... the farmer's dump." He climbs over
the battered five-bar metal gate, with the rest of the gang eagerly
following him along deep tractor-rutted tracks. Mickey leads them
to a large pond, which covers about a third of the field. The green
algae-covered water has congealed into a putrid stagnant ooze.
It has been used as a dumping ground for many decades, with a
medley of agricultural and private waste regularly thrown into the
filthy water. Old rusting oil and chemical drums, twisted barbed
wire and bent corrugated tin sheets are all tangled into a jumbled
mixture, along with remnants of old bicycles, rotting timber, paint
cans, spent washing machines, broken refrigerators, rusty wire
fencing and many other items of derelict junk.

"This is one of me special places," Mickey states proudly, spitting into the pond. "Sometimes I picks me self up a bit of scrap metal from in 'ere," he squints, scanning his coveted El Dorado, and suddenly spots something. "Hey look! See, what did I tell yer?" Kneeling down, he delves into the water up to his elbow, crowing triumphantly, "'Ere ya go, lads." He drags the remains of an old cooker from the stinking sludge, and in one fluid movement conjures a flick knife from his sleeve to slice off the electric cable. "We'll probably get two shillins' fer this old stove." On a roll now, he spies the remains of a child's pram. "We can drag it to the scrap yard on these old pram wheels." Mickey cackles like a witch preparing a potent brew. "Gotta improvise lads, name a' the game these days. Last resort is these slim pickins' though. Shit like this is only fer when we're 'ard up like and totally skint. We got bigger fish to fry, me boyos."

With a deft flick of his wrist the electric wire coils about his arm. "See this leccy cable, now this is the gear we're after mostly. We'll save up the wire until we've got us a big old pile of the fuckin' stuff, then set it afire and burn off all the rubber casin', until all that's left is pure copper." Grinning like a deranged alchemist at the thought of transforming junk into money, he elaborates further. "This copper wire, now that's the scrap metal wot's worth most fer the weight. If we keeps on like this, boys, we'll all be typhoons, I tell ya... fuckin' typhoons." Calum sniggers under his breath, before daring to correct his commander. "Tycoons, Mickey... I think you mean tycoons, my friend."

"What the fuck, clever guy?!" Mickey turns angrily, fists bunched, "we'll all be in the money, let's put it that way... if we all pulls together, I knows that much, dopey bollocks."

Calum is swiftly losing interest in Mickey's innovative business seminar, his attention drawn to the way the pond water seems to be moving and heaving of its own accord. He picks up a nearby stick, poking and probing in the murky quagmire, peeling back the sticky green algae, then gasps with amazement as he sees what's causing movement in the sluggish liquid mass. Looking across the lake, he realises excitedly, 'There are hundreds! No, must be thousands of newts, frogs and toads, crawling and tumbling all over each other as they come up for air. Wow! What an incredible sight.' He has never seen so many of these creatures together in one place, and wonders, 'How can they all survive together, crammed in here like this?'

Mickey grabs a large piece of ancient flint stone and throws it into the middle of the pond. The loud splash sends a family of moorhens skittering and screeching for the safety of a clump of tall reeds on the other side of the water. Laughing at the birds' distress, he wipes the knife on his jeans, before flicking it closed and sliding it back up his shirt-sleeve. "Over the road it's 'zactly the same, another lake, like this 'un... but bigger. Wanna see it, lads?"

"Surely do!" Pete is hooked. "Especially if there's more scrap metal in there." The gang retrace their steps and cross the road, and sure enough, behind the ragged hawthorn hedge and barbed-wire fence, there is another even larger expanse of water, forming a natural oval in the field, with lots more dumped junk, even an old rusty Standard motor van sitting nose-up in the water.

The atmosphere is different here, though, and the foul smell nausea-inducing. 'Something's not right,' Calum picks up instinctively as he prods again with his stick, finding nothing moving, no sign of life in here, except for, he notes with a shiver of dread, the many rats swimming to and fro. Many of these sodden rodents are gluttonously feasting on the bloated carcasses of unrecognisable dead animals, nibbling and chewing on the decaying corpses, some rats dining on the move as the cadavers go drifting in the breeze, cutting a macabre swathe through the lime-green sludge. The stench is over-powering, but it is not detering the clouds of buzzing bluebottle flies and tiny mosquitoes from gorging on the rotting decomposing body parts which are floating in varying stages of decomposition. A gust of swirling wind sends a rigor mortis cat gliding, to go prowling zombie-like across this contaminated wastewater. The splayed legs and stiff raised head of the lifeless creature sends a cold chill coursing through Calum. "This is so wrong lads... what the hell are all these dead creatures doing in there?"

"It's alright, keep yer fuckin' hair on, Cal, everythin's kosher," Mickey gestures to an adjacent piece of land. "See that place over there, that's Appleshaw Abattoir, the slaughterhouse, where they kills the farm animals and knackered horses." A stark windowless white-painted brick building stands alone in a barren stone-strewn field. Nothing grows near it, except one old beech tree... like Nature's memorial. Even the normally invasive native weeds and wild grasses seem to have recoiled in horror and disgust at this dark house of death. It seems as if all species of flora and fauna are keeping a dignified distance from man's desecration of all that is holy. "Me old man used to work there," Mickey lights a cigarette, "until his accident." Keith is interested in the gory details. "How do they kill the animals?" Calum glares at him, snapping, "Do we really need to know how?" Mickey splatters a fence post with a mouthful of blood-flecked phlegm, wiping his filthy pond-wet shirt-sleeve across his mouth before explaining. "First off they forces the critturs to walk up that long concrete ramp there, proddin' and pokin' 'em wiv sharpened sticks, and one of the guys, right sadistic little cunt, even slices 'em up a little fer fun, wiv a razor, tormentin' 'em, even as they walks to their doom." Mickey smiles smugly, as if revelling in the nostalgic notororiety and his audience's discomfort, before continuing enthusiastically, "Me old man, he sez the animals holler an scream fer fuckin' ages, strugglin' up to the very last, as if they knows, somehow, that they're soon gonna be dead meat," he draws a bony finger across his throat to emphasise and laughs gleefully, "ha ha ha." He points to a rusty iron staircase fixed against the side of the slaughterhouse. "When they gets to the top of that elevator, the slaughtermen prods 'em sum more wiv electrified poles, so as to force 'em into that iron cage. Even so it takes six or seven guys sometimes to drag 'em in there, they're so fuckin' terrified." His eyes widen, a grin creasing his face as he warms to his subject. "Then the buggers is stuck rigid in the cage, and cain't move, until the head man, he pulls out a big bolt gun, puts it to the crittur's head, and pulls the trigger." Sniggering, Mickey's relishing the moment, as he cocks an imaginary firearm to his head. "The iron bolt hits the brain, and that's it, bang, bang sucker, lights out, kaput. It don't always work first time though, and they just get stunned, so then they has to do it again and again... or sometimes they just slits their throats as plan B like... ifn the gun don't work, with the crazy dumb animal screamin' an' screamin', over and over, then they–"

Calum has heard enough. "So you think that's clever, do you Mickey, you cruel bastard, to treat innocent creatures in such a depraved barbaric way?" Raging inside, fuming at the injustice, he is shocked to his core by this horror tale. "How could anyone with any feelings for a fellow living being do such a terrible terrible thing? They must have cold hard hearts, those bad bastards?"

Mickey throws up his hands. "Whoa! Hold up now, tiger. Don't shoot the fuckin' messenger. It ain't like it's me done it personally, is it geezer? I'm just tellin' it like it is."

Calum rounds on him. "Oh yeah! That's as may be, but you sure seemed like you enjoyed recounting the full sick and sorry tale."

"So fuckin' what if I did!?" Mickey shouts in retaliation, "Free country innit, mate? Last time I looked anyways. Don't get yer fuckin' knickers in a twist, pal. Calm down now, after all they is only stupid dumb animals, when all's said an' done."

"What happens to them after they've been killed then?" Pete's query briefly breaks the tension. Mickey sighs, directing a withering look towards Calum. "That's wot I wuz just gettin' to, before saint fuckin' Cal here butted in on me verbals... now look, 'ere's the thing guys," he resumes enthusiastically, "after the slaughterin'," he pauses to grin slyly at Calum, "which also involves beatin' em first wiv iron bars, in front of the other waitin' animals," he chuckles before continuing, "tuh get 'em movin' along the line, yuh unnerstand... sorry... as I wuz sayin... back tuh the end game... after the killin', they sends the dead carcasses off to the butcher, where your ma an' pa buys the meat." Mickey points accusingly to the assembled, "that you lot then has fer yer poxy dinners, so just remember that, me boyos, before you all gets so holier than thou wiv me." He gestures expansively, "Yer all involved to some degree."

"Mickey's got a point there y'know fellas," Rod agrees. "True, of course, it's really gross, like Cal says, but we're all caught up in this, one way or another, guilty through association like."

"Yeah, you got it Rod, and as I was also gonna say, before I was so rudely innerrupted," Mickey glares again at Calum, "any animal parts that is startin' to go off a bit like, or has the pox, and cain't be sold, is chucked in this 'ere pond."

Calum realises now why nothing else lives or grows on this hellish site. The place is cursed. Damned, he is sure, for all eternity.

"Now, course, evry' one knows, that the dead animals shouldn't oughta' be dumped in this pond," Mickey jerks a thumb towards the slaughterhouse. "The waste products is s'posed go in them big steel bins with lids, that yuh can see outside, and then be incinerated of in a furnace, burnt to a crisp like, in case the critturs is contaminated with foot n' mouth or summat. But it costs the company money, does that. So to save some dosh, they chucks the remains in this stinkin' pond."

Stevie feels angry about this. "What say we go tell the villagers? Bet they'd be mad as fuck about this going down on their doorstep."

Mickey shakes his head, chuckling worldly wise, "Yer 'avin a fuckin' laugh matey, them bastards knows about it alright, make no mistake. They even dumps their own animals in 'ere, like the unwanted kittens they've drowned, cos they cain't be bothered to look after 'em, and the dead mice, rats 'n moles they've caught in traps, flings 'em all in, even their family pets. Cats 'n dogs, rabbits, all sorts mate, to save the bovver and cost of buryin' or disposin' of em... oh yeah... and one old geezer I knows catches squirrels in wire traps, then drops the trap in his water butt, and sits wiv a cup a tea an' a biscuit watchin' 'em drown before bungin' 'em in this 'ere pond."

Calum takes a long hard look at Mickey, no longer angry at him, but suddenly overwhelmed by a strange emotional amalgamation of loathing and great sadness. He wishes there was some way to help change him, to divert his destiny, but knows that there is a greater power at work here. Nature would administer karmic payback for all atrocities committed in these slaughterhouses and would also condemn those that celebrate and glorify the depraved abuse. 'It has to be so... it's the way it works... this cosmic retribution stuff. A dead man walking is our Mickey, his fate pre-ordained, complicit, condoning, condemned. Karma will ensure he is doomed for his involvement.'

Mickey persists in elaborating on his theme, blissfully unaware that he is just digging a deeper hole for himself. "Me old man, he told me one time, of a farmer he knows, that used his Land Rover to stampede a herd of his own cattle into a brick wall."

Pete is shocked, "What the fuck's that all about, mush?"

Mickey laughs again. "To save the farmer money agin' my mate, by doin' away wiv the cost of taking the cows to be killed at the slaughterhouse."

Calum looks over at the evil house of death. The clouds directly above the abattoir appear darker than elsewhere in the sky. Like Auschwitz, the shameful carnage carried out here, over many decades, seemingly engendering a permanent depressive gloom to hang heavy about this evil place. No birds fly near, until suddenly, from out of nowhere, a kestrel hawk swoops close by, dropping silently from the sky to alight on a nearby fence post. The Great Spirit speaks through the bird of prey. "Do not be surprised, Calum, by this house of death. If some humans are capable of constantly administering the vilest of atrocities to their own kind, then this decimation of Nature's animal family will be of little consequence to them. The murderers will be devoid of compassion for innocent creatures, even though they share the same DNA. So one will encounter murder, depraved abuse and cannibalism on this farm, in this accursed pool, and the adjoining slaughterhouse. It is noticeable, should one study the perpetrators, that these individuals of non-existent spiritual intellect often move in a lethargic manner, led by karmic justice into the environment they have themselves created, invariably appearing clumsy – mentally and physically – walking with a lumbering gait, their movement reminiscent of slow clunky automatons. Like the rats in this poisonous pond, they live constantly amongst a man-made contaminated concoction of death, blood, slurry and excrement. The karmic consequences these humans ironically self-administer eventually consumes them. Some become afflicted by nervous tics to their faces, are often prone to stomach and intestinal illness, and many more become susceptible to respiratory ailments caused by frequent exposure to, and ingestion of, the toxic chemicals, pesticides and insecticides they use on their farms, fields and crops. Here in England, for example, wildlife habitat has rapidly declined in the last fifty years, due mainly to over-intensive chemical farming methods, destruction or contamination of natural ponds, and the ripping out of most natural hedgerows. When karmic retribution bites, humans still fail to grasp the reason. They will attempt to divert blame, so will then accuse some innocent creature, like the badger for example, for the TB outbreaks amongst their cattle. Regarding animal welfare, expecting industrialised livestock farming and animal husbandry organisations to show compassion is akin to employing King Herod as a babysitter. Granted, there are some farmers who work diligently to incorporate organic measures into agriculture, to try to replenish and improve the soil and land conditions for the benefit of future generations. Some replant hedgerows, trees and wildflower meadows to conserve and preserve Nature, and some humans treat animals with kindness and dignity, using a slaughter-free policy. But these spiritually aware, enlightened ethical people, as with the rest of mankind's caring, compassionate peacemakers, are in the distinct minority at this present time. Unlike those with cold, dark hearts who, in their base form, are executors of mass cruelty and suffering. The crimes they commit against Nature are of their own free will. The fact that these acts are of premeditated intent, and that some humans actually enjoy and gain pleasure from causing the innocent animals pain and torment before killing them, is even more abhorrent to the divine ethical truth codes of the universe, and so compounds the severity of karmic retribution."

Calum understands. It is exactly how he feels. The past recriminations with Gaia are put aside in this moment. This latest connection is far more important; a seminal moment, as he experiences a sense of heightened perception, akin to a revelation. The power of Nature is indisputable. This is followed by the overwhelming realisation that mankind, despite all their egocentric posturing, their weapons, the need to dominate the weak and innocent, their wars and cruelty, will eventually face the ultimate reckoning. The egotistical belief that they are all-powerful is their biggest mistake. A karmic armageddon is inevitably building in retributive intensity, the forces of good against evil, with the spiritual warriors of the greater good eventually annihilating the perpetrators of the countless crimes against divine Nature.

The Great Spirit agrees with Calum's thoughts. "Yes, an accurate observation, but also be aware, cruelty and suffering in the farmed food industry extends far beyond what goes on in that hellish abattoir. Producing milk, butter and cheese from dairy farming involves artificially inseminating a cow. She's virtually raped by humans, before becoming pregnant for nine months, producing huge amounts of milk. The newborn babies are then snatched away from mother shortly after birth, leaving her grieving, crying for her children, breaking her heart. The infant calves are then killed for veal, before the farmer sells off the mother's milk for unnatural human consumption – milk that was intended for the baby cow – before the farmers restart the whole process again. Year after year the animal is used as a money-making machine. It's no wonder the cow is left exhausted, emaciated and permanently depressed.

Eating eggs or poultry is also not cruelty-free… on the contrary, the chickens are kept in industrial-sized buildings, left to live out their short lives cramped in tiny cages, with hardly any space to move, no natural light, never seeing daylight, and all to make them unnaturally produce eggs, which are the chickens' menstrual cycle. When the birds can no longer lay, they are killed and ground up, and used for cheap takeaway food. The male chicks are exterminated immediately after they hatch, and thrown away like so much trash."

Calum shudders. He had not known this. The horrific human cruelty and abuse in the farming industry is much worse and more widespread than he thought. He remembers Eleanor feeding the cats a vegan diet, and her dire warning for mankind. Although Calum is vegetarian, the horror of the abattoir only strengthens his resolve, knowing he will never, ever, eat meat, poultry or fish again, but after today, also no dairy products. Truth be told, he had never felt comfortable with consuming dairy anyway, realising now, with disgust, that in his younger years he had been force-fed by the people purporting to care for him – just another example of selfish humans forcibly influencing the vulnerable and innocent. He determines here and now to always strive to protect innocent creatures whenever possible, accepting it's his moral duty. This heightened sense of awareness creates a radical transformation. Just as the Cat Woman had said, the decision to become vegan elicits an immediate and profound change in one's consciousness, an amazing awakening, his soul instantly elevated to a new level of perception.

Gaia acknowledges his pledge. "Yes, this is a profound move forwards in your decision-making, Calum, but be aware it will take at least thirty days to reset your palate after stopping the consumption of meat and dairy. This is a major step, although one will never truly attain the highest level of enlightenment available to the soul until giving up all leather, wool, skin, and any other animal by-products."

"Yes, mother, the Cat Woman said similar, I get the message."

"On the contrary... I think you misunderstand. There is no message. Not from myself, or indeed from anyone else on the universal panel. No influence from Nature whatsoever. We do not preach. The evidence is merely presented to mankind. It is then up to each individual how they react; remember, how one implements one's free will is a personal decision. Karma then interprets the reaction in terms of consequence. This is a cosmic fact."

Mickey picks up a sharp piece of flint stone and flings it at the kestrel. The bird has flown effortlessly before the stone lands harmlessly against the post. "Why you talkin' to a fuckin' bird?" He mocks Calum, "you've lost it big time, you."

The kestrel soars high, before returning silently on a low flight trajectory, homing in directly on Mickey, who sees the screaming blur of high-speed bird at the last moment, throwing his hands up to shield his face, but too late to prevent the hawk's sharp talons from raking deeply across his cheek. Falling to his knees, wide-eyed with shock, he screams in pain, blood streaming from the razor-sharp incisions, frantically peering up and around, before his panic subsides, realising the hawk has gone. "See! That's what yuh get from fuckin' animals." Holding out his bloodied hands, he yells, "yuh cain't trust 'em. They're evil bastards, fuckin' evil, I tell yuh."

Calum ignores Mickey and speaks directly to the rest of the gang. "See that godforsaken place lads?" Gesturing towards the abattoir, "It's like the concentration camps in the holocaust. Nothing grows near. No birds fly overhead. The sky above is permanently dark and foreboding. The crimes committed there are so horrific that the Great Spirit of Nature will never forgive."

Everyone looks down, struck silent, avoiding eye contact with Calum, as they ponder this awful truth; all except Mickey, that is, whose bravado has quickly returned. "Come on, lighten up now, snap out of it youse fuckin' sissies. After all's said and done it's only stupid critturs we're talkin' about here, ain't like it's yer fuckin' folks died or summat, is it?" He winces as he gingerly strokes his wounds. "Look, let's all meet up in a few days to see what we've managed to scrounge or thieve in the meantime."

All of a sudden a large grass snake shoots across the pond, skimming over the water with head raised, cobra-like, as if preparing to strike. Mickey sees it coming towards him and runs away screaming. The snake chases him as far as the road, before slithering away into the hedgerow. "Wow! Would you believe that?" Pete shakes his head, "that snake seemed to be chasing after Mickey." Calum smiles grimly, "It was."

Dusk is altering the sky dramatically as they head for home. Mickey is nowhere to be seen. The boys seem deeply shocked by recent events, quiet and subdued. No one speaks as they walk on. The fast-fading daylight entices the odd inquisitive bat to swoop about them before they arrive at Meadow Bank. All swear secrecy and arrange to meet tomorrow. The last of a fading sunset is burning glorious red and orange above the railway embankment as Calum slips indoors.

Janet turns from her chores at the kitchen sink, pausing briefly from washing up. "Oh, hello, son."

"Hello," he replies, quietly.

Jim is snoring loudly in the armchair, half-empty whisky bottle at his side, while The Mike Sammes singers croon out their 'Family Favourites' on the radio, releasing harmonious melody from the 'His Master's Voice' music centre in the corner of the room. "Have you had a nice time with your friends, Calum? You must invite them round to play sometime."

He feels like shouting down her naive stupidity but keeps a hold on his thoughts, thinking incredulously, 'Play, play? Invite them round? Are you for real, woman? You don't have a fucking clue, do you?' He groans inwardly, imagining Janet meeting Mickey. He keeps his cool though, he can't be doing with bickering tonight. Surviving his first day at the new school, and Mickey's revelations, has exhausted him. "Yes, thanks, Mrs Brown, same old same old, just been playing football with the lads." She hands him a mug. "Here, take this cup of hot Horlicks, and off to bed with you now. You must be up bright and early for school tomorrow. Don't forget to clean your teeth."

"Yes, sure thing. Goodnight Mrs Brown," suddenly he stops in his tracks as he wonders… 'Horlicks…?' Before questioning, "Uhho… is there cow's milk in this?"

"Yes," she smiles, "of course, son… warm and milky, will help you sleep." Calum hands it back to her. "No more dairy products for me, from here on in, thanks all the same." Janet looks dumfounded, "But whyever not, what's wrong with milk, it's so good for you?"

"Yeah yeah, if you say so, you drink it then. You've force-fed me enough bad karma already methinks, no more." Janet stands in the hall, hands on hips, and shouts after him. "Well, I've heard it all now, thats ridiculous, absolutely ridiculous." His legs feel heavy, like lead weights are attached. Too tired to argue the point, he trudges to his bedroom, feeling so down, his positivity unusually suppressed. He pulls back the bedclothes and is soon drifting into deep sleep. Despite the horror of the abattoir, he is so glad Gaia had come back to visit him. As shocking as tonight's revelations are, Calum feels warm reassurance, so pleased the divine spiritual presence is once more a part of his life. He has advanced one step closer on his journey of the Sacred Path. But isn't that always the way of it... just as this harmonious reunion beckons, true serenity and peace of mind are again to prove elusive, as this evening the gorilla nightmares begin.

After being lulled into the false security of slumber, Calum is led forcibly into the darkest sleep dimension by shadow figures without face or form. They hold him fast while the nightmare begins. Alone in a white sterile room, he is forced to sit, anxious and fearful, staring at the large round clock on the wall, tick tocking methodically, black-arrowed hands dripping blood as they move anti-clockwise across the roman numerals on the clock face, as if present time is retreating in fear of the future. Waiting helplessly for the horror to start, as he knows it surely must. Calum is edgy and tense, wondering what form the terror will take, from where and when it is to appear... then suddenly... CRASH! The white concrete wall is demolished as a gigantic gorilla breaks through, its explosive entrance showering the room with masonry and dust. The raging creature lumbers forwards, halting directly before him, its muscular arms outstretched. Bubbling saliva runs from the snarling mouth as the monster roars in pained anguish. The massive hands close into threatening balls of angry fist, and although the creature stops short of physically attacking him, the presence is so frightening that Calum screams uncontrollably. The next thing he knows, he's being gripped and shaken roughly as the fearsome image of the enraged gorilla fades vortex-fast into that subtly warped twilight zone betwixt consciousness and sleep... until the urgent tugging of the shadow beings make him aware of Janet Brown's strangely distorted face looming above him. "Wake up, son, it's all right now, you've just been having a nightmare." She covers him with a blanket before leaving the room.

Breathing hard, heart beating fast, tremors of relief course uncontrollably through his body as a big glowing moon casts forbidding shadows throughout the room. "Just been having a nightmare," he scathingly repeats, chastising Janet for her casual observation and general lack of basic awareness. "You have no fucking clue, lady." Although extremely shaken up by the unexpected visit of the gorilla and these dark shadow beings, at the same time, strangely, he's experiencing an overwhelming sense of empowerment coursing through him.

CHAPTER
TWENTY-SEVEN

The mind-numbing boredom of living with the Browns, and the torture of school, continue for another three years. The disturbed nights persist. If it isn't the nightmares disrupting his sleep, then it's Jim Brown, who continues on a regular basis to wake Calum and Janet, so as to extol his great virtues, ranting and raving until falling into a drunken stupor in the early hours of the morning.

Calum has taken to writing his own sick notes for the school activities he hates with a passion, passing the letters off as if written by his foster parents. This crafty deception enables him to get out of sport and games, or PE, as the teachers called it, 'Physical Education.' He smirks scornfully at the nonsensical notion of this sweaty masochistic group activity, so beloved by the self-styled macho sports teachers. He scoffs, 'What ridiculous rubbish, I can get all the exercise I need by connecting alongside Mother Nature in the great outdoors. I've no need to jump through human hoops, like some poor abused circus animal.'

Calum is not connecting or conversing with the Great Spirit, though. There had been no verbal contact since that dreadful evening at the abattoir. 'No matter, I need no one,' he thinks, resolute, sure of himself. 'I have learnt enough from the hidden laws of Nature to keep one step ahead of the hateful humans.'

Calum and his classmates are informed one morning that they are to be taken by bus on an educational visit to a factory, a school initiative to help prepare them for finding jobs when they leave school. He is excited by this news. Anything to escape lessons!

'Barnetts Meat Factory' is the destination. Calum smells a rat, and death, a mile before the coach reaches the factory. Arriving at lunchtime, they are led by Mr Braun, the deputy head across the car park towards a big square grey concrete building. The stench of murdered animals is immediately overwhelming, but no one else seems to notice. The kids are laughing and joking around as normal behind the deputy head's back. They are all pre-conditioned, Calum realises, indoctrinated to believe this is normal, which for most of them it is, as the majority of children are all fed dead animals from birth by their parents. The teacher stops at the shop door to shake hands with a big burly white bearded man. He's wearing white overalls with abstract crimson blotches, and totally red sleeves.

'Strange uniform,' thinks Calum, 'like a clown's outfit,' until, on closer inspection, he can tell it's no Pollock-esque fashion statement, it's not paint, the red... but blood. The gore-splattered fat man invites them all into his gruesome grotto, with Calum thinking, 'like some alternative Father Christmas... the one from hell.'

"Welcome boys, name's Stuart, I'm foreman here at Barnetts Meat Factory." He gestures theatrically, "Come now, come see our operation. I hope this visit is as inspirational to you as it was for me on my first day." Becoming misty-eyed in fond recall, he sighs, musing emotionally, "been here over forty years now, man and boy... man and boy."

The deputy head graciously leaves him to his nostalgic reminiscences and addresses the assembled pupils. "Now then, before we go in... does anyone have any questions for Stuart?"

Calum raises his hand. "Yeah, I don't understand... sir... why they call this a factory. Surely things are made at a factory... one can't make meat... you have to murder innocent creatures to get meat, don't you?"

"Oh, yes, of course, obviously animals have to die, but that's not done here," the foreman answers cheerfully, chuckling 'ho ho ho' jolly, "but murder, that's a bit strong lad." He turns to Mr Braun and smiles, "morbid little bugger, ain't he? But yes, the animals are slaughtered at the abattoir and then brought here to be butchered... if that's what you mean?"

"Same thing, you still have their blood on your hands," Calum points accusingly, "literally, in your case." The other kids giggle as Mr Braun intervenes, "Cut that out, Connor, that's enough. Stuart has been kind enough to facilitate this visit, now show some respect."

Calum ignores him and addresses the foreman once more. "How can you stand the constant stink of death, mister, it's vile."

Stuart smiles, "Oh, you soon get used to that, son... after all, it's only food... just uncooked food is all." Calum snorts, "It's more like a Nazi death camp for animals." Stuart sighs, becoming irritated now by the unrelenting interrogation. "Look, the job's not for everyone, granted, but all who work here seem content with their lot in life." Calum sneers, "So is Lucifer... I expect." Stuart has had enough of this sniping inquisition and doesn't answer, instead leading the boys inside, pointing to a row of rubber boots. "Wellies on, please, lads... hygiene rules." Mr Braun comes up behind Calum, pinching the back of his arm spitefully and whispering close up in his ear, "I've told you once already, now cut it out, you little bastard, or you're back on the bus, and up before the Headmaster upon our return." He twists free and scowls back, "Yea teach, I'll take the bus option." The deputy head pushes him roughly ahead, causing him to stumble. "Yes, you'd like that, wouldn't you, to skive off, but no Connor, you will endure, and like it."

The disgusting smell is now intensified, as they get to the business end of mutilation, where the factory floor is a bloodbath of almost unrecognisable body parts, torn apart, cut, ripped and discarded. The twenty or so workers, trampling back and forth, squishing and squashing over the animal remains, seem not to notice the karmic stink of murderous activity as they chatter and banter, about Man United beating City, or the various ways they would 'give one' to the blonde secretary in the office, while others lean over long stainless steel benches like pre-programmed robots, all with the same intense fixed expression, as if driven by some deep genetic desire to abuse and mutilate, programmed to cut, hack and slice with cleaver and hacksaw, until these formerly alive fellow Earth dwellers are totally dismembered. Tearing away flesh and sawing through bone, throwing skin and hooves, heads and trotters, wings and claws, livers, eyes, tongues, kidneys, brains, entrails... tossing the offal all over the floor. Like lowly minimum-wage workers casually sorting through rubbish at a landfill dump, whilst blood drips on them, and the tiled floor, from the whole sides and carcasses of dead pigs, cows, sheep, lambs and deer, all hanging suspended from the ceiling on steel hooks. A little further along, row upon row of dead chickens, ducks, geese and turkeys hang by their necks on long wheels along metal frames.

"The best cuts are packaged and boxed for retail, and the left--overs," the foreman informs jovially, gesturing to the mangled remains of the corpses, "go in that big mincer over there, for your mince meat, pies and sausages... and as a special treat for today," he beams at the boys, "samples of our delicious products will be available for you all from our butcher's shop on your way out." He walks on, his boots squelching in the blood and guts.

Calum's mind is reeling. The walls seem to be closing in. He feels faint, sick, needing to get out... 'Breathe... breathe through your nose... regulate... just concentrate on breathing... quell the inner panic... switch off... calm yourself...' he repeats, over and over, until a state of spiritual slow motion gradually envelopes him, the Great Spirit's protection from the inevitable karma associated with setting foot in this hell-hole.

While the kids are in the butcher's shop receiving their gruesome gifts he runs behind the bus and is violently sick, eyes streaming, stomach aching, before reflecting... 'This is just one such meat factory, in one small village, on the outskirts of one small town, in one small country.' The scale of cruelty, abuse, death and destruction towards animals in England alone is enough to leave him stunned and staggered at the heartlessness of man, but it becomes mindboggling as he thinks of how many such places exist all over the world, 'And that's before one takes into account the atrocities the humans perpetuate against their own kind.' Calum sees no hope for those involved, or mankind in general, having been taught by the Great Spirit all about cosmic retribution. 'But even if one were not aware, or involved spiritually with Nature, there is an undeniable truth to be felt in places such as this meat factory. The actions and depraved behaviour of the humans is so wrong, there must surely be karmic consequences. There will be no escape from that, be it in this world or the next.' He is sure of that as he gets on the bus and heads for the back seats. Although deeply disturbed by what he has seen in this hell on Earth, he feels a profound sadness for those involved in such desecration, knowing that many children have been brought up believing that to commit these atrocities to a living sentient being is normal behaviour. That what the adults are doing is just gainful employment. Brainwashed and indoctrinated by parents and school, by government and the powers that be who rule over the susceptible masses.

The deputy head and the kids return to the bus, gorging on their freebie pies, pasties and sausage rolls. All in high spirits on the journey back to school. The young humans seem to have thouroughly enjoyed their day out.

CHAPTER
TWENTY-EIGHT

Every evening after school and at weekends, the Weyhill Wanderers continue to meet and practise their solemn vows. These oaths of allegiance are sworn before the gang set off to pilfer scrap metal from the local farms and factories.

One Friday evening Rod calls for Calum, asking, "Fancy coming to the youth club tonight, pal?" He grabs his coat, excited, welcoming any excuse to escape the foster parents. "Yeah, and why not? Come on, then, what are we waiting for, Rodders, dear chap?" They walk the mile or so to the local youth club, held once weekly in Thruxton War Memorial Hall. Calum smirks as they go in. "Don't you just love the humans, forever erecting monuments to celebrate their wars and violence."

They play table tennis and tune in to the latest top ten hits playing out. Local Andover group the Troggs' big hit 'Wild Thing' is followed by the Rolling Stones belting out 'This could be the last time, maybe the last time, I don't know.' Constantly replaying on the club's old record player, these rocking tunes suit Calum's current mood... he's feeling like a 'Wild Thing,' living for and enjoying the moment to its full capacity, squeezing every last drop from the here and now, consumed totally by the hedonistic adrenaline rush of not knowing when 'the last time' may be.

His gaze is drawn to the girls dancing up on the stage. A cute young thing catches his eye. She is about his age, fourteen or fifteen he guesses, pretty, slim, with long dark hair framing a cheeky pixie face. Rod notes his interest and nudges encouragement. "Hot, hey man? Her name's Coral, shall I introduce you, Cal?"

"No you're cool, Rod, I'll make my own move, if and when I'm ready." Her green eyes catch his open appreciative gaze. She is offering him the come on. Calum knows she could be his tonight should he make a move on her. But he hesitates... and the fleeting possibility is lost.

As he steps outside for a cigarette Rod shakes his head. "She was there for the taking my man. Are you mad or what?" He laughs, "Jury's still out on that one, friend." The quip comes easy and dismissive, but he's not sure why he did not pursue Coral further, allowing, 'Certainly pretty and cute', but he isn't feeling any immediate stirrings of passion or excitement, 'maybe she's too tame for me?' That's all he can put it down to, as there was no other obvious reason to reject her.

They hide from view inside a small wooden outbuilding attached to the hall before lighting up. Smoking is prohibited in the club, especially at their age. As Calum takes a leisurely puff, his attention is drawn to the reams of thick copper wire running across the walls. Some of the wire is exposed from the black plastic coating and hanging detached from the main junction box. Assuming this old electrical supply is disconnected, he resolves to return for these rich easy pickings. Rod has failed to notice the opportunity, so Calum keeps schtumm, reasoning, 'It's every gang member for himself when it comes to scavenging.' He determines to come back tomorrow at first light...

Awakening early next day to a bright Saturday morning, Calum dresses quick and quiet, then creeps silently along the hall. Entering the kitchen, he gulps greedily from a jug of juice, before lifting a sharp carving knife from the cutlery draw. Jittery with excitement, he leaves quietly by the back door, grabbing a small axe from the garden shed, stashing it and the knife into a hessian sack. Grinning, he imagines the forthcoming plunder and booty coming his way. Running away up the drive, he knows the earlier he gets to the hall, the less likely anyone will be around to thwart his plans. Jogging along Dauntsey Lane the early morning air feels cold on his face, making him squint with headache, but the burnished fiery orange sunrise promises a warm day. Leaving the road, he slows to a brisk walk, striding across swaying breeze-rustled corn fields, dodging the roads and any possible prowling policemen, heading for Thruxton.

Calum arrives ten minutes later at the perimeter of Mullen's Pond. He stops and breathes in the fresh clean air, feeling it purify his whole being as he strolls across the surrounding meadow. A flock of grazing sheep eye this stranger warily, while resting ducks take little notice of his approach. A snapping twig underfoot disturbs a crouching heron to flap away silently on the languid beat of prehistoric wing. Coming upon a burbling stream he crosses over on moss-encrusted stepping stones, probably set there by shepherds, centuries past. This sparkling brook predestined by Nature to constantly replenish nearby Mullen's Pond with sparkling clear spring water.

"Uhhh… what the..?" Calum is suddenly stopped in his tracks. He curses aloud, "For fuck's sake!" His breathing on hold… his previous relaxed ease instantly terminated. An adult swan lies dead before him, a crossbow bolt through its neck. Judging by the advanced state of the decomposing remains the corpse has lain in this spot for some weeks. He takes a deep breath, picks up a scent, his feral instinct detecting the lingering odour of depraved human activity.

Calum wonders, 'What would Gaia make of this wanton act of violence against one of her own?' This mindless destruction reinforces his previous conclusion. 'No matter where one travels on planet Earth, there is no escape from the overwhelming evidence of mankind's abuse and cruelty.' He shakes his head, cursing aloud, "Man kind! Kind man! What kind of preposterous misnomer is that?"

Suddenly, a large toad plops into the stream, clambering onto a rock, before turning to face Calum. The Great Spirit speaks, "Rarely will one find my offspring after they succumb to natural death. Most sacred souls are swiftly transported when they die. Millions of creatures pass over daily on planet Earth, yet only a minute percentage of their corpses are found by humans. These exceptions are some of the murdered animals, such as this swan, which are left as an example and a warning." Calum shakes his head. "But this is so wrong, there is no need of a warning, surely it should just feel abhorrent to kill an innocent life form."

"You must be aware that most people on planet Earth do not connect with or care for wildlife like you or I. Some humans are capable of many variations of deviant evil, and so it follows, animal welfare does not figure highly, if at all, on their radar. Many humans lack any sense of care and compassion for their fellow Earth dwellers, even though all life forms, including man and animal, share the same DNA. Examples of bizarre cruelty such as you have just witnessed comes easily to those that harbour a morbid fascination with the death and destruction of living things. This begins for some at an early age, with the destruction of insects. For example, young children pulling the wings from butterflies, the legs from spiders, and pouring boiling water on ants. This malicious mutation then graduates as the children grow to adulthood, escalating into advanced levels of cruelty and abuse. Barbaric behaviour such as this leads ultimately to the gratuitous defilement of their own; even the human's own children are not immune from being subjected to physical, mental and sexual abuse."

"OK, Mother. That's a fact. I see where you're coming from there... lest you forget, I have just been on an educational trip to a meat factory! So what's to be done to stop these crimes against Nature?"

"Perpetrators of this cosmic criminality are forever prevented from experiencing the euphoric feeling of wonder, of seeing the beauty integral within the precious universal gifts of flora and fauna. This is a classic example of the universal karmic power of cause and effect. As I have explained to you previously, an irreversible spiritual lobotomy is performed upon those who are guilty. There are some humans, granted, who care for and respect all life. These altruistic souls shall be part of the higher order. Their status shall be elevated to that of enlightened beings."

The toad hops back into the stream, sending basking water voles scurrying away into their nesting holes along the riverbank. The little creatures all settling simultaneously, poking tiny heads out from simple homes, silken ears twitching, as if waiting to hear more. The Great Spirit leaps to the bank before continuing, "The violence against the swan was the result of a lurking rogue gene mutation in humans from when planet Earth first exploded into life. It was thought that all human life had been erased in the destruction of your previous host planet. But alas, no, some human DNA, present in a skeleton encased in a hollowed fossilised tree, somehow found its way to Earth. Not all inhabitants of this universe, or indeed planet Earth, have been exposed to this ominous human transformation. Some are fortunate to be blessed with the pure genes of the Aurora universe, whose frustrated souls weep for the innocents... such as this once beautiful dead swan." Calum is shocked by this revelation. "So OK, tell it like it is, then, Gaia, as I'm part human I need to know the truth... in which category do I fall?"

"You, because of my intervention at your formative stage, are blessed with the Aurora gene." Mightily relieved, he sighs. "Thank you... now everything makes sense. This is why I feel such an aversion to cruelty and violence, persecution and injustice."

"I think that you already possessed that altruistic attribute, it was part of your core character, from your Earth mother's side, and naturally instilled, before our connection."

"That's nice of you to say... but I'm not as pure as you might think... trust me. Anyway, whats to be done about the cruel ones?"

"Those who abuse and prey on the vulnerable are nothing but sophisticated savages. Despite their false niceties, fake manners and smug displays of social etiquette, they have not advanced spiritually since your planet's Stone Age. It was not so long ago that some humans were killing and eating owls and mice as supposed cures and remedies, and burning to death innocent pagan herbalists as witches."

"I hear you, Great Spirit, but what happens to these evil people? What is their payback for these atrocities? Surely they deserve far more severe punishment than being denied the spiritual enlightenment to experience or appreciate the wonder of your world, as you say the more attuned do?"

"You are correct in your assumption, Calum. Allow me to elaborate... there is a race of karmic beings, from a planet many millions of light years away, who wish to wipe out man, to cleanse the scourge. We are in constant negotiation, in a bid to save those of you who are in tune with the hidden laws of Nature. Compassionate human beings are as precious as the animals to the great scheme of universal enlightenment expansion. There are only three other planets in the seven universal galaxies that can support the life of man or creature as they live here on Earth. There were many other habitable planets, but these have all been destroyed by meteorite showers or climate change in the continuing expanding evolution of the universe. A cosmic conglomerate has previously evacuated some flora and fauna to the three receptive planets. Knowing of man's propensity towards evil we chose only non-human flora and fauna for the mass migration."

Calum raises his hand. "Excuse me, Great Spirit, but you said we, who are the other members of this conglomerate?"

"There is one representative for each universe, so seven individuals in total."

"Are they human, animal, or just disembodied spirits like you?" The toad chuckles, "Disembodied spirit, hey... is that the sum of my parts? A little harsh... don't you think? You may meet the others on your travels along the Sacred Path, but that's for another time, another place. The most important aspect of universal enlightenment is that we, you and I, and other kindred spirits, are operating, functioning, creating, existing, in the here and now. Now is where the power is concentrated for change, creation and truth."

"Yes, I get that, sorry if I'm getting ahead of myself, but you did say before that you would enlighten me in the future, Gaia. It all seems extremely interesting. You can't blame me for wanting to know more."

"No, I understand, Calum, more is never enough though... is it? This is a common human trait. The more one has, the more one wants."

"Hang on there, don't get me wrong, in a material sense greed is bad, I get that, but I'm greedy for knowledge, that's only a positive, isn't it?"

"That depends on what you seek at any given moment. Truth and learning should be filtered, a stream of consciousness, and unconsciousness, flowing, meandering, absorbed or relinquished. Some information should be retained, but most released, and never accumulated by gluttony. Facts gathered without understanding, words spoken without thought, are just so much mind clutter hindering true transcendental spiritual illumination... I digress... we can only surmise that fortunately some positive human DNA also escaped from an exploding meteorite on impact with planet Earth. Perhaps this is why there is a compassionate caring presence on this planet. We have identified these benevolent souls, and although in the distinct minority, they, like you, have been blessed with the Aurora gene."

"How did you integrate this gene within me, and to these others?" Calum probes, "And who else is helping you?"

"Aurora is linked to celestial light beings. Born of stardust, they have been instrumental in nurturing an amalgamation of the sun, moon and planets, thereby creating an atmosphere where the sun's exact proximity to the moon and planet Earth encourages life to form."

"Wow!" Calum is impressed. "It seems that these prerequisites of life have fortunately fallen neatly into place as far as humans are concerned."

"Hmm.... Do you really think it is a coincidence that Earth orbits at exactly the correct distance from the sun and moon, so allowing water to exist in the exact three states of gas, solid, and liquid... with these three ingredients being the precise essential formula to create life?"

Calum is captivated by the enormity of this extraterrestrial intelligence, but now feels a little foolish. "Well no, forgive me. I had not really thought that through properly. I can see now how complicated the magnificence is. Please tell me more, Mother, so I may grasp and digest the complexity of these revelations."

"Love energy is the prime cause motivator and is not given or blessed to any one individual, nor instilled or integrated. It is a natural process which is there for all to access... but one must already possess and retain the spark of pure unconditional love... that is a core free will soul choice... Everything else is connected to nature and the power of numbers. The universe unfolds and expands based on a cosmic geometric grid. You can learn a lot from a spider's web, that's sacred super nature geometry. If you are patient all will become clear during your evolutionary development. When this radiance will illuminate your soul I cannot predict, as spiritual progression depends to a large extent on one's free-will choices."

"OK, OK," Calum groans in frustration. Although disappointed, he knows better than to push the issue. "I realise I will have to be patient, but what happens to the evil ones in the meantime?"

"Because of their cruelty and evil intent towards my creatures they will gradually be poisoned – poisioned by their own mind, in a spiritual sense, until to all extents and purposes they are dead inside, their souls burned out by hate and blood lust. At their physical passing over, which is inexorably linked to one's free-will chosen path, their souls shall be disconnected by karmic intervention and spiritually sterilised, before being transported and deposited into a cosmic black hole. Any evil essence is then transformed into dark matter, before being despatched to the grey Planet of Bones. Here the infected souls will remain for eternity in perfect isolation, their contaminated psyche forever segregated from the remainder of the cosmos, because mankind and evil are forever tainted by association." Calum is fascinated, and unable to contain his curiosity. "Why is it called the Planet of Bones? What happens there? Where is this place?" The Great Spirit bounds away. "More of this later, another time, another place."

"Come back," Calum pleads. "Please, tell me more." But the toad has gone. En masse, the water voles retreat backwards into their nests.

Calum squeezes through a gap in the hawthorn hedge, pausing to curse... 'Shit... I meant to ask the Great Spirit about the gorilla nightmare." Kicking out at a fence post, he's exasperated by too many questions and not enough answers. He climbs over a barbed-wire fence, balancing briefly on the swaying metal strands before jumping down onto the pavement. He heads towards the centre of the village.

A few strides on he hears a mumbling and cursing coming from the water-filled ditch to his right, where an old man is struggling to get up from the dirty water, but so drunk he's unable to stand. His jacket is coated in wet mud, fresh vomit, and liberally festooned with old food and beer stains. He waves a bony fist and shouts, "Get I outta here, young whippersnapper! Do ya hear me, yuh fuckin' long-haired hippy, get me out."

Despite the insulting tirade, Calum is about to help him, when Gaia speaks. "It would be wise to be selective in your sympathy for elderly humans... If Adolf Hitler were alive today he, too, would be an old man, would he not?"

Smiling at the simplicity of this wisdom, he declines the offer of the drunk's outstretched hand, walking away, leaving him raging in frustration, spitting and cursing, and still trying unsuccessfully to get to his feet. 'Strange old world, this... ain't it just?' Calum reflects on the last ten minutes or so, reinforcing his open-minded attitude of always expecting the unexpected where humanity is concerned.

The wizened filthy old reprobate in the ditch, and a rumbling electric milk float trundling through the village, are the only sign of life in Thruxton Village at this early hour. Whistling cheerily, Calum walks on, stopping briefly at the post office stores, taking a peek at the latest pop music albums on sale in the window, admiring the psychedelic artwork on the sleeve of the new Pink Floyd offering, before running the last few yards to the War Memorial Hall car park. Taking a precautionary look around, making sure he has not been followed, he tugs hard on the ramshackle wooden doors of the smoking shed. Once inside, he removes the tools from his bag and starts cutting the thickest wiring. The carving knife is sharp, quickly sawing through the thick black rubber cable, until, BANG! The metal blade strikes bare wire, causing a tremendous crack of diverted current. The powerful electrical discharge creates an ear-splitting explosion, sending a huge voltage of raw power coursing through Calum, throwing him backwards to go crashing through the wall of the timber shed. He lays sprawled on the grass, concussed, out cold, flat on his back amidst the shattered timbers. Such is the damage it looks as if a bomb has scored a direct hit. The shed has totally collapsed; shattered and splintered wooden planks protrude at odd angles from under the twisted tin roof. A bitter acrid smell of burning rubber drifts about him as he slowly comes to. He has landed heavily at the foot of an ancient gravestone leaning at a forty-five degree angle against the foot of the surrounding flint wall. Winded, his head swimming, the truth slowly dawns on him as he gradually comes round. "Fucking hell! That cable must be alive and connected!"

Shocked and still, he notes that the tombstone he's lying against is one of perhaps a dozen similar ancient memorials leant against the old wall. 'Strange,' he ponders, 'that I've never noticed these old graves until now.' The crumbling headstones are chipped and cracked, with some broken clean in two. The stonemason's engraved words so eroded and covered with orange lichens and dark green ivy as to be barely legible. It is obvious no one has visited or tended these graves for many years. Clearly they are relics of an old human burial ground. It seems no one remembers or cares any longer about the people interned here, it's as if they never existed.

'Very apt,' Calum allows, contemplating on just how close he had come to becoming one of these faded and long forgotten statistics, and musing philosophically, 'Father Time, and his indomitable henchmen, the universal elements, have patiently erased any past memory of these human lives from history. Such is life, such is death.'

CHAPTER
TWENTY-NINE

Several weeks later, Calum is still being haunted every night by the same terrifying gorilla nightmare and getting very little sleep. The situation has become even more intolerable as Jim Brown has taken to awakening him abruptly from the horrors of the dreadful dream by sadistically whipping the backs of his bare legs with a birch wood cane.

Early one evening, Calum snaps, so incensed by this deplorable situation he decides on a desperate revenge mission against the shadow beings. Believing them to be hiding in the nearby hedge, he takes a can of Esso blue paraffin from the back of the bungalow and sets fire to the tall native hedgerow that grows alongside Dauntsey Lane, all the way to Whitey House. Standing back, he smiles at his handiwork as the flames take hold, sending red hot sparks flying up into the sky like a mass migration of angry fireflies. He prays that somehow the shadow beings are trapped within the raging inferno, hoping their malevolent intent is consumed in the ferocious blaze and despatched straight to hell. Shaking his fist at the dark matter offenders, he laughs at their demise. "Ha ha ha, take that, you evil bastards, you won't be coming for me again."

"Proud of your work this night, are you boy?" A stern voice booms from above. Startled, Calum spins round... no one there..? He looks fearfully about him. "No, you don't see me."

"Great Spirit... is... is that... you?"

"Yes, of course it is I... now listen carefully, I shall say this once, and once only. Whilst I realise that you are enduring mental pain and anguish, you must never ever vent your frustration and anger on Nature's own, or I will sever all ties with you, cut you off dead, do you understand?"

Calum knows that what he has done is terribly wrong. But his Chi is in such a fragile scattered state at this present time he won't admit to this grim truth. The hedgerow is now fiercely ablaze, crackling and spitting, showering the cold black night with red hot embers. "Leave me, Mother! Go, please!" he screams. "I will just have to deal with my demons and accept the terrible consequences of my actions. It hasn't been easy, you know. You have often deserted me in my hour of need. Why come to me now? Where were you when the gorilla threatened me every night? When the shadow beings came for me?"

"I am always near for those in tune with Nature… and also close by for those that would harm my creatures," the Great Spirit replies ominously.

Sirens wail, louder and louder, as the emergency services home in on their duty. Calum sees the flashing blue lights of police cars and fire engine as they speed along the main road from Andover, no more than a mile away now. He's suddenly worried, sensing correctly that they are heading his way. Self-preservation kicks in, and he runs down the driveway of Meadow Bank, hiding behind the tall shrubs.

The fire engine arrives first, screeching tyres and locked brakes bringing the red Dennis tender squealing to a halt just yards from him. The water hose quickly deals with the blaze and the firemen leave soon after. The fire is reduced to smouldering ash, sending dense grey clouds of vapour and smoke spiralling up and away into the atmosphere.

The police stay a while longer, searching the area with long black torches, poking and prodding with pointed metal poles and rakes, sifting through the glowing remains, hoping to discover some clues. Finding no such conclusive evidence they leave, with one muttering "Senseless bloody vandals, bring back corporal punishment, a dose of the birch, that's what the buggers need."

Calum remains hidden, breathing heavy, fearing capture. "Are you pleased with the desecration this night?" The Great Spirit's voice breaks through the dense blackness. He shrinks further into the under-growth. "There is no point in cowering there. One cannot hide from universal truth. After all I have shown you, are you still so lacking in natural awareness not to realise the hedgerow is a sacred home for many families?"

Calum knows he has done a real bad thing here and feels guilty, sad, ashamed. "No... yes... oh Mother... I am so sorry... I really don't know what came over me." Hanging his head, he continues, "I did not mean any harm to your creatures, I love them all, they are my family, how could I do such a thing?"

"My patience is not inexhaustible. I can help you with this, but you must learn from Nature, or I shall move on to those more deserving."

"Yes, yes, I understand... Please give me another chance," Calum implores. "I beg of you, Gaia, don't leave me alone any longer with the shadow beings."

"Fear not the dark shadow sentinels, or the gorilla. They visit you because you are an Aurora child of Nature. They are but reality reflectors conveying a cosmic truth. The gorilla is raging in helpless torment... not at you per se, but at the grim reality of his species' forthcoming extinction at the hands of man."

Comprehension and enlightenment comes in an overwhelming rush. The shocking truth of the shameful situation engulfs Calum, mourning from his soul for the gorilla... before further realisation hits home. 'Oh my god! What of the wildlife consumed by fire in the hedgerow?' The sadness of this moment, the consequences of his actions, creating a cataclysmic void of anguish that he feels may haunt him forever. "I must leave you now, child, but I shall always be with you... if you stay true to the Sacred Path."

"Thank you, Mother. I will never let you down again. I under-stand the implications of my actions now... but... but what of the poor creatures in the hedgerow?" Suddenly weeping, from his heart, inconsolable, "How can I ever compensate for their demise?"

"Your remorse I feel is genuine," the Great Spirit's tone softens. "My creatures are akin to cosmic children, meaning the spiritual essence of their psyche is sacrosanct, holy. These sacred souls do not prepare for any concept of future. They live only for the now, with no illusion of time. The souls of these innocents are being reborn and repatriated to another planet, even as we speak."

Calum looks to the sky, hearing only the hum of perfect silence as a bright moon intrudes on this darkest of nights, incontrovertibly uniting the seven universes, combining seamlessly in creation, bestowing birth to sparkling stars. He shivers, walking away, so grateful for this reprieve, but feeling mournfully desolate as he heads back to the bungalow, alone again.

CHAPTER
THIRTY

The next day, Calum wakes full of retrospective regret. His actions the previous evening were a wakeup call for his soul. He decides to leave the Weyhill Wanderers, aiming to distance himself from the shallow activities of the group. He had been thinking of going forwards alone for some time now, but his decision has been greatly influenced by the gang now being armed and dangerous. Mickey had supplied each member with powerful air guns, bought broken from the scrap yard. He had managed to repair the weapons, and with ingenious malevolence had made them even more powerful, by increasing their original velocity specification and compression, before selling them on to the other gang recruits. Mickey was adept at fixing damaged goods, like these rusty old rifles and pistols, always trying to get more mileage out of other people's cast-offs. Calum's allocated weapon was a short black snub-nosed Webley 1.75 air pistol, and yes, for sure, he had enjoyed some fun with the other guys, shooting at old bottles, baked bean tins, and Mickey's pilfered fairground rifle targets. That was until Robbie, a new member of the gang, having run out of pellets, had inserted a tiny piece of sharp flint into the chamber of his gun. He fired this at Calum, hitting him right between the eyes, the flint shaving embedding sharply into his forehead like a karmic Hindu bindi. This was stark warning enough, but the final straw came when Rod informed Calum that some of the gang were firing at live targets, following Mickey's cruel lead, using the guns to kill or maim wild creatures such as birds, squirrels, mice, and even local domestic cats.

Calum finds this abhorrent and distressing, knowing bad karma was already preordained for Mickey, an unavoidable collision course waiting to happen. But now the prospects were, he felt, of a distinctly negative nature for anyone else choosing to remain too closely acquainted with the doomed one. He swore to himself from this moment on he would always distance himself from the pack. This would be no great sacrifice, as he had never felt comfortable with most of the humans he came into contact with anyway.

One boy that he had a fragile connection with was Cleeve, his fellow rebellious classmate at school. He lived with his parents, three elder brothers and two sisters, in a rented local authority dwelling at a small hamlet called Quarley, in Hampshire. It was rumoured that the family were descended from Romany travellers. No one knew for sure, but it was an unlikely tall tale, not least because the current generation of Cleeve's family had certainly never travelled anywhere further than their immediate surroundings.

Conscious now of dissociating himself from the gang, Calum would regularly bike the three miles over to visit Cleeve. They would cycle together around the local villages, play football, go exploring, all the while constantly on the lookout for scrap metal or any other booty they could salvage and sell on to fund this fun lifestyle.

Calum liked Cleeve, but had nothing in common with the other members of his family, and deliberately avoided getting into conversation with them, especially as they had a penchant for hunting and killing Mother Nature's creatures. These country men ate their kill and lived off the land as their forebears had done. Calum understood and accepted this, as it had also been the way of the Native Americans and many other primitive races. But he felt there was no longer any need to hunt and kill animals, not in this day and age, particularly so for those who lived in the modern western world. He was of the opinion that if one were so inclined to be a carnivore, then there were many supermarkets, factory farm outlets and butcher shops pandering to those specific needs.

To Calum the rose-tinted nostalgic connotations of 'living off the land' was just an excuse to kill and destroy Nature's creatures for fun. He was well aware, living in the countryside as he did, and through kosher information provided by the Great Spirit, that many humans, especially those with power and privilege – the so-called landed gentry – blatantly murdered animals for what they called sport. He could not imagine, on any level, the fun or pleasure to be gained in the wanton ending of an innocent being's life.

Cleeve seemed different, though. 'OK, so he's a bit rough around the edges, loud and brash, swears a lot, and is forever fantasising like he's a real Romany,' Calum allows, knowing this charade is mostly bravado. And most importantly, Cleeve did not strike him as being a cold-blooded killer.

One evening, whilst cycling over to see his friend, Calum comes upon a tramp sat on the grass verge of the road. Slowing to take a closer look, he is amazed to see the old man has hundreds of tiny coloured patches sewn into his raggedy green corduroy jacket and tatty trousers. Frowning at the perceived intrusive rudeness, the tramp takes offence at being scrutinised, booming haughty and indignant, "And what, pray, do you think you are gawping at, my boy?" Calum is surprised that he is so well-spoken. "Sorry to stare, sir, it's just that your clothes, um… look a little peculiar."

"Hmm, you think so, do you? Perhaps you would care to relay that criticism to the dark matter witch, as it was she who carried out the cosmic alterations?" Calum leans forwards to take a closer look at the strange hieroglyphics on each of the patches. "Never heard of a dark matter witch, mister?" The tramp laughs. "Then you've never travelled, my boy, for they are ubiquitous throughout the cosmos… if one only knows where to seek." Calum points to the patches. "What are those strange signs, sir?"

"How perceptive of you, they are mystic symbols, have you not heard of sacred geometry?" Suddenly he leaps to his feet, startling Calum with his agility, looking fearfully to the sky, before chanting, "Kill a cat, shoot a dog, burn a bat and squash a frog," then spinning on his heels, faster and faster, whilst repeating the demonic chorus over and over. "Kill a cat, shoot a dog, burn a bat and squash a frog." With his wild-eyed unblinking gaze, foaming spittle running down his chin, and him grinning like a maniac, the old man appears as if possessed by demons. Sure the tramp is about to have a fit, Calum panics, riding away fast down the lane, skidding to a halt outside Cleeve's place. He's in the yard splitting logs, and he turns at the squeal of bicycle brakes, calling out cheerfully, "Hiya, mush."

"Come quick, my mate!" Calum splutters breathlessly. "You won't believe what I've just seen."

Cleeve buries the axe in a large beech log, before wiping dripping sweat from his brow with the back of a 'Love'-'Hate'-tatooed hand. "Dunno chavvy, I'm sure, but go on then, I guess yer gonna tell me." Calum points back up the road, "There's only a mad old tramp up there, dancing around like a right mental case." Cleeve is curious, smiling as he grabs his bike, "Dordi, come on then chav, dik eye, let's go take us a gander at what's trashd yuh so." Calum smiles, shaking his head as they cycle away. Cleeve makes him laugh, 'always trying to talk traveller language, like he's a true Romany'. They skid to a stop at the top of the road, finding another boy talking to the old tramp. A local lad who lives with his well-to-do parents in the nearby manor house, Phillip is thirteen, a wan, pale-looking boy, his eyes often shut with conjunctivitis, or 'rich folks' pox,' as Cleeve sneeringly termed the sickly malaise.

"Hi there, silly Philly," Cleeve laughs, "see yuv made yerself a friend then."

"Oh gosh! Yes, chaps," Phillip gushes excitedly, "this gentleman is a bonafide professor don't you know." Cleeve snorts, "Ha ha! Yeah, like fuck he is, and I'm Mahatma fuckin' Ghandi."

"No really, it's true, Cleeve, won't you tell them, sir?" Phillip tugs on the old man's coat and urges, "Please tell them, professor." The tramp groans, shaking his head in obvious irritation at this rude imposition. "Must one repeat one's self? How tiresome..." Several long seconds pass before he responds. "Oh, very well then, I shall relent, but this once only. One is feeling a mite peckish, you know. Some sustenance is required, I feel, before one can elucidate and elaborate more fully on your proposed topic, my boy."

"Yes, yes, certainly sir, of course, forgive me," Phillip grovels, "what would you like to eat professor?"

"Why, some buttered rolls and salad, of course!" The professor states sternly, glaring, as if sorely irritated Phillip has not read his mind. "Yes, certainly, I will see to it immediately, sir," he replies subserviently. "But are you sure... just salad... will that be sufficient? Maybe I can provide a nice hock of ham, a leg of chicken perhaps... or maybe some rare roast beef to complement your meal?" The tramp is outraged and snarls, "How dare you! Brainless little bastard, do you think I rose to such universal prominence by eating one's fellow living beings? I am a vegetarian. Eating meat will restrict and retard your spiritual development and give you such a karmic kicking... and often when you least expect it. Do you think one will ever attain the highest stage of spiritual enlightenment whilst killing and eating animals?" Phillip shakes his head emphatically, "I don't kill animals, sir, and can categorically state I never would."

"Oh! How very noble I'm sure, but you eat them, don't you, dullard?"

"Well... yes... I suppose... but–"

"No buts, imbecile, by eating murdered animals you are complicit in the cruelty administered to an innocent life form. Do you know that many of those who work in the meat industry enjoy the cruelty? They actually perpetuate the suffering by tormenting the creatures before killing them?"

"Are most not just doing a job, though, professor?"

"Pah! Bullshit, those wicked monsters love their job, would toil at torture and abuse every day for no pay, most of them, the sick psychopaths would even pay for the privilege. Some humans get the same satisfaction from abusing defenceless creatures as they do from beating their women and abusing their children after a night out on the booze. Any life form that is weak and vulnerable, that cannot fight back or defend itself, is of course all fair game to the depraved desire of these sick cowards. I have had the grave misfortune to come into contact with some of these vile ghouls. I have seen the fur farms, where animals live out their lives in tiny cages before being skinned alive for their pelts. I've seen trappers torment a trapped animal for hours, sometimes days, until dead, or starve the creature to death out of callous spite. I have passed the cattle trains at the railway yards, smelt the stench of frightened, desperate animals, lowing and bleating, waiting in dread for their last journey to the slaughterhouse. So cramped in the sweltering wagons that they cannot move, here they are left for days, without food or drink, so the farmers can save money. After all, what's the point in feeding and watering them if they are soon to be slaughtered? This happens every day, every hour, every minute, all over the world. Yea, such is life with the humans, perpetuating death and cruelty. Without going into further detail, believe me when I say there is no compassion in farming, animal husbandry, or indeed the slaughterhouse. Compassion and love must begin at the very lowest denominator of Nature. It has to start with children, and with respect for insects. Unless such a sea change occurs, humanity is doomed."

Phillip attempts to calm the professor. "I beg your pardon, sir, I had no idea. Please don't go anywhere, I'll be right back." He cycles away at speed to raid his mother's kitchen, calling back over his shoulder, "Keep him entertained chaps, I won't be long."

Cleeve laughs. "Stupid dinlo chavvy that silly Philly, he'll believe anythin' any fool tells him," pointing to the old man, "even a dirty old hedge hopper like this'un." Calum pulls him to one side and whispers behind his hand, "I should be careful what you say, friend. He knows all about witchcraft, this guy. Dark magic and such like. I heard him casting a spell earlier." The professor cackles witch-like, chanting once more, right on cue, "Shoot the dog, kill the cat, squash a frog and burn the bat."

Cleeve looks rattled, and makes the sign of the cross. The tramp puts up his hands, as if to shield his eyes. "Now dik 'ere, old 'un,"

Cleeve snarls, "us Romany gypsies knows a thing or two about t'other side, fer instance, me auntie Ellen, she reads the runes and tea leaves. Even me father, he can tell from the lines on yer palm what yer fortune's gonna be." The professor stares him down, the intensity of his pale blue eyes causing Cleeve to blink and look away. "How dare you use the sign of the cross against me! I am a free man who shows no allegiance to your Christian ideals, idols or brainwashing dogma. I, whose magical influence comes directly from the Great Spirit of Nature," pausing, he grins wickedly. "Oh yes, and lest one forgets, the dark matter witch."

"Hey look guys," Calum breaks the standoff. "Here comes Phil with the grub." Phillip rushes back, carrying a basket on his handlebars, breathlessly keen to ingratiate. "Here you are, sir. I've got everything you asked for, with one exception, the bread rolls. But I've some lovely homemade walnut bread to accompany your salad, and a slice of mother's delicious Christmas cake for desert."

"Harrumph," the professor looks disdainfully at Phillip's offering, whilst scratching his head urgently, in an effort to be rid of the hordes of biting bugs entangled in his matted hair. "Well, hand it over then, boy! Don't stand on ceremony. Man cannot live by bread alone. I suppose if this is all you can muster, it will have to suffice, needs must and all that."

He snatches the wicker basket of food from Phillip and gorges like a starving wild animal, stuffing his mouth full with both hands, tearing the bread to pieces, butter and salad cream running down his chin, coating his thick white beard and dripping down onto his grimy shirt front. After swiftly devouring the main course, he holds up the cake, inspecting it suspiciously, before nibbling cautiously.

"Fer fucks sake!" Cleeve chides, "Just eat the fuckin' stuff yuh ungrateful old fucker, it ain't poisonous y'know." Phillip looks worried. "Is it the marzipan on the Christmas cake that troubles you sir? Shall I remove it?"

The professor gives him a withering look. "What troubles me boy is not marzipan, but you, you idiot. Christmas cake? Pah! For you to place such an inappropriate title on a basic piece of confectionary irks my sensibilities mightily. Now listen, allow me to educate and enlighten you." He stands and grabs Phillip by the shoulders. "It is cake! Nothing more, nothing less, Mary Antoinette, for instance, she said let them eat cake, did she not? Not Birthday cake, nor Christmas cake, just cake boy, just plain and simple fucking cake! There is no such event as Christmas. That preposterous fantasy event exists only in the minds of babes and idiots. It is but a fairy tale for the young, with not a smidgeon of reality involved, you gormless simpleton. Do not, I implore you, ever pin false and fanciful labels on something so base as vittles."

"Begging your pardon, sir," Phillip replies warily, "but I believe the good lady's name was Marie... Marie Antoinette... not Mary. And Christmas... is it not the season of goodwill to all men?" The tramp pushes Phillip hard in the chest, sending him staggering backwards, sudden shock registering on his face as he falls over a fallen tree branch. "Pah! Braindead hogwash, and even if it were so, what care I for goodwill to all men? What of the millions of animals slaughtered and devoured, the trees felled and destroyed, to celebrate the greed and gluttony of Christmas. Haha... the festive season? I fail to see any goodwill extended to those innocent beings... do you? So no, most of humanity matters not a jot to me. The money orientated, materialistic masses, can stew in their rancid, festering sewage pool of existence."

Phillip scrambles to his feet and backs away, cowering, "I have never looked at it in that way, sir, I am sorry to offend but—"

"No! You won't grasp the implications. Those of low intellect who have been indoctrinated and pre-conditioned to eat our fellow Earth dwellers fail to make the connection between animal cruelty and eating meat. Ignorance and apathy thrives among the masses. Children would be better served by not attending school or worshipping dogmatic religion, fawning over royalty or recognising the government's self-serving laws. Synthetic education breeds artificial intelligence. The more youngsters learn from humans the longer they will remain blind to the hidden laws of Nature. Look, I will spell it out for you, simpleton. There are differing levels of karmic retribution. If you eat meat, poultry or fish you will receive the karma which that free will choice entails, and it is no joke, believe me, health-wise or spiritually. But if you show the animals a lack of respect, dignity or compassion and treat them cruelly before slaughtering them, then you will attract the most severe form of karmic justice. The same is true for those that hunt for sport, for fun, that evil bloodlust craving. The big game hunters, the killer poachers of rhinocerous and elephant for their ivory tusks, those who hunt fox with hounds, the killers of sharks and whales for fins and trophies, baby seals clubbed to death, bears trapped and shot, bullfighting, dog fighting, cock fighting, badgers slain for no reason, cats and dogs skinned alive to produce clothing and knick knacks from their fur, or boiled alive by demons to eat, the list goes on and on. This world is insane... and all because of human interference. But Nature will reclaim, after the scourge is cleansed, by order of karmic overlord Krale."

Cleeve grins at Calum and elbow-nudges him in the ribs, "Cheery old fucker, ain't he, mush?" The professor looks to the ground, bemoaning sadly, "I have seen too much... too much... One underwent a cosmic ego deactivation operation many moons ago, a long drawn out, but thankfully irreversible procedure, and so I am more than ably equipped to decipher what is right and wrong here on planet Earth." He sits again, his eyes glowing blacker than coal. "Truth be known, I despise the majority of mankind. They will be judged. You mark my words. There may be justice in the next world, but in this world we have only the law."

"Yes, yes, I know of that quote, sir," Phillip exclaims enthusiastically as he dares to creep closer. "Is it not attributable to Seneca, the famous Greek philosopher?"

"I know of that quote, sir," the professor imitates sarcastically, before shaking his head furiously. "No! No, not Greek, he was a Roman, you dimwit." He looks wistfully to the sky, "but Seneca... yes, correct, that indeed was he. I knew him well, before his untimely demise…" All of a sudden he leaps to his feet and claps his hands. "Well done, boy! You have actually deduced something correctly today, all hail hallelujah."

Phillip, taking this as high praise, confidently continues. "One other thing sir, in my humble opinion, I do not believe Marie Antoinette actually uttered that oft-repeated statement about cake."

"Fuck you! And your worthless opinions." Phillip averts his gaze from the mad staring eyes. "Sorry I'm sure, professor, if I've upset you, it was unintentional, I can assure you. Would you like a drink, sir? I've brought some of mother's homemade lemonade." The professor scowls, smacking his head with the flat of his hand over and over, as if sorely pained by the offering, muttering under his breath, "And fuck your mother too… useless spawn of bitch. A crystal-cut glass of chilled Chablis would have been eminently preferable, but yet again, and at the risk of repeating oneself… if that's all you have, boy," gesturing impatiently for the lemonade, he raises his hands to the heavens before closing his eyes, as if in anticipation of the forthcoming ordeal. "Oh well, when in Rome," grimacing, he snatches the bottle, gulping it down in one, before expelling a burp so loud it startles the cows in the adjacent field to stampede away. He throws the empty bottle carelessly over his shoulder and away into the hedgerow.

"Did you enjoy your meal, sir?" Phillip asks, hesitantly optimistic of receiving a positive reply. The old man strokes his beard. "Hmm, well, whilst the food was, I'll grant you, edible, I do not think that enjoy would be the correct terminology to describe such a lamentable dining experience. As one who has dined in the most salubrious of establishments, more often than not as the guest of highly respected, celebrated and eminent practitioners in the field of quantum physics, psychology, medicine…" His words trail off… gazing ahead, his eyes glaze over, lost in detached, nostalgic reverie. "Why, even heads of state have craved my company at their presidential banquets. One is therefore reluctant to critique your meagre offering as little more than adequate, dear boy, oh, and lest one should forget, it's only fair to warn you, I deemed it necessary to activate a small cosmic curse against you," he smiles at Phillip, "due to the lack of buttered rolls, you understand." Cleeve points to the empty basket, "Yuh soon wolfed all that grub down yer fuckin' gullet though, dint ya, bread rolls or no?" He tosses the basket to Phillip, "Look silly Philly, not a bloody scrap remaining!"

The professor gets to his feet and advances menacingly towards Cleeve. "How dare you! Although it was sub-standard fare, it would go against the very essence of basic dining etiquette to leave any morsel remaining. Are you so uneducated as to be unaware a multitude of unfortunates elsewhere in this world are starving to death, even as we speak?"

Cleeve sniggers. "Yeah, that may well be so Dr fuckin' Dolittle, but it ain't likely that you'd ever be one of 'em, is it my mate? Not judging by the way you just stuffed all that scran down yer scrawny neck."

"Uncouth lout," the professor admonishes, in a pitying tone, waving a thin bony hand dismissively in Cleeve's direction. "Such is life when one is in the presence of the underprivileged low intellect. No social skills. One shall refrain from attempting to enter into any meaningful dialogue with a wretch so coarse, vulgar, and unrefined."

Something has been bugging Calum, and he feels he must speak up. "Excuse me, sir, at the risk of further attracting your wrath, I note you are vegetarian, and applaud you for that, but I wonder if you realise that the buttered bread you ate and the cake made with eggs and butter, is not cruelty-free, as chickens, cows, sheep and pigs, in fact all farmed animals, suffer the most horrific, inhumane treatment. They are literally used and abused as food production vessels until worn out, and then killed for meat."

The professor glares hostilely, seeming, most unusually, lost for words momentarily, before cursing venomously under his breath. Calum is sure it's the C word, and aimed in his direction. "None of us is perfect, boy," pointing and challenging them all, "come on then, you trio of fallen angels, who's going to cast the first damning stone?"

Calum holds up his hands, "Sorry I'm sure... just saying."

"Yes, hear hear, not all of us are bad people you know," Phillip chips in bravely. "I for one do not condone cruelty. My family hunt, but I don't like it. What you have told us is horrible, horrible. I love animals."

"Ha ha, hee hee, is that so? Don't make me laugh, you silly little cunt! You love animals? You love eating them, more like." Phillip ponders before answering gravely, "Yes, you are right, of course, and I don't know why I eat them sir, I know it's wrong... I can see that now. But it's difficult to imagine not eating meat, poultry or fish... at home we eat some form of that food at nearly every meal. I am not allowed to leave the table if I don't eat it."

Cleeve cuffs Phillip around the head. "You're fucking mental mush, even givin' that old crackpot the time of day. No meat! I ask yuh, me, eatin' vegetables? No fuckin' chance, thats fer nancy boys is that."

Calum feels sorry for Phillip and tries to inject some positivity into the atmosphere of doom and gloom. "Come on guys, give Philly a break, not everyone is as condoning towards animal slaughter as most adults, especially children. If they were brought up knowing what happens to animals before they eat them, then I feel sure a lot of kids would be vegans if they had the choice, growing up, and would hopefully choose kindness and compassion towards creatures. It's down to the parents, and schools, to educate them and give them the option."

The professor pulls a small book from inside his jacket. "Allow me to enlighten you by reading an excerpt from this psychology textbook. In a strange twist of fate it was given to me by an ex-soldier, a man not unaccustomed to violence and death, but for all that, an animal lover, and I quote... 'Killing animals for pleasure is psychologically linked to the following... psychopaths, sociopaths, child molesters, serial killers, sexual dysfunction including erectile problems, frigidity, micro-penis syndrome–'"

"Ha, ha, ha..." Cleeve guffaws, turning and pointing to Philly, "he means little pecker mate... like yourn, ha ha."

The professor glares witheringly at Cleeve before continuing... "'And animal maltreatment is also linked to sexual sadism, genital mutilation eroticism syndrome, and several other sexually related conditions. Such participation in hyper-masculine activities like killing, abuse and cruelty towards the weaker and vulnerable is often used to compensate for feelings of sexual inadequacy, repressed homosexuality or an inability to achieve social integration.'" Cleeve sniggers, "In other words, fuckin' losers then."

Calum laughs, and even the professor has a little splutter, stifling a chuckle at the crude but astute observation, allowing, "Hmmm... in a nutshell... yes," before reverting back to his frowning grumpiness, running greasy fingers through his food-encrusted beard and wispy white hair, spitting on his hands and wiping them vigorously on dirty torn trousers. He glances up sharply, raising an eyebrow at Phillip's look of disgust. "Well, sorry I'm sure, boy, but what else is a gentleman to do. Due to your base ineptitude, and general slowness of mind, you failed to provide the very basic courtesy of a table napkin, let alone soap and water. Hence your lack of refinement and sub-standard mental dexterity has impacted severely upon the implementation of one's usual exemplary table manners," pausing, he sighs deeply, an aggrieved expression creasing his face. "One can only work with what one has to hand."

"Oh gosh, sir, I am so sorry, please, please forgive me," Phillip sounds mortified. "I was in such a hurry to get your lunch, I clean forgot about a napkin."

"Tut, tut, elementary requirement," the professor waves him away, "spare me the excuses... please! I can't abide snivelling apologies. Poor show my boy, just damn poor show."

"Shall I go fetch a table napkin now, sir?" Phillip asks eagerly.

"No! No matter, too late now, the damage is done," the professor rejects the offer, muttering, "essential, rudimentary, basic hygiene, de rigueur when sitting at table."

"Begging your pardon sir, but how did someone like you end up as a tramp?" Asks Calum, hoping that changing the subject will get Philly off the hook.

The professor flashes him a scornful glance and replies haughtily, "I prefer the term Dromengro, boy, pray call one that if you must. At least that description evokes and conveys rather more subtle romantic connotations, don't you think?"

"Yes, of course, sorry sir."

"Would you prefer man of the road?" Phillip volunteers hurriedly, desperate to ingratiate himself back into favour. "Insulting, in fact damn rude I'd say. What I would prefer is for you to disappear... as in off the face of planet Earth. Do I look like I belong only to the road? Do no other redeeming features shine through, in your limited view, you odious little cretin?" Crestfallen, Phillip avoids eye contact. The professor continues. "I was once a multi-millionaire you know, but lost everything, all material wealth and possessions, through gambling on equine pursuits and the stock exchange." A faraway look clouds his eyes as he recalls this past veil of privileged life. "Yes, I was rich beyond most men's wildest dreams... owned exclusive property all over the world... Nice, Monte Carlo, Monaco... Ferraris and Maseratis were my playthings. I was married to a beautiful Italian countess, but as is the female's wont, when the money ran out, so did she, taking my two young children with her... never to be seen again."

He seems to be welling up with grief, gazing vacantly ahead, silent now, his thoughts drifting away to mingle morosely with his memories... Eventually he turns back to the boys. "I retained a large mansion in Verona, but alas, could no longer afford the upkeep. One began to drink heavily, and eventually I lost my palatial home," sighing, "Ah well, C'est la vie."

"Oh! What a tragedy, sir... to end up like this." Phillip is genuinely shocked by the professor's revelations. "No, no, not at all, no longer do I view it as any great loss, I am happier, content, in this, my present incarnation. More so than ever one was whilst in the demonic grip of the material world. Besides, the nostalgia and emotive feelings of those past events have been dulled somewhat by the grand illusion of time."

"Could you tell us in which medium you excelled as professor, sir?" Phillip asks meekly. Standing ramrod straight, he announces proudly, "I am professor WM Rogenharten, once esteemed world-wide as the one and only true master of parapsychology, revered throughout the western world, in fact, lauded even beyond the claustrophobic restrictive confines of this galaxy." Cleeve snorts. "That's a big statement to make, fella. How comes I ain't never heard of yuh then?" He glares at Cleeve as if a bad smell has just passed under his nose. "It's highly unlikely one so coarse, ill-mannered, so common, would ever move in such influential circles. A scoundrel such as you, sir, would never gain access to anywhere more exotic... than the gutter." Cleeve sniggers. "Yeah, just how I likes it too, my mate, keepin' it real, down and dirty in the gutter, not like you and yer poncy fuckin' poofter pals."

"What is parapsychology, sir?" Phillip is enraptured. "Please tell." The professor grumbles to himself, perplexed and irritated by Phillip's lack of basic knowledge, muttering, "Idiotic, base, stupid, dense," but grudgingly continues, "parapsychology is the only scientific endeavour which originates from the supernatural spiritual element of the universe. Consequently and paradoxically, fact and reason are intertwined within the imaginary realms of fantasy. The scientific studies undertaken here on Earth are somewhat flawed, though, because most scientists do not recognise that the Great Spirit of Nature is the one true overlord of the universe. This ego malfunction, common in our learned friends, leads them to perceive Nature's presence on Earth as little more than an inconsequential nuisance. To them the Great Spirit is seen merely as a meddling interference, a bind, an insignificant entity to be relegated almost to obscurity, and as such, to be barely tolerated. Ordained in heaven, but not here on Earth, is the sad truth. This is a popular misconception amongst those egocentric power-junkies that would rule absolute."

"Blimey!" Phillip is amazed. "How do you know all of these fantastic facts, sir?" He smiles wearily and jabs a finger at his head, "Professor... the clue is in my title... is it not? O dim one." Calum can't help sniggering at Phillips hangdog expression, before enquiring, "I bet you read a lot though, Prof?" He ponders this. "No... actually it has been so long since I read a book that I believe one has forgotten how... Who needs books anyway?" Gesturing dramatically to himself, "When moi is an abstract living art form. Always remember that the most authentic art installation is one's self, and the greatest masterpiece that one can create is to live to the full one's own life, with free will, extending grace and kindness to life's unfortunates and those sentient beings of the animal kingdom. Walk one's own Sacred Path. Be as lacking in ego as if you are just dust in the wind. By being involved in that creation, that truth, one will escape from the static social patterns so beloved of the masses and forge ahead into inspiring natural dynamics, which will in turn allow your mind to expand into a level of unconsciousness far beyond the capabilities of the average human. That is the elevation one should strive for in any form of art or creation."

Cleeve is not impressed. "You old fake... don't read books, eh? You just fuckin' read to us from a book, dint yuh?" He throws up his hands. I'm off home lads, cain't be listening to no more of this fuckin' bullshit," cocking an imaginary gun to his head as he walks away, "the old timer's lost it, big time." Phillip, hands on hips, calls after him, chastising. "Can you not show at least a modicum of decorum for our esteemed guest?" Cleeve laughs. "Fuck off, silly Philly, yer as mental as he is." Phillip stamps his feet and whines, "No I'm not, and don't call me silly Philly, you know Mother doesn't like it."

The professor stands, resting his hand on Phillip's shoulder, pointing a finger at Cleeve, as if aiming a weapon. "No matter boy, let him go. The retarded fool is a disbeliever. No good will come of that one. The stain of karma is ingrained within him... now... where was I before being so rudely interrupted?" His aged brow furrows as he addresses his audience, "Ah yes, I recall, there are no boundaries, boys, or indeed limitations, obstructing the soul from the pursuit of spiritual enlightenment. The possibilities open to all altruistic kindred spirits are of vast cosmic enormity. Any preconceived obstacles exist only within the mindset of those humans who believe they are superior to Nature. The attainment of true enlightenment is a monumental task as far as the majority of mankind is concerned. This is because everything that man holds dear, such as education, language, science, politics, warmongering, history, money, precious metals, material possessions, greed, egotism, sexual deviation, covert activity, philandering, plunder, saving, hoarding, jealousy, rage, abuse, persecution, slavery, death, deception, destruction, torment, murder, torture, people trafficking, animal cruelty..." He pauses to take a deep breath. "I could go on, and on and on. But to cut a long, depressing litany short, suffice to say these base human traits are alien to the universal spirit of Nature. These examples of scurrilous human endeavour here on planet Earth are hailed as an example and warning to other inhabited planets in the universe. But in the great scheme, all of mankind's activities are seen as just trivial punctuation marks amidst the cosmic flow of universal spiritual enlightenment. Even man's self-congratulatory highly overrated form of intelligence is synthetic compared to the authentic reasoning of Gaia. For the majority of human beings the soul atrophies to become but an incon-sequential vegetative component of their own damaged psyche. The karmic consternation at human interaction with the greater good and the subsequent deployment of man's base traits occurs because man constantly tampers with the universal natural order of Nature. This will not be tolerated by karmic overlord Krale."

Calum is interested now. "I know of the spiritual elements, and something of karma, sir." The professor strokes his beard. "Hmm... pray tell how you came by this knowledge, boy?"

"The Great Spirit of Nature often speaks with me, professor."

"Yes, I am aware of that."

"Really? Then why do you ask, sir?"

"Because I wish to hear it from you boy. I can then decipher from your vocal intonation, the level of your advancement, intent, and belief."

"But how... how do you know of my connection with Gaia?"

"Because the great one often converses on a personal level with WM Rogenharten." Calum is intrigued. "Great Spirit hasn't been around me for a while though, Prof... between you and me... I was beginning to wonder if she were for real...or maybe just–"

"A figment of your imagination?" The professor interjects. "Well... yes... I s'pose so."

"What is real shall be felt. That which is false will only be seen. Most human activities are nothing but egocentric drama, acted out on a stage of virtual reality. Self-delusion is all the rage here on Earth. Self-trickery concocted in homage to the ego. A lack of basic authenticity which eventually leads to identity crisis... or mental health problems... as the self-styled psychoanalyst specialists call it. Engaging in these materialistic scenarios distracts the soul from the meditative contemplation that is required for nourishment and enlightenment. If allowed to run wild, the ego will bombard one with constant subliminal interference. This intrusive mind chatter induces stress, anxiety, panic, irritability and depression, among countless other negative ailments. The key to cosmic clarification is learning to differentiate between fantasy and reality. Then, and only then, will you be able to tune in to the advanced universal frequency of the Great Spirit."

"Mmm... yeah... Gaia mentioned something like that," Calum agrees, though in truth he is more than a little baffled now. His brain is aching, admitting to himself, 'It's tough-going conversing with this guy, just listening requires so much effort.' The professor picks up on Calum's struggle to fully comprehend, and patronisingly elaborates, "Allow moi to simplify... planet Earth is over 4 billion years old, and although still enchanting to the naive, young and innocent, even the grandeur of the mighty peaks and valleys pales into insignificance to a weary universal traveller such as I. Even when taking the scenic route of the Sacred Path, Nature's magnificence becomes just diluted wonders to a frail old man. But when you reach the Beautiful Garden..." He directs a sneering glance at his rapt audience... "If any of you rapscallions ever do... now that's a different story. Anyone fortunate enough to be relocated there will be received with reverence, and will be greeted with the most vivid array of new colours and emotions, which will cleanse and refresh the soul. To put it in a nutshell, boys, be true to yourselves and Mother Nature, and then you shall want for nothing on your journey of the Sacred Path."

Phillip looks doubtful. "Is it really as simple as that, professor?"

"Yes, it is," he claps his hands loudly. "Bravo, you've hit the nail right on the head, boy. Even one so limited in natural intelligence as you understands, proving conclusively it really is that simple... simpleton... haha. As a great Zen master once confided in me, the essence of Zen is the art of looking into one's own soul, and thus escaping from bondage to freedom. Meditation will then have a serenity at its core that allows one a spiritual reflection of a material reality. Just simplify, simplify. Therein lies the answer. That's all you need do boys... search within."

Rising up surprisingly spritely from the floor, he extends a grimy gnarled hand. "Well, my work here is done. One must be on one's way. I have dallied here too long. Good to make your acquaintance gentlemen, I'm sure. Have a good life. Make hay while the sun shines. Precious are your young salad days. Be assured, they will soon disappear, as fast as snow in summer." He chuckles, "Excuse one's predilection to the cliché, but, as a clever man once said... youth is wasted on the young." He shakes hands with the boys, before pulling a small folded card from one of his torn and shredded lace-up boots, offering this to Calum who, surprised and excited, cautiously accepts the gift. "Why, thank you, sir." He opens the card, revealing six strange symbols drawn in black ink, recognising the signs as being similar to those adorning the professor's clothing.

"Ha ha ha, don't thank me, boy. I am glad to be rid, besides, I have a sneaking suspicion that they may come in useful for you... in the future." Smirking knowingly, he gathers up his few belongings, before walking away without a backward glance. Calum calls after him. "Hey, Prof... one more thing." The old man turns back, glowering world-weary... "Yessss?"

"If you're so into Nature and such like, how come you go around singing that 'kill a cat, squash a frog' kinda song?"

"Ahhh... That's the dark matter witch influence, I'm afraid. I came under her spell during a weak, low moment, many years hence, when she seduced and enticed one to her bed. The Great Spirit understands, though. After all, as I said before," staring pointedly at Calum, "none of us is perfect, boy... so the ditty, the song, is a cosmic curse, like a parasitic nervous tic, permanently ingrained within my core make-up. Let that be another lesson, boys, no matter how tempting the incentive. Never, ever, sell your soul to a dark matter witch." Phillip runs after him. "Please tell us more about this witch, sir, and the karmic overlord Krale." The old man waves him away, walking on. "Be gone boy, are you so dim as to not recall that I have already activated a minor curse upon you? Do not force me to increase the power; be assured, you will not like that, you tiresome whining wretch."

Phillip walks back sheepishly, muttering miserably under his breath, "I'll take that as a no, then." Calum grins. "You two sure hit it off, didn't you?" Phillip looks up, suddenly beaming. "You really think so?"

"Hmm..." stroking his chin, Calum feigns thoughtful musing... "Duh, err, no Phil." He picks up on the cruel sarcasm and sighs resignedly, "OK, point taken, Cal," before asking in wistful contemplation, "Do you think he really is an eminent professor?"

Calum laughs. "Yeah, of course... what other kind is there?"

CHAPTER
THIRTY-ONE

Calum catches up with Cleeve the next day. He has news. "Guess what 'appened to silly Philly this mornin'?" Calum senses bad tidings. "Go on, spill then, friend?"

"Only came off his bike, and broke his fuckin' leg," Cleeve chuckles. "The nutter kept sayin' over and over that it's the old tramp's curse."

"Yeah..? Well, he could just be right about that, pal."

"Nah, baloney, I told him to stop being a big Jessie and take it like a man. It's only an accident after all, just coincidence."

Calum shakes his head. "I wouldn't be too sure about that. I've found there's no such thing as coincidence."

Cleeve puffs out his chest, adopting an exaggerated boxer's stance, sparring at thin air. "The old git cursed me too, dint he? And I'm still standin' cushti, ain't I mush?"

"Shouldn't tempt fate though," Calum advises, "just in case."

"Bullshit! I got more power in me little finger than that old vagrants got in his whole fuckin' body, dark magic, ha! Don't make me laugh, chavvy." Calum holds up his hands in submission. "OK, OK, have it your own way."

"I fuckin' will, matey!" Cleeve snorts. "Don't you worry... Now look, don't get me wrong mush, Phil's an alright sort really, bit dim up top, and terrible accident prone," he sniggers. "All the inter-breedin' is that, but he's always good fer a laugh. These silver spooners though, they're all the same, fuckin' dinlos, the lot of em."

"Yeah, Phil's OK," Calum agrees. "He's harmless enough… don't get what you mean though, by silver spooners?"

Cleeve snatches up a long blade of grass and chews angrily. "Yuh knows, my mate, must a heard of that old sayin', ain't ya? Born wiv a silver spoon in his mouth… No?"

"Oh yeah, sure," Calum recalls now. "Well, that's silly Philly for yuh. His mum and dad is loaded, posh gaff, big motors, horses, land, the fuckin' lot, and never had to do an honest day's graft in their lives. So, only natural, they ain't got no street savvy, don't know what real life is, not like me and you, Cal. We've had to get by on us wits, us. Well-educated, that's as may be, but them lazy bastards ain't got an ounce of real life think on yer feet nous goin' on. They wouldn't survive a fuckin' week on their lonesome wivout all their creature comforts." Calum picks up on the jealousy in Cleeve's voice. "You may well be right, pal. But I shouldn't let it get to you, after all, you wouldn't want to be like them would you?"

"Well… err… no… course not… but it still ain't right though, is it chav? Fuckin' eejits like them, never lifted a finger, but they's got all that dough, and 'ere's us struggling to make a bar." Calum grins wryly. "Lots of things ain't right in this world, my friend." Cleeve, looking like he's carrying the world on his shoulders in this moment, sighs in agreement. "Yeah, true enough… we just gotta grin and bear it, I s'pose." Calum gives him the thumbs up. "Yeah, it ain't all about the money, honey. That's just a commodity. Doesn't matter how much dosh you've got, it's no guarantee of class or intelligence."

"Amen to that, bud."

They spend the rest of the afternoon on bike maintenance duties, making any urgent running repairs, before cycling into Thruxton early evening. Cleeve suddenly swings his bike in a wide skidding arc into the deserted car park of the George Inn public house. Calum rides in close behind. It's five-thirty. The pub doesn't open until six. There's no one about. Cleeve dismounts. "Let's take us a decko, chavvy." Calum follows him to the rear of the pub. "Dordi, dordi, dickety ki!" Cleeve always spoke in fractured Romany when excited.

Calum didn't get this, allowing, 'OK, for sure, it's a great thing to aspire to, the Romany and traveller lifestyle, not being a prisoner of convention, the freedom and independence, being your own boss. But why pretend to be something you're not? It must be hard work keeping up that level of pretence, and cringe-worthy embarrassing, as a real Romany would always spot that sham a mile off.'

Cleeve points to a pile of beer crates stacked against the wall. "Wow! Cacker, me chav, won't yuh just dik eye that little lot."

Calum looks at his friend in pity. "What's so special about a pile of old beer crates? You're losing the plot big time, my man."

"Spondulicks pajo, vonga a plenty," Cleeve rubs his hands fervently, "that's what's so special, chavvy."

Calum is not convinced. "How so? What money is there in junk like that?"

"It's the bottles, that's in them there crates," Cleeve perseveres, "that's where the money is, me boyo."

Calum picks up a beer bottle. 'Strongs of Romsey,' the legend reads, 'Finest pale ale.' He laughs. "Its empty, fool."

"Yeah, I knows that, don't I dinlo... Lookit, me pa drinks these back at home, then sometimes he gives me the empties, or else I chors 'em from 'im, when he's kippin' after a skin full, but either way, I takes 'em back to The White Horse pub, just down the road a ways, then Bob's yer fuckin' uncle, thruppence is paid to yours truly in a cash refund for each returned bottle."

"You're joking me?" Calum, now equally excited at the prospect of some easy cash, begins the calculation process. "That means... what we have here then... is... is," he gives up struggling with the mental arithmetic. "Oh fuck it! A fair bit of loot though, to be sure."

"Yeah? That's wot I bin tryin' to tell yuh, dinlo chavvy." Tucking his jumper into his jeans, Cleeve slides five bottles down the V-neck and gleefully rubs his hands together. "Come on then, pal, let's be jellin' on, next stop The White Horse."

Calum slips four bottles down his shirt-front before they ride away, extremely carefully, so as not to drop the valuable contraband.

Minutes later the pair free-wheel into The White Horse car park, with Cleeve turning around in the saddle to inform, "They opens at six 'ere, my mate." The boys get off the bikes extremely cautiously, with Calum giggling, "Careful now, don't drop the gold." Cleeve cradles his bottles protectively and laughs, "As fuckin' if, mush."

They stretch out on the cool grass, waiting expectantly for the pub to open. "We might even get us a drink 'ere tonight," Cleeve advises, "If Frankie boy is on duty instead of Moray."

Landlord of the White Horse, Mr Moray is in his early fifties, with dyed dark hair and beard. His ample girth is sustained by the frequent over-indulgence of his wares, an ever-present temptation, this occupational hazard of working in the licensing trade. He runs the pub along with his buxom partner Molly, a lady who likes her drink – a little too much, on occasion – and has a tendency to become bad tempered and volatile after one too many. Frank is head barman here. Aged forty, sharp-featured, a good-looking guy, slim, always smartly dressed. Divorced, he lives alone and rents a room in the village. Easygoing, Frank would occasionally allow Cleeve – or any other youngsters he knew well enough – to have a beer or two, even if they were underage. This happy hour treat was only on offer prior to Moray appearing in the bar at around eight each evening.

The White Horse is a 16th-century thatched public house, bizarrely painted bright pink by its flamboyant landlord. The interior dominated by big open fires, old black-painted beams, and much crude hanging horse brass. The large car park and overgrown beer garden is enclosed by a curved whitewashed cob wall. A popular pub for holidaymakers, it is situated right next to the A303 main road to the West Country. Moray is a canny entrepreneur who has his irons in a number of fires – one of which is 'Moray's Bar', a single-storey rough house of a nightclub based in an old warehouse on Thruxton airfield.

CHAPTER
THIRTY-TWO

Calum hears the distant roar of motorbikes a long way off, gradually becoming an ear-splitting roar, as a rough tough-looking gang of bikers come cruising into the car park. These leather-clad greasers and their girls, aka the 'old ladies,' are members of the local motorcycle club. The White Horse is well known as a bikers' pub.

Cleeve lets out a long low whistle. "Dordi my mate, won't you just look at them machines."

"Yeah, something else," Calum agrees.

The convoy of twenty heavily chromed motorcycles rev loudly as they park up. A mixture of BSAs, Norton Commandos, Triumph Bonnevilles, a pair of AJS, an old Ariel and several old Japanese Kawasakis (or 'Kwakkers', as the bikers affectionately called them). Dismounting and removing their helmets, some of the guys light up cigarettes, or joints of cannabis, before strutting about the car park with the assured swaggering arrogance of outlaw power in numbers. These guys made their own rules and did not live by society's convention and laws. Most wore their hair long, with their lower faces and necks covered by dust- and bug-repellent bandanas. Heavy greatcoats over leather or denim jackets, with silver studded leather waistcoats worn underneath, oil- and grease-encrusted Levi or Wrangler jeans (sacrilege to wash them) or leather motorbike trousers. Steel toe-capped boots complete the bandit dress code. Some sport the bikers' club colours:

ANDOVER AVENGERS
MC
HAMPSHIRE

stitched onto a denim waistcoat, worn over the ubiquitous leather jacket.

The 'old ladies' are all donned in similar gear. The majority wear jeans, with some clad in short denim, suede, or leather mini-skirts. After removing their helmets, several of the girls shake loose and brush out their hair, while others adjust their make-up aided by the mirrors on the motorbike handlebars. Two of them spot the lounging boys on the grassy bank and pose provocatively before the mesmerised pair.

"Phwoar!" Gasps Cleeve.

"Wow!" Calum agrees.

The shorter of the two, a petite curvy blonde, struts confidently over to Calum, a self-assured smile on her pretty face. "Hi honey, I'm Chrissie." She sits down close to him. Chrissie smells strongly of petrol and cheap perfume, this heady fragrance fusion serving only to further entice the already smitten teenager. "What's your name then, handsome?" He sits up eagerly, smiling. "Hi'ya gorgeous, Calum is the name, and lovin' is my game." She laughs at his cheek, "Is that so?" Chrissie's wet pink tongue flicks and licks contemplatively over garishly rouged lips, while her pale blue eyes look him up and down. "Hmm, well then, Calum, my boy, as you're such a little cracker, you'd best give me a snog, dont'cha think?" Not waiting for an answer, she pushes him flat out onto the grass, straddling expertly, treating him to a long lingering French kiss before getting to her feet. The bikers cheer and cat-call her, "Hey, cradle snatcher, put him down, you'll be locked up fer fuckin' child abuse, so you will." Chrissie pouts back at the banter, poking her tongue out at the mob, turning her back on the jeers, and pulling down tight blue jeans to wiggle a shapely bare bottom at the accusers. This is greeted by shrill wolf-whistles and more lusty cheers from the throng. "Fuck you all," she shouts, giving her comrades a two-fingered reply. "Don't care how old he is, I'll have whoever I fucking fancies, me." She gets back on top of Calum, knees on his shoulders, tickling him under the chin. "And as this one's such a cutie, I'll come back for him later, but right now I need me a stiff one." Another roar erupts from the boys. "Drink that is, ya sex mad buggers." Chrissie laughs sexy dirty as she rolls off her willing captive. Strutting off to the bar, she elbows her way through the rowdy bikers. "Come on, then, you dozy bastards, get the fucking beers in." The gang whoop and holler as they follow her in to the pub.

Calum is dumbstruck and hooked by this, his first ever kiss, savouring the new taste of lipstick, wondering wistfully, 'Is this love?' Whatever it is, he sure wants in on more of the same.

"Wow!" Cleeve sighs, "You lucky bugger, you. Ain't she just sex on legs, that blonde rakli? Why'd she choose you, though? What's wrong with me?" He whines, insecure frustration eating away at him. "Life ain't fuckin' fair."

The obvious answer to Cleeve's jealous query, from Chrissie's point of view, is that Calum, at nearly fifteen years of age, is blessed with long blonde hair, blue eyes and nice white teeth. Allied to these desirable attributes, he exudes a natural feral wildness, a primitive attribute certain members of the female species seem to find irresistible. This alluring magnetic aura compels some girls, such as these rebellious bikers, to find him a tempting turn-on. Cleeve, by comparison, has not been blessed with this raw pheromone allure, often wearing the look of a lurking ferret, appearing untrustworthy and sneaky. The dark brooding eyes being set too close together not helping his cause, only adding to the general negative vibe lingering about him. He nudges Calum in the back and heads for the bar. "Come on, then, chavvy, let's get in that kitchima and cash in these bottles. I needs a fuckin' livna, so 'elp me gawd."

Captivated by this whole new world opening up for him tonight, Calum needs little prompting. Feeling dizzy with the rush of his first sexual experience, he enters the bar to be hit full-on by an intoxicating mix of swirling cigarette smoke, flowing alcohol and boisterous banter. Jethro Tull's 'The Witch's Promise' playing out from the jukebox only accentuates the alluring vibe. He recognises the old scruffy guy leaning against the bar as the drunk he had come across laying flat-out in the Thruxton ditch a while back. The room is buzzing as the bikers kick back. Calum is entranced by the raw scent of wild sexual excitement and fun atmosphere in the bar. It's a brand-new emotion. These sexy girls are addictive, and he wants in.

Cleeve squeezes through to the bar. "Hey Frank, got us some more empties here. Do us a favour, gis us a drink, my mate." Frank glances nervously about the room. "OK, lads," he whispers. "But be sure to take the liquor outside, mind. I'll get shot if Moray catches me serving you." Cleeve dismissively waves away the barman's warning. "Yeah, yeah, sure thing, Frankie, let's be having two of yer best barley wines then, pal."

Frank pours two glasses of dark liquid from a keg on the bar and shoos them away hurriedly. The boys take the drinks outside and sit on the low brick wall bordering the beer garden. Cleeve takes a long swig of the strong alcohol, grimacing as the syrupy brew slides down his throat. Calum swallows a mouthful and immediately feels the potent promise of the sour wine... his eyes stray back to the bar, all he needs now is more kissing. As if in answer to his prayer, Chrissie comes out, puffing on an oily reefer as she links arms with her girlfriend.

"Hey Calum, Val, me bestest oppo 'ere, fancies a little snog also. Can you oblige her, hon?" Chrissie tilts her head coyly, "Just for me, babe?"

"Oh yeah?" Calum, nervously excited, beckons Val, "Does she now? No problem, my love, c'mon then, the more the merrier, sweetheart." Val is taller and slimmer than Chrissie, but just as sexy, he reckons, appraising her attributes as she slinks towards him, flaunting her curves, posing seductively with hands on hips, jet-black hair hanging long and loose about her shoulders. He can't take his eyes off her long legs, sexily clad in sheer dark stockings. She turns and bends over provocatively before him. He gasps as a brief flash of tanned silky thigh is tantalisingly exposed by the riding up of the tight leather micro-mini. She comes up close, pressing against him, glossy lips parting in anticipation. "Like what you see, lover boy?" she whispers in his ear. "I'm always eager to please, honey." She steps back, resting her hands on his knees and leans forwards, brazenly exposing her cramped cleavage.

Val reeks of stale tobacco and beer, but to Calum, she seems mysterious and exotic. He couldn't have been more aroused had she been doused in Chanel No 5. She looks daringly into his eyes before kissing him, passionate and hard, her tongue wriggling and writhing like a rampant serpent in hyper-exploration of his mouth. He doesn't resist, surrendering meekly to the hardcore charms of this hot temptress.

Chrissie, suddenly jealous, snarls possessively, "Hey! That's enough, get off him you fucking nympho, he's mine, bitch, I found him first." She pulls Val's head back violently by the hair, and using a boot in the back, sends her sprawling across the lawn.

"Fuck you!" Val screams back as she slides over the damp grass.

An urgent primeval desire suddenly overwhelms Chrissie, kissing Calum so intently that he struggles to catch his breath. So powerful is her passion, he's sure she's attempting to devour him... Eventually relenting her administrations, she releases him, breathing heavy in short shallow gasps, backing away unsteadily, eyeing him mischievously, the dilated pupils of her wild sexual gaze confidently challenging him to take this further... he hesitates... she shrugs... the moment is gone.

Chrissie laughs in his face, sneering, "You had me going there, I was up and ready to fuck. Your loss, you bottled it, kid." She returns to the bar, leaving Calum stunned and tasting blood from where she bit deep into his lip. Flushed with renewed lust for these wild rebel girls, he downs the remainder of his glass, sighing, "Jeez!" Looking to the heavens, he gratefully acknowledges, "Yes! There is a God."

"You wanna watch out boy, or else you'll get a taste fer them dirty morts, so you will." Cleeve sounds angry and resentful. "You are not wrong there friend," Calum smiles, "I've sure got me the taste tonight all right."

"Them slags ain't no good fer yuh at your age, mush. Never know what you'll catch neither, besides, we got plenty goin' on wivout raklis bein' involved."

"Yeah, yeah, I hear you mate, but only a while ago weren't you saying how she's sex on legs, my little blonde cutie," Calum sniggers. "Come on now pal, make yourself useful and go get us both another brew. I'm mighty parched from all this kissin'." Feeling elated, on a high, the American gangster actor James Cagney's immortal line comes to him. "Top of the world ma, top of the world." He smiles to himself in recognition of that vibe, 'Yeah, that's how I feel tonight, top o' the world ma.'

Cleeve returns, looking surly, with refills. They savour the alcohol whilst listening to the music belting out from the bar. "A crackin' tune," Cleeve allows, relenting his obstinate jealous stance somewhat, clicking his fingers and tapping his foot to the number one hit single of the day, 'Spirit In The Sky', by Norman Greenbaum. The song feels like a token of unity to them both in this moment. Emotional, inebriated and excited, they decide on the spot to adopt this tune as their forever anthem, swearing solemnly that, 'Spirit In The Sky' will always remain their totem. Despite this harmonious mutual accord, glowering Cleeve still seems edgy and uptight.

'Something has changed tonight,' Calum can feel it. Carnal knowledge, that shady corrupter of innocence, is influencing a new dynamic in their friendship. His sexual initiation has altered things irrevocably between them. Darkness swiftly shrouds the beer garden, as if calling time on their adolescence.

"Time to jell on home I s'pose," Cleeve sounds unusually subdued, "got no lights on the old pushbike, so I best be makin' tracks."

"OK mate, been a good night though, enjoyed it, must do it again. We meeting up tomorrow?" Cleeve avoids eye contact and replies sulkily, "Dunno, mebbe... if yuh kin spare me the time, mush." Calum drapes an arm around his shoulder, slurring, "Course I can, come on, don't go getting all serious on me, old buddy, I'll be here, same time, same place."

Cleeve shrugs off the drunken embrace and shouts, "yuh kin please yer fuckin' self, chav, fer all I cares." He staggers drunkenly to his bike, before riding away unsteadily from the car park.

Calum hangs around a while longer, hoping that Val or Chrissie may need him for more sexual duties. The alcohol has boosted his confidence, and he's vowing not to let the opportunity slip next time, but the girls fail to reappear, so he leaves his bike at the pub, lurching away from the beer garden, swaying and wandering along erratically as the barley wine kicks in big time. Happy and carefree, he grabs at the foliage of the long hedgerow along Dauntsey Lane, trying to keep his balance, barely noticing the spiteful brambles and thorns ripping at his hands and clothes. He couldn't care less, though, allowing, 'What's a few scratches and scrapes?' He feels immune to life's minor irritations tonight, especially as the world is now his oyster. Calum feels wanted, for the first time ever, and the promise of this new life is suddenly thrilling. 'Those girls down The White Horse need me, adore me, most probably love me even? That's real, ain't it? After all,' he gloats smugly, 'are they not desperate for me? What a buzz'. His confidence sky-high, he feels certain he is now surely a man of some importance. No one can hold him back, nothing is off-limits or taboo in this exciting new adventure. There are no streetlights along the way, and frequently veering off course, he stumbles drunkenly through several gardens. But a full moon eventually guides him to his door. More by luck than judgement he has managed to find the way home, creeping indoors, feeling along the wall in the darkness, entering his room, before collapsing and flopping down on the bed. He's soon snoring, sleeping fully clothed, and dreaming of his next liaison with those sexy girls down the pub.

CHAPTER
THIRTY-THREE

Calum groans as he awakes to his first hangover, accepting, 'Hello…
here we go… payback time'. Feeling groggy, head muzzy, mouth dry
and craving water, lethargy feels just right, as hazy playback recall
of sexy putting-out girls, strong alcohol and loud loud music filter
through his fragile memory circuits.

Janet calls to him. "Calum, Calum, can you come for your breakfast please. We are off to town soon to get the weekly shopping."
Pulling the blankets over his pounding head he grumbles aloud, "Oh
yeah? Big fucking deal! I'm interested why exactly? I think you're
mistaking me for someone who gives a toss, lady."

"Can you hear me, son?" she continues.

"OK, OK, I hear you," he growls, under his breath, covering his
ears, before shouting back to her, "I'll be there in a while, but don't go
getting any ideas, I won't be coming to town. I'm not feeling too good
today Mrs Brown, bad headache, gonna rest up a while."

"Will you listen to that insolent lazy good for nothing," Jim
grumbles from the kitchen, "out until all hours, then expects to just
lounge around the next day. Now in my day–"

"Calm down, dear," Janet gently interjects. "Don't take on so,
you'll only bring on your indigestion. It's Saturday after all. Let's just
leave him be. He can have his day off. We can manage without him."

"Yeah, that's it, shut the fuck up, both of you," Calum curses from
under the warm blankets. "Just piss off and leave me be". Dragging
the covers back over his head, he moans, the slightest movement

making his head throb, waiting until they leave before emerging from his room to gulp down a glass of water and taking a strong hot cup of black tea back to bed. After slowly drinking the warming brew, he drifts back to sleep...

He is woken later by the sound of the Browns chatting. "Fucking hell, are they still here?" Through blurred vision he checks the tin-plate alarm clock on the mantle. "Oh my god! It's three o'clock... how did that happen?" He leaps from the bed, wondering, "Where's the time gone?" The long sleep has been beneficial though and, feeling refreshed, he's raring to be off down the pub again. Smirking arrogantly, the memory of last night is still imprinted in full colour as he heads for the bathroom. 'Those biker girls will be there again, waiting for me, can't keep their dirty little hands off can they? Best not keep them waiting too long then.' He splashes cold water over his face and has a quick strip-down wash, before lying down on his bed waiting for opening time.

"Dinner's ready, Calum," Janet calls, waking him from his dozing. He gets up, scowling at the sound of her voice, and mumbles to himself, "Yeah, yeah, cool it now with the whining, I'll be right there."

He dresses fast, hungry, but dreading the carnivorous karma created by one of Janet's meals. Once again the repugnant aroma of dead animals being cooked assaults him as he enters the lounge. He eats quickly so as to minimise the revulsion, devouring the vegetables and mash in double-quick time, hiding the chunk of dead steak and kidney pie under a large overcooked grey cabbage leaf. Janet notices and tut tuts, wagging a finger at him. He glances up sharply at her. "What! Come on now, how many times Mrs Brown, do I have to spell it out? I... don't... eat... meat... remember?" She looks offended. "Oh, I'll never understand this vegetarian business... I thought you were alright with steak and kidney pie? Are you staying in this evening, Calum?" He looks up in shock and horror at the very thought. "The fuck I am... uh... sorry... no... promised I'd meet up with a friend tonight."

Janet looks sternly quizzical. "Did I hear you swear just then Calum Connor?" He glances up, mock horrified. "No! As if... course not Mrs Brown... just mumbling away with my mouth full is all." She looks far from convinced, but lets it go. "Mmm... very well. I would like a hand with the washing up, though, before you go, if you don't mind, and please don't be late back tonight." He smirks, "No, of course not, Mrs Brown." Janet winces at his formality, desperately wishing he would warm to her, pleading hopefully, "Do call me Janet, dear... if you wish." Calum does not wish though, just wanting to keep things on a formal footing with the foster parents, with no emotional complications. He's not into any touchy feely creepiness going on, only hanging around until he can make good his escape. "OK, will give that some thought, Mrs B."

He goes to clean his teeth, then liberally dabs on Old Spice, before donning faded Levi jeans and his best Ben Sherman shirt, finishing off tonight's hot-shot look with a light tan waistcoat hung with Wild West tassels. Checking his look for the umpteenth time in the mirror, he finally deems himself ready for his adoring female fans, nodding in vain satisfaction at the smug reflection smiling back. After slipping on his light brown zip-up Chelsea boots, he smiles and whispers, "Fuck the washing up." He creeps silently along the hall, leaving the bungalow, ducking down below the lounge window ledge, escaping undetected. Now he is away, striding quickly up the drive, laughing out loud in joyous anticipation of another night of sexy fun and frolics.

Calum is consumed by bubbling excitement. Eager anticipation of the sexual delights in store for him at the White Horse power him purposefully towards Thruxton. He pauses after a while to light his first cigarette of the day. Inhaling deeply, he sighs in satisfaction. It tastes good, real grown-up good. 'Ain't this the life', smiling at his good fortune, 'not a care in the world'. But he knows it is imperative now to get away from school, and the fosterers, if he is to take advantage of the freedom that this new lifestyle opportunity offers. Life would then be complete... Ambling on, deep in thought, devising his next move...

"Hey there, chavvy!"

Caught unawares, startled by the close-up shout, Calum spins round to see Cleeve cycling towards him. "Just been up to your gaff to call for yuh, mush, right old ruckus goin' down. The old geezer was cursin' you summat chronic." Calum laughs, "Fuck him." Cleeve checks out his dressed-to-impress look before throwing his bike clattering to the ground and demanding, "Now, now, tell me friend, where is you jellin' to then? All got up in yer best gear 'n all." Calum picks up on the accusing tone, feeling a little riled, but lets it pass. "Just off to Thruxton, on my way to meet you, thought we'd get us some more empties and then–"

"Meet me! Pah! Like fuck you was," Cleeve cuts him short, in his face now, jabbing a finger in his chest. "Don't give me that bullshit," sneering, "Oh, now don't tell me, let me fuckin' guess, yer off to see them dirty morts again I'll wager, yuh don't take notice of anythin' I says, do yuh, dinlo chavvy?"

Anger rises instantly in Calum at this suspicious hostility, and he pushes Cleeve away so roughly that he stumbles backwards over his pushbike and goes sprawling to the ground. "So what if I am? Your tone's sounding kinda threatening, man." Standing over him, fists bunched, he shouts, "I don't need this hassle from you, or anyone else for that matter. I've had a gut full of people telling me what to do. It's my life, get it? I'll live it how I damn well please."

"Yeah... yeah... course... course it is, me old mate." Cleeve's suddenly doe-eyed submissive as he gets to his feet, backing away, arms outstretched in surrender, shocked by Calum's vitriolic tirade. "Ain't tryin to tell yuh what to do wid yer life bud," he pleads, "Course I ain't. But listen up, friend, it's just that we got things goin' on that raklis cain't be involved with. Just the way it is me chavvy, 'orses fer courses like."

Calum sighs, realising that the relationship between them has been further soured in this moment. "Now see here, stop fucking whining at me, all I get is people moaning in my ear, it's doing my head in. Look, I'm gonna say this once, and once only. You've been a good pal Cleeve, no denying, but I'm sick of people always getting on my

case. If you don't like my way, then best we call it a day as friends...
Anyways, I reckon you're just jealous man, cos those girls can't get
enough of me," he grins at the recall. "You saw them yourself last
night, fucking gagging for it!"

"All right my mucker," Cleeve concedes reluctantly, "you 'ave it
your way, be it on yer own 'ead then, pal." His eyes narrow to slits.
"I kin tell yuh straight up though, I ain't jealous of them dirty VD
carryin' slags. I just don't wanna see yuh taken fer a fool by some
old prossie, is all." Calum eyes him coldly, "Don't call them that...
anyways, you've no need to worry about me, I've got it all sussed. I'm
cool, man." Cleeve looks to the heavens, exasperated, but accepting
he is fighting a lost cause. "OK, OK, let's just ferget it mate, you'll
just 'ave to learn the fuckin' hard way," he says, suddenly clicking his
fingers. "Got any toovlers on yer, chav?" Calum smiles and throws
him a cigarette. After lighting up they walk on towards Fyfield
village, passing a long windowless farm building, and straight into
a stench so foul it almost causes them to retch. "Fucking hell! What's
that stink, Cleeve?! Is it a sewage works or something?"

"Nah, that's the Canni farm. Battery chickens kenner, they keeps
the poor bastards in there wivout daylight, cramped up in tiny compartments. Do yuh know, they cain't move or even turn round, stuck rigid
fer life, the poor bastards, just to lay fuckin' eggs. I knows a guy works
in there, wanna know what his job is?" He doesn't wait for an answer,
"The sick git has to kill all the male chicks, cos obvious they don't lay
eggs when thems grown up like, so the cruel cunt chucks 'em on a big
conveyer belt that dumps 'em alive into a big mincer." Calum shakes
his head. "There's some real evil bastards about, Cleeve. The human
has to be the cruelest species of life in the universe."

"Hey... hold up there, chavvy, don't tar us all wiv the same brush
now. When me and the family kills the canni or shoshi fer our scran,
it ain't cruel, not like what them fuckin' farmers does. Our kill is
quick 'n clean. We don't make 'em suffer like this. Even when we goes
coursin' wiv our Juckals and long dogs, leastways the rabbit and hare
gets a sportin' chance."

Calum stays silent... despite the fact he is totally anti-animal cruelty in any form, he has to agree with Cleeve. No one is as heartless as those depraved ghouls that farm these poor creatures. Cleeve continues, "Then there's them factory farmers, they does the same to their hogs as well y'know, keepin' 'em in tiny compounds, or in wire body casts, where they cain't move around, so gettin' no exercise, just to fatten 'em up quicker afore they slaughters 'em."

"Yeah, I know only too well what most farmers are about, Cleeve. There's no love or compassion for animals in that profession. Look, I understand your way, but I don't personally agree with killing any innocent creatures. I reckon that if all humans could live as vegans then there would be no cruelty, or bloodlust... so no aggression."

Cleeve spits on the ground and grins, "Ha ha, yer a strange one Cal, you is. At least us travellers don't stand all day in the fields like the fat fuckin' farmers and their Hooray Henry mates, shootin' and maimin' the pheasants, partridge and rabbits in their thousands, just fer the fuckin' fun of it. Yuh know mush, we've bin out wiv the long dogs after them cruel bastards 'ave 'ad their fun, and seen pheasants and grouse lyin' all over the field, shot full a lead, and left flutterin' and squirmin' in agonies... seen 'em on the roads too, wiv their guts blown out, some still alive, even watched 'em strugglin' floatin' down the river, injured so bad they is drownin' cus they cain't walk or fly. Them landed gentry fuckers don't eat many of 'em neither, that's just a bullshit excuse," he laughs heartily, "after them poor critters have been filled full a lead shot there's fuck all left to eat. They just luvs the killin' my chav, and that's the truth on it."

"Well there you go then Cleeve, so now you know where I'm coming from." Calum kicks hard at the door of this locked animal torture chamber. "These poor chickens don't ever even see daylight... you never know, though, maybe... just maybe, one day, someone will come along... and set these poor buggers free."

"Cushti, my mush," Cleeve smiles knowingly, "and I got me an idea on just who that someone might be?" A thoughtful smile plays on Calum's face. "Watch this space, friend. I'm sure, before too long, the Great Spirit will do what needs to be done." Cleeve looks to the heavens, offering up his hands in prayer mode, and declares solemnly, "Amen to that, bruv. Amen to that."

They head on to Thruxton, calling in at the George Inn, to collect another crate of empties. The White Horse is open when they arrive, and buzzing, with quite a crowd already in the bar. Four biker girls are sat on the wall outside. Calum swaggers over, calling out cheerily, "Hiya ladies," as he spies Chrissie and Val, sexual allure personified, oozing easy temptation in oh-so short denim miniskirts. He makes a beeline towards them, grabbing Chrissie roughly by the shoulders and clumsily attempting to kiss her. She pushes him away abruptly. "Get off me! You silly little prat, what yuh think you're fucking playing at?" Unperturbed by this ice-cold rebuttal he moves on to Val. 'Surely she'll be up for it.' But she turns away to avoid his lips as he lunges open-mouthed at her. Their heads connect, painfully hard. She screams, falling back awkwardly and landing heavily on the lawn. He tries to help her up. "Get your fucking hands off me, you weirdo pervert," she screams, struggling to her feet, brushing mud and cigarette ash from her laddered nylons. "You'd best stay away from us, you sex-starved nutter!" Spitting venomously, "You hear me, or else we'll get the boys to sort you out good and proper, fucking mental kid." The girls storm off into the bar, still raging and ranting, leaving Calum shaking, shocked and embarrassed at this stinging public rebuke.

"You all right, buddy?" Barman Frank is out collecting glasses and has seen it all. Calum struggles to hold back tears. The barman puts an arm around his shoulders. "Don't take it to heart, son. Try to see it as a life lesson."

"But I don't get it, Frank, they were so up for it last night, couldn't get enough of me... what's changed so sudden?"

"Hard to figure, I know, kid, but last night you were fresh meat, and those chicks, being sexual predators, they wanted a piece of you. It's just the Yin and Yang of things. Because you didn't make the first move last night, there was an air of mystery about you. That mystique drew them in, like moths to a flame, and so they were red hot for some fun and frolics with you–"

"I tried tellin' 'im," Cleeve interrupts, "but would he listen? Would he fuck as like." Frank ignores him, and continues. "Women can be fickle creatures, Calum, especially the damaged ones. Granted, sex is wilder and more exciting with their kind. But it's a short-lived buzz. Those girls are not for real, and so they can't sustain the illusion. Take it from someone who's been there son, and learnt the hard way. In their world, what's hot today can quickly cool by tomorrow. The biggest turn-off for them is desperation. It's not sexy or a turn-on, and... sorry to say this... but boy, did you come on desperate tonight, fella." Stung by this, Calum yells, "What you mean?! Desperate? I just wanted to carry things on from last night. They sure wanted me then, didn't they?" Frank tries to console him. "Shouldn't worry yourself too much, and don't dwell overly on tonight. You'll find plenty more opportunities soon enough, a good-looking kid like you. Try playing a little hard to get though with the ladies. Like the old adage advises, treat 'em mean, keep 'em keen. Take my word for it, son, they'll love you for it."

"OK, Frank... thanks mate. I'll try and remember that... umm... look, any chance of a quick drink? My nerves are shot to pieces." Frank is caught in two minds by the request... "Uhh... yeah, well... OK Calum, but stay out here tonight please... Landlady's on the warpath. She's been on the sauce all day. I'll bring you a drink out in a while."

As Frank goes back into the bar Calum glances over to Cleeve. "OK, come on then! Spit it out, mate! I just know you'll have something to fucking say." He holds up his hands and grins knowingly. "No, not me chavvy," drawing a finger across his lips. "I'm keeping this zipped from now on. Yuh don't listen to fuck all I says anyways."

Calum turns on him. "And don't keep calling me chavvy! No more, get it, I'm no kid y'know, just like you're no traveller. You've never travelled further than your own fucking back yard. I've got connections with real travellers, believe me, so cool it already with all the fake Romany spiel." Cleeve looks hurt, scowling at the spiteful insult, but thinks better of replying. Calum already feels bad, regretting his outburst and realising he has hurt his friend's feelings. Frank returns with two pints. "Dry cider OK tonight, boys? Barley wine is off I'm afraid." Cleeve gets to his feet. "Cheers, Frank, anythin' will do to take the edge off, as long as its booze, ta very much." Calum lights two cigarettes, and hands one to Cleeve, who snatches it sullenly. They drink and smoke in stony silence, and are almost done when landlady Molly staggers out the back door of the pub's kitchen, tottering, unsteady on her feet, almost falling, clearly drunk, and cradling a double-barrelled shotgun against her impressive cleavage.

"Who the hell's that, Cleeve?"

"That's Molly," he whispers, cowering behind Calum. "Mental Molly, they calls her, Moray's bit a skirt." Calum's feral radar advises flight as her wide-eyed bloodshot gaze clocks them. "She looks out of it, mate. What's with the gun, do you think it's loaded?" Cleeve backs away slowly. "Dunno friend, but I ain't 'angin' around to find out, let's get the fuck outta here."

Molly notices the boys retreating and aims the shotgun in their direction. "Hey, you no good bums," she slurs, "what do you think you're doing? Drinking alcohol on my premises, and both of you underage? Get goin' now before I teach you a lesson you won't forget in a hurry." Cleeve's scared and grabs Calum's arm. "Dordi, my mate, the crazy mort's lost the plot big time, move yerself fer Christ's sake, let's jell on outta 'ere, afore she uses that yogger agin us."

"What's the hell's a yogger, Cleeve?"

"Fer fucks sake! Gun, shooter, my mush, don't you know nothin'? Calum can't help sniggering, thinking, 'Even in these dire straits Cleeve won't give it up with the fake Romany lingo'. They put down their glasses, backing away slowly into the car park. Molly raises the shotgun to her shoulder and, staggering off balance, she accidentally pulls the trigger. The close proximity of gunshot is deafening as the discharge of both barrels blasts a fusillade of lead pellets and scattered shot just above the cringing boys. The recoil from the explosion jars the stock of the firearm hard against Molly's shoulder, spinning her around before she falls backwards in a moaning crumpled heap. The shotgun clatters to the ground, sending acrid grey smoke swirling lazily skywards from the twin barrels.

Moray comes running from the kitchen, cursing as he sees Molly, glancing around furtively before hoisting her under the armpits, dragging her backwards to the kitchen. "For god's sake, what have you done now you crazy, crazy woman, whatever next? You'll be the death of me yet." He reappears quickly, panting breathlessly, and grabs the shotgun, before scurrying away with the incriminating evidence.

"Oi, you!" Cleeve stops him in his tracks, "Not so fuckin' fast Mr Landlord." Moray turns to see Cleeve and Calum emerging like avenging nightmarish figures from the dark shadows of the car park. He holds up his hands, knowing the game's up, but thinking on his feet. "So sorry gents, the lady's had a little too much to drink, you understand," he says, winking at them as if they are all old pals. "No harm done though, hey lads?" Pressing a finger to his lips, "mum's the word... please." A crowd is gathering, the sound of the loud gunshot bringing customers spilling from the bar. Moray is sweating as he waves them away. "OK, OK, come on now, funs over, boys and girls, back to the bar please... drinks are on the house." The punters cheer as one as they file back inside.

Moray turns to Calum and Cleeve. "As for you fine gentlemen, come back tomorrow, and your drinks will also be on me." He turns his back on them and starts walking away. "Not so fast, man!" Calum is still shaking after the close shave. "She could have killed us both, and all you offer us is a poxy drink?" Moray turns back, hands outstretched. "As I said, I'm deeply, deeply sorry lads. I cannot apologise more profusely. She's going through a rough phase at present, time of the month and all that... affects her strangely... you know how it is boys," he says, smiling insincerely, "us all being men of the world." Cleeve is not to be placated so easily. "We coulda fuckin' croaked it tonight, mister."

"Won't happen again, I can assure you, young sir." His hand on heart, "you have my solemn word, gentlemen."Calum points and sniggers, "You're having a laugh, mister, if you think we'd take your word on anything. Just like your fucking name, Moray, as slippery as an eel, I'll wager." Cleeve, sensing a ripe opportunity, nudges Calum in the ribs before whispering, "Don't be too hasty here, chavvy... let's take time out to consider this some." He moves up close to Moray. "How would it be then... Mr Landlord... if, fer instance... we was persuaded to mebbe overlook this evenin's diabolical events..." he pauses pointedly... "And I'm sayin' only mebbe, mind... let's just say we were to accept yer offer of them drinks on the house... then just how many bevies would that be in total, 'xactly?" He pauses again, before delivering his coup de grace. "That is, if we decides not to call in the gavvers to deal with this very serious situation, like."

Moray looks stunned now, eyes full of fear and a nervous tremble to his voice. "You... you... mean... get... get the police involved?" Cleeve laughs. "Yeah, you got it in one Mr Respectable." He turns to grin at Calum, "quick on the fuckin' uptake, ain't he mush?"

"Come, come now gentlemen," Moray pleads, perspiration leeching from the pores of his brow. "Surely there's no need for that. We can sort this out, can we not, man to man."

"Hmm," Cleeve rubs his chin, as if deep in thought. "Ain't so sure about that? Does the lady 'ave a licence fer that shooter, I'm wonderin?' Cos I knows that me father, he needs a firearms certificate fer his piece, fer killin' his game an suchlike." Looking flustered and uncomfortable now, but never one to miss the opportunity of a deal, Moray opts for damage limitation in this instance. "Look... if it's the barley wine you like lads," smiling sickly false and tapping his nose knowingly, "and I've heard on the grapevine that you're both partial." (He's well aware that barley wine is the least popular drink in the pub and fast becoming corked.) "I'll see you both alright on that esteemed beverage for the foreseeable future, if only you can find it within your hearts to keep schtumm about this whole unfortunate episode."

"Hmmm..." Cleeve takes his time deliberating... before finally accepting. "OK, matey, yuh got yerself a deal," spitting in his palm before offering the landlord to shake on it. Moray grimaces, but thinks better of declining this age-old deal clincher. "Good man, good man." Smiling, he grasps Moray's hand tightly. "I knew you'd see sense, see yuh tomorrer, then... nice and early mind?"

"Yes, yes, of course lads," he replies, forcing a weak smile, but his disgust evident at the exposure to Cleeve's regurgitated saliva. Recoiling, with a fixed grimace of revulsion, as though he is now infected by some deadly incurable disease, Moray wipes the contaminated hand on his trousers, over and over, before backing away, muttering, "Must go now gents... see to... to the wife... you understand."

"Yeah, we get the picture... only too fuckin' well, mister," Cleeve sneers. "Go on then, on your way, run along now to the good lady." Moray stops and stiffens, clenching his fists, about to react angrily, but thinks better of it as he notes Cleeve's cold-eyed glare, a grim forewarning of the consequences of crossing this young blackmailer. Hurrying away into the kitchen, he slams the door behind him.

Cleeve punches the air triumphantly. "What d'ya think a that then, chavvy? Look at him, trash'd scared, scuttling away with his tail between his legs." Calum is not so easily enamoured. "Yeah, gotta hand it you, great negotiation technique I'm sure, but the bastard got off lightly in my book. We could be dead meat right now."

"Yeah, but we ain't is we? Lighten up, me old mate, name of the game is makin' the most of every gainful situation in this poxy life. One door closes, another fucker opens." He chuckles at fate's unpredictability. "Bet the fat bastards shittin' hisself now... don't seem to be frettin' too much about us being underage now does he? No sirree. Listen, my mush, I might 'ave been born at night, but it weren't fuckin' last night... I'm wise to his sort, got him well sussed, so I have." He smacks a fist into his palm. "Well and truly fuckin' sussed."

"OK, if you say so." Calum suddenly feels exhausted, delayed shock swiftly zapping his energy. "I'm wrecked man, getting off home now. I've had enough excitement for one day."

"Amen to that, me old mucker, see yuh then, same time tomorrer'?"
Calum perks up a little now. He can't help but grin at their stroke of
luck. "Yeah, be a real shame to miss out on Mr Moray's kind hospi-
tality." Cleeve smiles. "Attaboy, that's the ticket. Keep yer pecker
up me chavvy," he grins and wags his finger at Calum like he's a
naughty child, whilst gyrating and thrusting out his hips in sexual
simulation. "And not like that mind. Ferget about them pox-ridden
morts, yuh knows it makes sense." Calum shakes his head and smiles
grimly. "Can't let it drop, can you. You're a right old misogynist,
ain't you Cleeve?" His eyes narrow sharp and sudden, "A fuckin'
what?! I ain't no miss anythin' pal, straight as a die me, I'll 'ave yuh
know," thumping his chest defensively at the perceived questioning of his manhood. "You sayin' I'se a sissy queerboy or summat?"
Calum sniggers at Cleeve's misinterpretation. "No, not saying that,
friend, it just seems obvious you're none too fond of the females, is
what I meant, at least not by the way you're always running them
down." He looks wounded by the accusation. "Not so, my mate, far
from it, I'll 'ave yer know I've got page three babes stuck up all over
me fuckin' bedroom wall, worships 'em most evry other day..." his
hand miming frantic masturbation. "If yuh gets me drift?" Calum
frowns, forcing away the distressing image, raising a hand in protest.
"Hold it right there, man, too much information already." Cleeve
continues, "Look, I ain't got nothin' personal against the raklis...
long as they knows their place, mush." Calum laughs, "Oh yeah,
and where's that then, chained to the stove, or flat on their back,
when master wants his wicked way?" Cleeve offers no argument
with Calum's summing up, "Well... yeah... pretty much, I spose...
lookit, no point in gettin' all sentimental over 'em, bottom line is
they gotta earn their corn, the females, they ain't never gonna be as
strong or as clever as us men, is they mush? Ain't never gonna rule
the world like a man does. It's like me pa always sez to 'er indoors,
when him and me ma has a row... I fucks yuh, don't I, so I must
love yuh, don't I?" Calum sniggers, "Sounds a right charmer, your
dad... bit of an old romantic is he?" Cleeve narrows his eyes and

bunches his fists, "What yuh tryin' to say now, dinlo chav?" Calum holds up his hands "Me... nothing friend... just interested in human behaviour is all."

"Well, strikes me yuh got a lot tuh say about others, mebbe yuh should concentrate on getting yer own fuckin' house in order mate, and give them sluts the old heave ho, afore yer so quick to go round castin' judgement on others."

"I'll be sure to give that some thought, Cleeve... um... look... what I said earlier about you not being a true traveller... didn't mean it, I was just pissed off mate... with the biker girls, you dig?"

"Yeah, well... spose yer head wuz fucked up by them dirty raklis..." Cleeve allows begrudgingly, "but no sweat, Cal, yuh wouldn't know the fuckin' difference anyhow, with youse bein' a gorger an all... But we is proper travellers my lot, make no mistake, goes back genera- tions in our family, it's in our blood," he says, tapping his fist proudly on his heart, "always bin Romany gypsies, us, my mate... and always fuckin' will."

"Yeah, sure Cleeve, course you are, no offence... look, what do I know? Oh, and by the way, what's a gorger, when he's at home?"

"Non Romany... a pikey... a didi coi." Calum bristles at the damning condemnation. He knows Cleeve's being confrontational, but lets it go. "Oh, OK pal, that's me told then."

"As yuh said to me, friend... no offence, it's like, just the way the cookie crumbles, how the cards is dealt, how the dice rolls... yuv either got it or yuh ain't, son, no two ways about it." He groans disparagingly at Cleeve's multiple analogies. "I'll try and remember that profound life lesson, my friend... see you around," walking on a few yards, before turning back. Calum can't resist calling out, "Oh... I forgot to mention... my old man – my real father – was an Irish travelling man, from Connemara... so let's see now... I would say that gives me real Romany blood running through my viens?"

Cleeve stands and stares with a vacant expression on his face, briefly lost for words, before laughing out loud and shouting back, "Yeah... like fuck he was, mush, ha ha ha, yuh fuckin' dinlo gorger."

Calum turns and waves him away dismissively. He's had enough, feeling like going back and punching Cleeve's stupid leering face, but washing his hands of him now... before things turn nasty. Trudging wearily home, with this evening's bizarre events slowly sinking in, he mulls over the frightening shotgun incident, rendering the altercation and subsequent shaming by the biker girls to now appear almost trivial in comparison. He smiles ruefully, concluding that matters of life and death will have that effect. Just as Frank had said earlier, it all comes down to the Yin and Yang, the universal power of fate giving positively with one hand and taking negatively with the other.

Calum sleeps poorly this night, the disturbing nightmare replaying, as the shadow beings come for him again, leading him once more to confront the raging gorilla.

CHAPTER
THIRTY-FOUR

Calum is up next morning at first light. Last night's close call at the pub and the recurrence of the bad dream has left him feeling edgy and uncomfortable. Leaning over the kitchen sink he gulps gushing cold water from the tap and splashes a handful over his face.

A shrill whooo-whooo whistling startles him, ear-piercingly loud, heralding the first rumblings of a steam locomotive. The seismic train tremor through the soles of his feet reminds him that Jim Brown, last week, was telling Janet that today was to be the old loco's last run. The government was phasing out these big beasts and replacing them with ugly dirty diesels. Most of the old steam trains were doomed to be scrapped, with just a small percentage allocated for preservation. It was reported in the local paper that the covetous scrap metal dealers, for once, were surprisingly outbid by a hardcore band of determined enthusiasts hell bent on saving some of these old steam engines.

Running outside, he's just in time to catch sight of the last run of this sleek black beauty. Leaning out from the cab of the steam engine, driver and stoker wave their caps furiously, with the stoker whirling a tied up grey blanket about his head, releasing it with a "whoopee" as they power on by. The package lands amongst the tangled under-growth of the embankment. Intrigued, Calum climbs over the fence and finds the make-shift parcel lodged in the forked branches of a young sycamore sapling. He carries it back to the garden before untying the tightly knotted white string. The coal dust-covered grey blanket falls open, to reveal a cardboard box containing packets of crisps, salted nuts and assorted sweets.

Sitting in the rusting old Mercedes sports car, enjoying the dawn chorus, tucking into this early morning feast, he's impressed by the efforts these strangers have made to bid him a last farewell. Their fleeting goodwill gesture, like the old steam engine, now swiftly consigned to history. Calum smiles warmly at this rare example of human compassion in a cruel unforgiving world, allowing, despite his inherent pessimism of the human race, 'Mmm... maybe there are some decent people around.' This tolerant appreciation of mankind is short-lived though, as his thoughts turn to Jim Brown and the old mobile home parked in the garden. He ponders, 'The old phony spends a lot of time in that caravan, always alone, with the curtains drawn.' Curiosity gets the better of him, and he ambles over to Jim's secret study. 'Hmm, wonder what he gets up to in there?' Trying the door, it's locked, so he peers between a gap in the curtains, but no joy, it's too dark inside. This is bugging him, and he's feeling compelled now to find out the secret of this mysterious space, then he suddenly remembers. 'There's an old screwdriver in the outside toilet'. Checking that the Browns are still asleep, he goes for the screwdriver and sneaks back to unscrew the square latch plate that holds the brass Yale lock in place. It comes off easily. Calum enters cautiously and shivers. It's cold inside, and smells stale and musty, the hardboard walls bowing and bending with age and damp. He gazes about, before gasping in surprise. There, on prominent display, in the corner of the caravan, is a re-creation of the memorial of the deceased Brown twins. The scene is set exactly as before, although the age-related yellow tinge and slight curling of the fading photographs is now more pronounced. Calum feels a little guilty at intruding once again on this sad altar, until he clocks the many photos of nude young women, in various erotic poses, decorating the walls. He lets out a long low whistle, cursing aloud, "Fucking hell," before probing further and finding piles of pornographic material under a long table. *Penthouse* magazine, *Playboy*, *Hustler* – the porn stacked high and wide in incongruous adornment to the shrine.

'The pervy old bastard is into young girls!' Calum judges, flicking through *Playboy*, his gaze lingering over the naked blonde centre-fold... before condemning Jim. 'He probably tells Mrs Brown he goes in here to pray for the boys' lost souls.' Grinning smugly, he leaves the caravan, convinced he has Jim's number now. After carefully replacing the lock, Calum stands back, pleased with his discreet DIY. "There, good as new."

He spends the rest of Sunday lazing in his room, listening to the pop music chart countdown on the radio, singing along to the current number one, 'All Right Now' by Free, before rousing himself at six, in readiness for another evening at the White Horse. Slinking out without a word, he cannot bring himself to speak to – or even look at – Jim, especially after this morning's porn mag discovery.

Strolling out of the drive, hands in pockets, he's in no hurry as the pub won't be open until seven. It's dark and chilly tonight, stars and moon seemingly reluctant to put in an appearance. The only illumination infiltrating the deep gloom is the gaudy multicoloured Christmas lights adorning the houses and bungalows along the way. He moves in stealthily to one, creeping across the garden, keeping tucked in close to the hedge. Liking this feeling of power, of going unobserved in the cold black night, just like a wild creature... he creeps closer... closer... until he's at the window, spying a young couple watching TV.

A Christmas tree in the corner of the room is hung heavy with shiny tinsel and baubles, with sparkly wrapped presents stacked at its base. Two small children sit on the floor, gazing up at the wonder of the glittering decorations, safe and secure, cocooned in this make-believe world.

A brief smile plays on Calum's face, the whimsical scene unexpect-edly causing a nostalgic lonely pang to tug at his heart. The love and innocence of this moment brings him close to tears. He's surprised at these conflicting emotions coursing through him. He imagines how his life could have been so different. 'But no! That's ridiculous,' he thinks, snapping out of the melodramatic revelry, 'how could it ever be so, I hate Christmas, and all the so-called "festive season" stands for. Especially the humans' celebratory mass massacre of animals, just another excuse for them to gorge on the dead flesh of my innocent relatives, no way!' Resolutely regaining his composure, he knows it is only right and real for him to be on the outside, looking in, musing, 'How peculiar that these people, some of whom hardly pass the time of day to each other normally, can have this Christmas goodwill to all men vibe going on for December only, oh well,' he thinks. Smiling grimly at the irony, 'I never could understand the crazy humans.'

He continues on his way, arriving at the White Horse just after seven. The old ditch drunk is again slumped over the bar. He looks up and nods as Calum enters. "All right young'un?" He nods back curtly. Moray is serving in the public bar, and true to his word, pours Calum his first free barley wine of the evening. He's liking this empowerment, having such a hold over this pub landlord. Gazing about the bar, he notes, 'Not so many bikers in tonight, no Cleeve either, so what, I need no one.'

He growls under his breath as he notes that the fickle biker chicks are in. Chrissie and Val are entrenched in the far corner, deep in conversation with an older man with long, slicked-back grey hair. The stranger is wearing a dark cowboy hat, black leather trousers and matching waistcoat. 'And a false smile,' Calum intuits, 'you would trust at your peril.' After a while the stranger heads for the toilets, limping away with the aid of a silver-topped cane and dragging a withered leg.

"That be Tom," whispers the drunk, noting Calum's interest, and nudging him in the ribs. "He be a dirty junkie pusher. Likes gettin' the young'uns hooked up, then 'avin his wicked way with 'em, get you your drugs he will, boy."

"Who says I want drugs?" Calum snaps back, annoyed at the old man's judgement. "You saying I'm a junkie?" He smiles toothless. "If the cap fits, young'un."

"Fuck off, you brain-dead wino," Calum snarls, poking him hard in the chest. "Don't you ever speak to me again, you hear?"

"Oww, that feckin' 'urt," the drunk moans, massaging his pain and glowering. "Assault is that, I'll have you up fer GBH, ya feckin' hippy girly." His grating nasal whine and stale beery breath annoys Calum even further. "You think that's assault, just keep on pushing my buttons, mister, then you'll find out what GBH really is." Scowling, retreating to the far end of the bar, he can't resist one more dig. "OK, keep yer stupid long hair on then... hippy girl."

"Why don't you just drop dead, you useless bastard," Calum shouts back. The drunk is about to retaliate, but sensing the hostile atmosphere increasing in intensity, he wisely resists the impulse.

The biker girls turn at the raised voices, waving, smiling and giggling behind their hands, as they spot Calum. He blanks them, still angry at their cruel rejection the previous evening, swearing under his breath, "Dirty prick teasers, you bitches won't be catching me like that again."

Their lame companion returns. Studying him, Calum makes an instant evaluation. 'This Tom fella has a presence about him, no denying, but it's not a good look, this furtive, fidgety persona of the archetypal drug pusher.' Downing his drink in one, he bangs the glass loudly on the bar, bringing Moray to reluctantly refill, glaring silently as he pours the drink. 'Ignoring me, as if I'm lower class, like dirt on his shoe,' Calum surmises, picking up on the landlord's reticence to converse, goading him to provoke a reaction.

"How's our mental Molly tonight then, Mr Moray... still mad as a bag of fucking snakes?" He sets the glass down so hard on the bar that some of the alcohol spills. "Now! Just you see here, boy," his face takes on a mottled flush of purple. "That matter is finished with. We have all moved on. Do you hear? We have an agreement, do we not?"

"Yeah, course we do, old chap, won't mention it again." Calum grins, before adding the caveat, "so long as the booze keeps flowing freely," looking the landlord straight in the eyes, making sure he understands the underlying threat.

Moray seems about to explode with rage, barely containing himself, before turning swiftly on his heel, slamming the heavy oak door as he storms from the bar. Frank appears soon after, alarmed by Calum's blatant breach of house rules. "Hey, come on, son! What you think you're doing, drinking at the bar? Who served you?"

"It's OK, Frankie boy, calm down, pal. Let's just say, me and your boss, we've got what you might call an understanding, an arrangement going on."

"Oh, OK, I get it," Frank looks a little less concerned now. "Because of last night, is it? I heard what happened with Molly."

"Yeah, damn right because of last night! It's sure not out of the goodness of his dark heart, is it Frank?" Calum chuckles at the memory. "We compromised though, and settled on free drinks for me and young Cleeve... for an unlimited period."

"OK son, that's as may be, but you gotta keep a low profile in the bar please. I don't want to get done for serving alcohol under age. It'll be my sorry ass on the line if it all comes on top."

"Yeah, sure thing, I get that." He likes Frank, doesn't want to cause him problems, so moves away from the bar.

Rod comes in a little while later, making a beeline for Calum. "There you are, mate! I've been looking all over for you."

"Hi'ya Rod, what's the craic then, my friend?"

"Me mate Paul, his parents are away for a few days, and he's asked me to get a few people over for drinks and stuff, tonight like." He is immediately suspicious, knowing that Rod likes his drugs. "Oh yeah? And what kind of... Calum's fingers indicate inverted commas. "Stuff"... exactly, dear Rodders?"

"Paul's got a pal coming over with a Ouija board."

"What's that all about then?" Looking around fearfully, wide-eyed, Rod whispers, "He sez they can contact... dead geezers... through the Ouija board."

"Is that right? Ha ha, seems like fun... OK, count me in then, those ghosts can't be any worse than some of the bastards in the here and now." Rod grins, "Tell me about it, Cal!" Calum finishes his drink and slaps him on the back. "Come on then, pal, lead me to the ghouls and ghosties." Rod looks up apprehensively. "Shouldn't take the piss though mate, it's no laughing matter, this is kosher... or so they says." Calum smiles at Rod's worried expression. "Think I'll be the judge of that, my friend."

They walk the short distance to Paul's place. It's eight o'clock when they arrive. The sky is overcast with massive grey clouds, provoking feral unease in Calum. Rod leads them in to a small block of prefabricated bungalows situated at the bottom of Stanbury Road. There are eight of these detached sectional dwellings crammed into a small plot. They were built just after the Second World War for local affordable housing, and although very basic, they are still owned and let by the local authority.

Paul welcomes them in to a small cramped lounge room, before introducing a long-haired hippy guy and a pretty young girl, both sitting cross-legged on the floor around a low coffee table. "Rod, Calum... meet Roger, and this is the lovely Coral." Calum recognises the girl as the young cutie from the youth club. Smiling down at them, he asks, "Hi, you guys, what you got going on here then?"

"We are about to contact someone from the other side, with the help of the Ouija board," Roger replies gravely, pointing to a brightly coloured, oval-shaped board on the coffee table. Decorated with many different symbols, strange signs, and all the letters of the alphabet, and the numbers 0 to 9 painted around the edge.

"What's the story, then, guys?" Calum asks, as he and Rod join them on the carpet.

Paul comes through from the kitchen with a glass tumbler and turns it upside down on top of the Ouija board, suggesting, "Let's all have a beer first, hey?" After handing round cans of lager, he lights a patchouli joss stick, before setting a Pink Floyd album to play on the Garrard turntable. Rod gets a joint together, Paul turns down the lights. The scene is set.

Roger leans forwards. "Right now, everyone touch this upturned glass, ever so lightly, with just a fingertip mind, no pressure needed, the spirits will control all movement."

Calum smirks at Rod's fearful expression. They all follow Roger's lead, placing thier fingers on the glass. He looks to the heavens before asking, "Please, almighty spirit of all dead people, allow us to make contact through your divine presence, with someone who has passed over to the other side." Coral shivers and snuggles into Calum. He can feel her soft warmth and anxious breathing through the thin cheese-cloth dress. "You okay, babe?" He whispers in her ear. She looks nervous but smiles and nods up at him. "Shhh now," Roger puts a fingertip to his lips. "Someone's trying to come through."

The glass starts moving around the board, seemingly of its own accord, sliding first to one letter, then to another. The interior lights start flickering with pulsating ultra-violet light, before growing dimmer and dimmer. Calum trembles involuntarily as the atmos-phere turns icy cold. Coral jumps with fright, and snuggles in closer, as a deafening clap of thunder explodes outside. All of a sudden, fork lightning bursts from the sky, with rain and hailstones pounding so hard against the windows it seems as if the raging elements are trying forcibly to break in.

Paul jumps to his feet. "I don't like this, something's not right here, guys. I think we should stop. Roger! Cool it man, like now!"

"No no, we're almost there," he pleads. "Look! The letters are spelling out a word... a name." The glass moves slowly to H... pausing at I... before sliding to T... then L... on to E... finally stopping at... R. HITLER.

The glass is now skimming back and forth across the board. Calum panics and tries to remove his finger, but he's stuck fast, like the others. Suddenly, the tumbler shoots away across the room to smash hard against the wall. Coral screams. A strong smell of sulphur fills the room, bizarrely reminding Calum of Mrs Brown's cooking of dead animals, and the resulting vomit-inducing charred flesh smell.

Roger looks badly shaken, gazing at his outstretched hand, wincing at the sight of the shrivelled strip of burnt skin torn from his index finger. "This can happen on occasion folks... w... w... when an evil spirit gatecrashes a séance."

"Stop then! Right now!" Paul orders, ashen-faced with dread, "Cos if that really is Hitler then that's about as evil as it gets, pal."

"Yeah, this sure is a bad vibe, man," Rod agrees. "It don't feel right to be messing with this far-out stuff." Roger doesn't answer. He's shaking now, convulsing, as if possessed by some invisible force, scratching and scrabbling at his clothing, wild-eyed, staring up at the ceiling, moaning, "Too late... too late now... I don't know what to do... argghh!" He's reaching for his throat. "The evil spirit is within me," he lets out a strangulated cry. "Mnnngh... I can feel it... inside... eating at my insides... arrrgh... oh my god, please... someone help me... help me... please."

Thunder booms and Roger expels a long high-pitched wail, like a dreadful drawn-out final breath. Neither animal nor human sound, Calum knows it's an evil paranormal force, as an icy chill shivers through him. Suddenly the lights go out. Lightning floods the building with brilliant white energy. Blood trickles from Roger's eyes. His long hair is standing on end and his feet are off the ground, as if he's being yanked up by some vengeful retributive dark power. Everyone else is rooted to the spot, unable to move. Roger clutches at his neck, like he's trying to exorcise invisible strangling hands, suddenly projectile vomiting blood-flecked green-yellow bile onto the far wall. The demonic force then bundles him up in a tangle of arms and legs before flinging him with great force through the open door. Scrambling to his feet, scratched and grazed, he runs screaming from the prefab, down the garden path and away down the hill.

Coral has been screeching hysterically for some time. Paul slaps her face. She stops. The storm dwindles away. Lights flicker back on.

Calum looks around. "Are you all OK, guys?"

"What the fuck just happened here?" A bewildered Rod asks.

"Don't know mate," Paul says, hurriedly folding shut the Ouija board. "But I'm never trying that shit again."

"Nor me!" Coral states emphatically, sitting down heavily on the sofa, rubbing her reddened cheek. "That was terrifying... c... c... can you walk me home, Calum? Now please... I'm really scared." He cuddles her. "Yeah, sure thing babe... but shouldn't we go find Roger first, check he's OK, he looked in a bad way, all that blood and stuff?" Paul leans over and gently strokes Coral's face. "Sorry to slap you love, but I was worried you were having a seizure or something." He turns to Calum. "Why don't you take her home, pal? Me and Rod will go and find Roger when we've cleared up here."

"OK... if you're sure you don't need me to help?" Calum adeptly hides his guilty relief at missing out on searching for Roger in the demon-infused dread darkness, adding as a warning aside, "but let this be a lesson to you all, don't ever mess with the dark side of the supernatural." Paul is shaking, all colour drained from his face. "Don't you worry, that's some heavy shit man, never again."

Calum's itching to get away from the alarming scene, knowing this is bad business going down here. He takes Coral's arm and heads for the door. "OK then, guys, I'd best get the lady home then?" Paul ushers them out. "Yes, yes, you two go on. Take good care of her, Cal."

"Sure thing." He walks Coral to her house, just up the road. She looks up into his eyes. "Thanks lovey, will you be OK to walk home alone?"

"Yeah, don't worry about me babe, I'll be fine."

"That séance was really horrible, Cal," she gazes at him wistfully. "I wish you could stay with me tonight," grasping his hand tightly, and pointing upstairs, she whispers, "but the parents, really strict... perhaps we could go to yours?"

"Nooo! No, sorry, that's not an option, babe... mine are worse, trust me."

"Awww... OK..." she says, cuddling in closer to him, looking up longingly. "Maybe we could just go into a warm hay-filled barn somewhere? And just cuddle... that would be so romantic." Calum dismisses this idea instantly. He's not looking for romance or cuddling, not tonight, life's too short. Imagining wild gratuitous biker girl sex is now his default turn-on remedy in dangerous close-shave moments, and he knows Coral won't be up for that, especially so soon after the séance, or if ever at all, she doesn't seem the type.

So he mumbles a wilting loser's acceptance speech. "Yeah... me too... would love that babe, but so cold tonight, honey, and then there's the rats...big ugly buggers in the barn... sneaking around in the dark..." She glances up sharply, terror in her innocent eyes. "Crumbs! Ugggh, no! Rats, gosh, not likely, Cal." He nods gravely. "Mmm, afraid so, love," leaving that scary scenario hanging. He hugs her, feeling the first oddly exquisite stirrings of sexual arousal deprivation, cursing inwardly at the restrictive ache of denied lust. Ironically acknowledging, "It seems, weirdly, a more potent fix of heightened awareness this, when one knows sex ain't gonna happen just yet... this energy somehow tantric in its vibe." She pulls away, asking, "maybe we can catch up tomorrow Cal? Would you like to come with me to my friend Lambert's place, we can just chill out... maybe listen to some sounds?"

"Yeah, OK, why not, hon?" He tries to sound enthusiastic. "We could all do with some light relief after tonight's shenanigans. Where's this guy live, then?"

"In Fyfield Village, just down the road, in a wing of a big mansion house, he's got like his own apartment." Standing on tiptoe, she kisses him lightly on the cheek, looking up, tears clouding her misty green eyes, whispering softly, "tomorrow then, Calum, please... just me and you... after lunch?" He squeezes her hand, carnal desire evaporating in tandem with each rapidly dropping degree in temperature on this bleak freezing night. "Yeah, sure thing, I'll call for you tomorrow babe."

Walking briskly back home, he looks up and realises the storm clouds have disappeared. The universe is visible again in all its sparkling glory. Nature's natural sedative. Immersed in the pure glow of a full moon, he gasps as a shooting star streaks across the black void of night, fizzing away across the cosmos, dispersing stardust, creating new life, millions of light years away.

CHAPTER
THIRTY-FIVE

Calum calls for Coral the next day. It's a biting cold afternoon. He smiles when she answers his knock on the door. Her pretty face, framed in a faux fur hat, is even more attractive today. She's wrapped warm, big scarf and grey mittens, cutely accessorised with dangling fluffy white dice. Noting the mournful expression, he kisses her cheek and puts an arm around her slim waist. "Why so sad, babe?" Coral's tearful snuffles tremble through him, the close proximity of her exposed vulnerability setting off confusing sexual emotions in Calum. "Oh my god, Cal! Terrible, terrible news to report, did you hear about Roger?" He struggles to stifle the inappropriate urges, holding her away at arm's length. "No, I've not seen anyone yet, came straight here. Did the boys find him?"

"Afraid not, no, so they called the police, who, after a brief search, found Roger... hanging... dead... from a beech tree... in that copse behind the church."

"No! Really?" Calum is shaken, remembering the Browns' son. 'Another hanging! What is it with all these suicides?' He hugs her tight, kissing the salty tears away. She looks up, pressing herself tight against him, her innocent eyes so alluring. "Can you believe it, Cal? Not suspicious though, or so the police think... Roger took his own life, is their verdict."

He struggles to concentrate. 'Uh oh, please god, no, not arousal, please, not now...' Sighing, he relinquishes the last vestiges of self-control, shuddering blissfully inside... knowing that taking advantage of her warm intimacy is so wrong in the context of this moment, but feeling oh so good, too... wanting her... now... badly... and trying to stifle the urgent craving demons... "Did the coppers know about the Ouija board, Coral?"

"No, Paul said he burnt it in the garden last night. He didn't tell the police that though."

"Yeah, I get that, suppose there was no point, they wouldn't have believed what happened, that a séance drove the poor guy to suicide, not exactly known for their spiritual awareness, the boys in blue." She nods in agreement. "Do you know many spiritual people, Cal?" He laughs. "No, not really. I get my spirituality from Mother Nature mostly... I find that most people who eagerly lay it on you that they're, like, oh so spiritual, tend to be, well, like, you know, really not very spiritual at all?" Coral smiles. "Hmm... interesting hypothesis... but yeah, I get that, Cal... the more they profess, the less they are... is that what you mean?"

"Yeah... something like that, love."

They stroll, hand in hand, down the steep hill leading to the outskirts of Fyfield Village. Coral points to an imposing-looking brick and flint manor house, which stands alone, in a large plot, surrounded by lush paddock and pasture fields. "That's Lamby's pad, over the river there, up that long driveway."

"Strange," says Calum, pausing to gaze upon Nature's splendour... "Such an idyllic setting, and only a short distance from where the poor hippy hung himself last night... sadness and grief, those compatible cohorts, are never far away in the realm of the humans." Coral shivers, and hugs him tightly. "Yes Cal, horrid, truly horrid."

They walk on, both deep in thought over last night's shocking events, silent, save for their synchronised footsteps crunching reassuringly into the gravel of the long driveway. Four period terraced thatched cottages, sitting adjacent to Lambert's place, catch his eye. He stops to take a closer look. Coral, observing his interest, asks, "Have you been in one of those houses before, Cal?"

"No, never, love… but strangely, I feel like I have… it's a weird sensation." She giggles, linking arms affectionately. "That's déjà vu, honey." He shakes his head, "No… but you're close, babe… can't quite put my finger on it… but it… it's something else… more like the opposite of déjà vu, whatever that means?"

"Come on you!" She drags him away from his nostalgic contemplation, skipping daintily away up the drive, turning back with amusement twinkling in her eyes, before gaily dancing back to him. "You are a deep one sometimes, Calum Connor. Please don't dwell on the mysteries of the universe today, my lovely, plenty of time for that in the hereafter. Come now, come meet my friend Lamby, and let all your worries drift away." He laughs, thinking, 'Fuck Lamby,' feeling horny, wanting her right now, fantasising about getting her alone, somewhere in the big house, locking the door, and having his wicked way with her. "You got it goin' on, girl, lead me onward and upwards to Hedonista!" She grabs his coat lapels, pulling herself up on tiptoes, pouting, tickling his nostrils with sweet young breath, fun in her eyes. "Where? Hedonista… is that even a place?" Calum laughs. "It is in my world, honey." He strokes Coral's hair, before kissing her and probing his tongue through her slightly parted lips. She pulls away, wagging her finger. "Naughty, naughty boy!"

Giggling together, they run up the drive, hand in hand. Coral yanks down hard on a long brass bell cord, dangling tangled amongst the dense foliage of a large clipped bay tree – one of a pair – these dark green topiary specimens growing in huge ornate lead planters either side of the wide front door. The jangling ringtone summons a pale, slight man, flamboyantly dressed in tye dye t-shirt and maroon velvet waistcoat. Flicking long lank brown hair from dope-lidded eyes, he smiles in fond recognition and gushes in girlish greeting. "Oh my, hi, if it's not my darling Coral…" He looks Calum up and down. "And welcome… to?"

"Lamby my love," Coral stands aside. Allow me to introduce Calum… Cal, to his friends."

"So pleased to meet you, my man." Lambert extends a thin bony hand. "Any friend of Coral's is a friend of mine." Calum accepts the limp handshake. "Likewise." Then it's over-the-top hugs for him from Lambert, and 'mwah, mwah' kisses, on the lips for Coral. The pair clinch so passionately that Calum intuits, 'these two are either an item, or have previous history in the romance stakes.'

"Come hither, yon good people, please, please, follow me." Lambert mincingly leads the way up a curving flight of dark-stained oak stairs, before ushering them into a large high-ceilinged room, which once was, obviously in a previous life, plush and opulent, bordering on ostentatious, but now run-down minimalist in a hippy chic dismissive kind of way. A big fur rug dominates the large expanse of otherwise bare, polished oak floorboards. So worn and moth-eaten is this tatty animal skin, it is impossible to deduce which unfortunate creature was slain to provide the vulgar Victorian floor covering. Several scruffy faded beanbags are strewn about the floor. Standing tall in the four corners of the room is a quartet of identical 1940s stand-alone Bakelite ashtrays, casting long dark shadows like grim health warning sentinels.

Calum is drawn to the massive bay picture window that takes up almost the length of one wall. He gazes out over neatly fenced fields and a meandering sparkling stream where winter sunshine shimmers on the water. A line of coppiced willow trees, old and hollow, lean from the river bank, with chestnut horses idling beneath the twisted and contorted branches. Calum is impressed. "Wow! Nice scenery."

"Yea, tranquil, is it not, my man?" Lambert concurs, as he nimbly rolls a long fat joint. "Yep, that's the word… tranquil," Calum sighs dreamily, realising, 'that's what's missing from my life, peace and quiet… too much crazy bad-assed stuff always going down with me. I could get used to some of this tranquillity vibe'.

Lambert passes the spliff to Coral, before flouncing over to a large black-stacked music system. "Cool rig, hey Calum?" She points to the stereo, before taking a dainty little puff on the pungent hash. "Pioneer, latest technology," Lambert advises proudly, as he fires up the big black beast. Brand names go over Calum's head; it's the sounds, not the system, that do it for him. He tries to sound enthusiastic, though. "Yeah, far out guys." 'All Along The Watchtower' suddenly startles Calum, exploding without warning from the four huge speakers set high in each corner of the room. Lambert swoons, "Dig that grooving quad sound, man. Never was much of a vocalist, our Jimi, but what an axe man, hey people?" Calum has to agree. "Yeah, right on, Hendrix is the main man on guitar."

Lambert goes to the fridge. "Beer, anyone?" Calum is thirsty. "Yes please La..." Unlike Coral, he cannot bring himself to call this weedy fey-looking man... 'Lamby!' Sneering dismissively, thinking, 'Come on! What kinda name's that for a guy?'

Lambert hands out the cans. Coral offers Calum the joint. He hesitates briefly, before accepting the sickly-smelling spliff, thinking 'What the hell', giving in and taking a small puff. It tastes better than he thought it would. So he draws deeper.

"Take a pew, guys." Lambert flops down on a bright red beanbag and gestures for Coral and Calum to join him. She runs to him, blurting out, "We went to a séance last night, Lamby. There was a Ouija board. It was really horrible... someone actually died..." Coral cries "m... my friend... Roger."

"Oh baby, my poor baby, why didn't you say?" Lambert moves in close, comforting and cuddling her. "Don't ever get involved with anything like that again, promise me baby girl, please please promise."

"Don't worry, we've learnt our lesson," Calum states adamantly, cursing under his breath, 'fucking fake, creepily taking advantage of her grief,' seriously irked at Lambert's touchy feely groping of Coral, suddenly feeling like dragging him around the room by his stupid long hair, and then tying him to the banisters with it, before making love to Coral in one of the bedrooms... with the door ajar... so that false fake Lamby can hear them! But he switches swiftly from this sado-masochistic erotic fantasy to snap irritably, "We didn't know what to expect, did we, man? Never been to a séance before, thought it was just gonna be some kind of clairvoyance... by a medium or something?" Coral is sobbing and wringing her hands in anguish. "That poor man died horribly, Lamby. The police found him hanging from a tree in Thruxton."

"I'm so sorry, my poor, poor, baby girl." Lambert strokes Coral's hair before cradling her face and peppering her forehead with dainty little pecks of kiss kiss kiss, "my poor baby waby girly."

Calum's anger and frustration bubbles up until his head hurts, knowing, 'there won't be any stolen sex with her now, not now she's consumed by more sadness over last night! This Lamby prick is just making things worse.' He suddenly feels light-headed, reality tilts in a split second, triumphing over demonic fantasy. Now feeling guilty for his callous coveting of Coral, he assumes it's the hash making him angry, emotionally scattered and wickedly confused, cursing the insidious nature of mind-altering substances. He's desperate for something to concentrate on, quickly, to divert his mind from the weird vertigo feeling of this spiralling disconnect from reality. He heads to the music centre, selecting a single by Joni Mitchell and setting her to play before going back over to the big bay window. He stares out over the hypnotic fields of peace as Joni warbles harmoni-ously about 'Woodstock,' her summer of love anthem, while Coral and Lambert remain entwined like a living sculpture, rocking gently back and forth together.

Calum knows she could be his if he were to make a move. 'That weed Lambert wouldn't stand a fucking chance!' The bitter bile of jealousy rises instantly to the back of his throat, catching him unawares, but immediately recognising the destructive symptoms, he deploys feral free will to curtail the negative vitriolic flow before it should gush forth and taint this moment. 'Wow! Where did that outpouring of hate come from? This isn't me, come on, cool it man,' he chastises himself. Calum hates feeling like this and is bewildered at his antagonistic feelings towards the harmless hippy. But then he blames Lambert and his narcotics for altering his personality so dramatically. 'He said it was home-grown weed, but I bet the prick has added chemicals to the hash.' Playing tricks on him, his mind switches back and forth from animosity to benevolence. He admonishes his unsavoury alter ego, 'hey, cut it out, dude, you're not interested in her, except for maybe a quickie, so just let them be,' before allowing magnanimously, 'don't begrudge them their bit of fun.'

He has taken a shine to Coral but tries to convince himself she's more of a friend... maybe a possible one-night stand... certainly not serious long-term item material. 'Then why,' he wonders annoyingly, 'is Lambert's loose familiarity with this pretty girl bugging me so?' Deciding to leave them to it, he slips from the room just as the music fades, feeling spaced out and paranoid now. This isn't a good feeling, this sluggish lethargy, and he's now unsure whether it's the hash affecting him or his bitterness at losing the girl. 'Fuck this, I can't be doing with all these human mind games.' Calum bounds down the stairs two at a time before letting himself out, sighing in relief as the cool evening air fills his lungs and refreshes his skin, welcoming the natural upgrade from the stale marijuana fug of the apartment, feeling better with each deep inhalation of Nature's narcotic, and quickly realising, 'This hash gear don't work unless you're calm and relaxed, has the opposite effect otherwise.' After several more deep breaths of fresh air, he's good to go.

As he heads back to Weyhill, a blood-red dusk, spiritually smudged with burnt orange, is encroaching into the dying embers of the day. All of a sudden he's strangely weary, his energy zapped, leaden legs plodding on, a repetitive throb at the back of his head rendering his mind tired, so tired, leaving him wondering, 'perhaps it's due to my first time on the pot... or maybe the after-effects of the séance? Takes it out of you emotionally, all that psychic stuff... I'm ready for an early night, me.'

CHAPTER THIRTY-SIX

Calum doesn't sleep well, tossing and turning most of the night, his mind heavy with obligation, agonising restlessly, 'Why have I been given this pure, perfect knowledge by the Great Spirit? I am not worthy. After all I'm only human, just seeking a carefree hedonistic lifestyle these days. Surely that's not too much to ask. I'll still do my bit, and look out for Mother Nature's creatures, but this spiritual stuff, it's all too much for a mere mortal sometimes... But hey, hang on, has Gaia not informed me that other humans also hold the knowledge? OK... so how do they handle it?' Suddenly it hits him, a true eureka moment, the sudden rush of clarity causing him to leap from his bed as if beckoned seductively by wild biker girl sirens. 'That's it, I get it now, I must get out more, move in different circles, meet and greet with similar like-minded obligated souls. Not just the drunks and pot heads of this world, but those on the same spiritual wavelength... on a similar Sacred Path as myself.' But the wave of euphoria quickly subsides, as he remembers that the Great Spirit had also said that these empathetic souls were in the distinct minority, and spread very thinly throughout planet Earth. 'One could spend much precious time searching them out...' shaking his head, swiftly abandoning this altruistic plan, he murmurs to himself, "No, no way, fuck that! Life is short enough as it is, without wasting serious party time."

Next up on this self-flagellation, beat-himself-up night, is the thing with Coral. He muses, 'she's delightful, granted, and cute, and thoroughly decent, caring, genuine, and would make great girlfriend

material... then why isn't that enough for me?' Even after being belit-
tled and humiliated by the sexy biker girls, Calum knows deep down
it's their wild unpredictability, that rebellious uncertainty, the excitement of never knowing what's going to happen next, that really turns
him on. 'Perhaps Frank's right, maybe I am irresistibly drawn to these
unstable personalities... the damaged ones. Is it because I'm damaged
myself? Is it any fucking wonder though?' He thinks, recalling bitterly,
'taking into account the life I've led with the humans so far.'

His conundrum remains unresolved. The lure of the natural world
is strong, and he knows that, if he could get past the temptation of
lusting after the allure and mystique of the BAD girls, then the purity
and uncomplicated truth taught by Gaia really would be all-pervading, and all one needed to attain complete fulfilment and peace
of mind. 'If one could stay the course as a true spiritual being... is
it possible, that a flawed loose cannon like me can accomplish this?
To be zen-monk-like disciplined?' Sighing wearily, he pledges, at
least, to give it a try, in the morning, before drifting off, emotionally
exhausted, to sleep at last...

Calum is awake at six o'clock, feeling jaded and out of sorts. His
mojo has deserted him big time. This is much worse than he thought,
this feeling of isolation in a spiritual no-man's land. It's a dilemma, an
emotional challenge that has to be resolved, one way or another. 'How
crazy for me to have downloaded all of this monumental wisdom
from the great universal spirit of Nature, and then be so weak-willed
in resisting the seduction of the dark side of the female psyche.'

It's a puzzling anomaly, a spanner in the works of his journey on
the Sacred Path. He concludes, after much soul searching, that he has
experienced enough drama and excitement for a while and needs a
break from human interaction. 'Too high-maintenance, the ladies,' is
his damning verdict. Calum makes an on-the-spot decision to retreat
into a hermit-like existence, at least for the remainder of winter.

So, making a conscious effort, over the next six months, he with-
draws into himself, welcoming the peaceful isolation and soulful
solitude of being in spiritual retreat, keeping his head down at school,

staying quiet and withdrawn, avoiding Cleeve. 'Defo avoiding Cleeve!' And even forgoing football with the lads. Instead he spends his days exploring the surrounding villages, walking many off-the-beaten-track miles, along footpaths and bridleways, through meadows and woodland, communing with stones, plants, creatures and insects. The natural world becomes his world. He comes across many insects and small creatures in perilous situations. Removing all manner of bugs, birds and other animals from the path of traffic, even wriggling worms and slow snails on the roads are saved and placed in the fields, saving insects trapped in spider's webs, or those marooned on rocks in the middle of ponds, rescuing other unfortunate beings from drowning in rivers and streams. Extremely unusually, Calum also finds a stranded mole, blindly zig-zagging this way and that, on the road outside the White Horse pub. He catches the mole in an old paint tin and returns it to the soft churned-up earth of the horse paddocks opposite. With great care and consideration, he moves each and every creature from peril to safety. This practice becomes second nature. Guided by Gaia to seek out the vulnerable and endangered, constantly alert, and always on the lookout, he rescues these innocents from any location where they may be in danger of being trampled on by lumbering clumsy humans or attacked by natural predators. He does not feel this kindly disposed towards humans though, and wonders how he would react if one of the abusers among them needed help. He does not ponder long.

Calum builds his strength by lifting heavy forest tree branches repetitively and hones his fitness by incorporating running and walking into this altruistic daily routine. Nutrition is provided by dining out on any available seasonal fruits of forest and hedgerow. He's preparing mentally for his spiritual escape from human reality and he spends his resting time meditating on the divine mysteries of the seven universes.

Janet notes the change in him and makes Jim aware. He is unconcerned, but she is worried enough to consider psychiatric analysis for Calum. "It's not right, Jim, for him to be moping around, to be so strangely quiet and subdued at his age." He waves away her worries. "Leave him be, woman. It's just his adolescent phase; lots of youngsters go through it, and besides, I'm enjoying the peace and quiet, without his whining and demanding." He laughs, "long may it continue, say I."

Janet decides the next day to get a pet. She thinks this will be beneficial for them all, and may bring them closer together as a family, informing Calum at breakfast. "Son, I have a lovely surprise for you," beaming in anticipation of his reaction, "can you guess?"

'Surprise, surprise!' He's so, so close to letting her know exactly what he thinks of both her and Jim, 'now, that would be a fucking "surprise"… for them.' He lets it go though, pretending to be interested. "Nope, haven't a clue, Mrs B. My clairvoyant skills are not that finely attuned… as yet. But go on, what's this big surprise, then?" Jim looks up from his paper, scowling. "Doesn't sound very excited, does he? Told you it was a bloody stupid idea, pandering to him. Pets! I ask you, who's going to look after it, that's what I'd like to know?"

'Pets! Oh my god!' Calum is horrified. "Oh no, Mrs Brown, please tell me it's not true, not after the dogs." Jim peers over his spectacles and directs a warning glare. Although taken aback at the lack of enthusiasm, Janet continues, upbeat. "It will be lovely, a little kitten I was thinking, maybe two, even three. We have the space. They will become a part of our family and—"

Calum butts in. "Please, Mrs Brown, I strongly urge you to reconsider, it's… umm… not really the right time… or place… currently I feel, for you… us… to take on the responsibility of domestic animals," he points urgently at head-in-the-paper Jim, while silently mouthing at her, "No! No! No!"

She smiles and ruffles his hair. "Aww, but they are so delightful Calum," her eyes wide with excitement. "You will love them when you see them son, they are so cute, one is black and white, one ginger and the other pure black, they—"

Jim cuts short her animated chatter. "Never thought I'd hear myself say it, but I'm with the boy on this, woman, no pets…"

But Janet is not to be denied, and a few days later she brings home three eight-week-old kittens in a cardboard box. Jim won't have them indoors, so she buys an outdoor cage-and-run combination from the local pet shop.

Despite his reservations, Calum can't help but love the tiny playful innocent youngsters. He thoroughly enjoys the next two weeks, caring for the kittens, and watching them play and grow. Janet seems to love the kittens as much as he does, spending all her spare time cuddling and stroking them. Calum has warmed a little to Janet as they have both bonded with the cats, even occasionally sitting outside with her of an evening, with the cute little creatures on their laps, whiling away the time, watching the sun go down together. They chuckle at the kittens' antics whilst passing the mischievous youngsters back and forth. This was big; a new dynamic going on here, there was now something to look forward to for them both in this dreary planet Earth existence.

Jim mutters and moans in passing back and forth to the mobile home, replenishing refreshments mid-porn-fix. "Bloody cats have taken over, useless scrawny creatures, time and money wasted," he shouts at his wife accusingly. "It's affecting the housework, Janet. For god's sake, we need animals like a bloody hole in the head."

"Take no notice, dear," she tells Calum. "Jim loves them really, as much as we do. It's just his way, son, he finds it difficult to show emotion."

Calum sniggers, "yeah, too right he fucking does!"

CHAPTER
THIRTY-SEVEN

One evening a few weeks later, Janet and Calum are sat together on the veranda, watching the juvenile kittens tumbling and chasing, play fighting, mewing and hissing in joyous fun on the dusty ground. All of a sudden there's a loud yelping, accompanied by hunting horns, followed by a bunch of hounds rampaging through the garden. There must be twenty to thirty of the marauding dogs. Before Calum or Janet can move, the hounds have grabbed the kittens by their scruffs, throwing the squealing animals high into the air, ripping the skin from their backs, leaving them screaming and writhing in agony on the ground. The horsemen and women are now trampling all over the garden trying to round up the loose dogs. Janet screams. Calum is rooted to his chair in horror.

Jim comes stumbling out from the mobile home. "What in god's name is going on here?!" Calum can't speak, struck dumb by the carnage, he points to the badly mauled kittens. "Get me a bucket of water, boy," Jim shouts. "Now! Move yourself, quick, you useless bloody article." He runs to the back of the bungalow and fills a bucket of water from the outside tap, sobbing as he staggers back in shock, spilling some of the ice-cold water over his legs and feet. Jim snatches the bucket, grabs the kittens, and holds them down under the water. Calum can't cry out, his despair stifled, muffled anguish repelled by dry silence clogging his throat as he watches the kittens struggle briefly under the water, tiny streams of air bubbles bubbling to the surface as they drown. Feeling about to faint, he finally lets out a long wailing cry before collapsing, head in hands, onto his chair. Janet sinks to her knees, weeping and wringing her hands over and over.

The head huntsman dismounts and waddles over, a big fat man in red coat, black hat and riding boots. He puts a hand on Janet's shoulder. "I am so sorry, madam... terrible accident... the hounds got the scent of fox and just took off."

"You utter fucking moron!" Calum screams at him. "If you hadn't been out hunting innocent creatures for your bloodlust fun these poor kittens would not have died such a horrible death." Janet gets to her feet and goes to Calum. "Now son, you mustn't speak to your elders in that disgraceful manner. The dogs lost control. Although it's very distressing, it was not intentional. Now... apologise, please." He looks at her in astonishment. "Apologise?! You must be fucking joking, woman! I won't apologise to that fat useless oaf, no way, never!" The hunter moves in and puts his face close up to Calum. "You heard your mother, how dare you speak so disrespectfully to your elders. Now apologise! He leans in even closer, determined to intimidate. "I'm waiting, boy." Calum can smell alcohol on his breath and see tiny blue thread veins erupting all over his pale, flabby face. "You'll be waiting a long time, then, you gross piece of shit," he screams, before spitting directly in the huntsman's face.

Staggering backwards, open-mouthed in disbelief, he goes for his whip, raising it high, just as Janet wraps her arms protectively around Calum. "No sir, please, no, I will discipline him for that disgusting act, please don't harm the boy sir, I beg of you." Calum breaks free and runs to his room, throwing himself on his bed, overcome by uncontrollable shivering, distraught and howling into his pillow. A gruesome image is fixed in his mind of the horrible fate the poor kittens have suffered, knowing he will never forget their dreadful screams of distress and pain.

Janet knocks on his door a while later. "Calum... you must come and eat."

"Go away."

"But son, you need to eat." He feels strangely calm and measured, before replying, "You really think I feel like eating?"

"Well... no... of course not... but life must go on. It was a terrible tragedy, I know... but god will–"

"I said go away. Leave me alone. You and your fucking god. Where was he for the Bee Lady, and the kittens, come on, tell me! What kind of twisted sick god allows beautiful innocent beings to suffer and perish in such a cruel way? You know nothing... nothing worthwhile anyway. Now go... please." His tone is flat, devoid of emotion. She leaves him crying into his pillow, for hours, it seems...

It's almost dark when he emerges from the room. Janet comes rushing over. "No!" He keeps her at bay with outstretched hands. "Stay away... please." She backs off. "Alright son, but at least let me reheat your dinner, you must be hungry." He snaps, shouting at her, "I told you, no food! Leave me be. I'll just get some water, then I'm going outside for a while."

"Leave him alone, woman, stop bloody mollycoddling," orders Jim from his armchair. Calum goes into the lounge to confront him. "What have you done with the kittens?"

"Buried them," he replies without looking up. Calum is surprised, but glad at least for that small mercy. He was dreading attending to their burial. "Oh... OK... thanks for that." Jim throws his paper to the floor. "Don't thank me, boy! You think I enjoyed all the ruckus this afternoon, then having to clear up after you two idiots?" Glaring at Janet, he shouts at her. "And you, you stupid, stupid woman. I said it would end badly, but would you listen? Would you hell as like!"

Calum accepts he has a point, but he hates Jim even more now for his lack of basic compassion. He knows there is no use whatsoever in trying to domesticate animals on this cruel, horrific planet. Making pets of them only lulled the creatures into a false sense of security, and made them easy prey for hunters and hounds. When wild and feral they would not trust man, as the poor kittens had, and so would at least have a chance of survival if left to their own devices.

Janet wails, "Jim, how can you be so cruel, we only wanted to love and care for them."

"Yes, and look what happened. Do you call that love, is that care? I told you to leave them be! I said no pets, did I not?" Taking a long slug of whiskey, he points at Calum and sneers, "As for you boy, you think you know about Nature... you know nothing about how the countryside works, you are just an inconsequential nobody!" His voice rises, flabby face quivering. "You hear me, boy, a useless nobody!"

Calum refuses to be goaded and answers calmly. "How the countryside works! The countryside doesn't work, you fat useless fool. Nature goes about its business effortlessly, seamlessly, in perfect harmony... oh, and for your information, fatso, I'd rather be a nobody... than a never-fucking-was."

Jim, fuming, struggles to get up, but is too drunk, toppling back breathlessly into the armchair. "You'll pay for your disrespect boy, soon as I—"

Calum goes into the lounge, taunting. "Oh yeah, is that so, soon as you what? Soon as you sober up? Soon as you can get your fat arse off the chair... you shit-faced drunken obese lump of lard."

He goes outside, taking a deep breath, heart racing with rage... his gaze is drawn to the sky, where the moon presents as a golden half crescent tonight, stars glowing silver in the deep black backdrop of space. It feels as if the very atmosphere is charged with tension. Calum can sense the retributive undertones, karmic atoms fizzing and popping with malevolent intent, Mother Nature's condemnation preparing to be unleashed in one form or another. "OK, Great Spirit, I get what's going down, but don't visit me tonight please, no sermon, no lesson. This is so wrong, and I need space to get my head around this."

He walks over and slides into the damp passenger seat of the old Mercedes. Closing his eyes, he feels helpless, but already hardened to human reality, his psyche is conditioned now to this gruesome world. Pondering an escape, he tries to imagine the bigger picture. 'Yes, escape... but not just from the here and now... but away for good, before human evil finally incites planet Earth to implode in self-combustion.' He accepts that 'even the divine power of Nature will be unable to prevent mankind's forthcoming armageddon.'

Gazing up at far away planets, stars, the universe – that's where he wants to go, where he wants to be, in outer space, anywhere in the cosmos. But most importantly, somewhere that is far away from the depraved evil wickedness of man.

CHAPTER
THIRTY-EIGHT

Several weeks pass... Calum has remained in a deep depression and has not uttered a word since the death of the kittens... Until one evening when broken sleep introduces the Bee Lady to his dreams. He feels her loving healing presence infiltrating his heart, before suddenly awaking with the angelic being's gift of love carrying her blessing to him on this cold Saturday morning. He washes and dresses quickly, then walks towards Thruxton Village, catching his breath as a sudden feeling of renewal, a re-energising lightness of being envelopes him, the cloak of sad solitude finally lifting. He realises he is being healed of his grief, and feels ready now to re-engage and interact again with the world. 'And who knows,' he thinks generously, 'maybe even some of its kinder human inhabitants.' Gaia's voice carries on the breeze, "Nature is the greatest healer, the only natural healing essence."

Striding on, smiling, hoping some of his old friends will be out playing football today, his positivity is swiftly deflated by the disgusting smell coming from the battery chicken farm on the Fyfield Road. A revolting stench hangs in the air. Pinching his nostrils closed, he cautiously approaches. All the doors and shutters are open. This is puzzling. 'Strange... where are all the chickens?'

A red sign on the big wooden double doors answers his question:

CLEANING IN PROGRESS
KEEP OUT

Calum ignores the command and goes in. There are no live birds inside, just the loud buzzing of thousands of flies as they feed on hundreds of dead chickens. Rats are scurrying here, there, and everywhere, meticulously covering every inch of this house of death, feeding on the corpses that lie rotting in the cramped compartments. He thinks he sees one chicken move, but on closer inspection is horrified to see the illusion of motion caused by a multitude of white maggots squirming inside the decaying carcass.

'Cleaning in progress, what a fucking laugh,' Calum shakes his head in revulsion. 'This place has not been cleaned out for decades. It's only being done now because there is no room to move for chicken shit. Meaning the birds won't lay, no money for the farmer then, so the birds are left, dying, starved until all are dead, dumped here ready for one big clean-up. It sure doesn't take a genius to work out the priorities here. But animal welfare is certainly not number one on the list.' He looks around for any sign of humans... he is alone, and knows what must be done, muttering to himself, "I'll save you the job of cleaning, you cruel bastards." He strides to the centre of the building and commands, "On behalf of the Great Spirit of Nature, all living creatures must now vacate this place of evil intent." A large tortoise-shell cat ambles in and rubs around his legs. Calum leans down and lifts the cat in his arms. "That goes for you too, old fella."

The big tomcat looks up into his eyes, before speaking. "Do not fret, Calum, there is no imminent danger here for my creatures. They would not, free will, dwell in such an accursed place." He feels a flood of confirmation for his unfinished business. "Thank you, mother, just making sure, as I have plans." He gestures expansively around the grim interior of the building. "Big plans, and I do not want to make the same mistake I made with the sacred hedgerow."

"Most commendable, then I shall leave you to your work."

"But what about all these rats and flies? They are taking no heed."

"I shall refer you to my previous statement. They are not my offspring. My children would not live in such an environment by choice. To do so would be to condone."

"Ahh... yes, Gaia... now I understand."

The cat leaps from his arms and runs outside. Taking this as approval, Calum goes to the far end of the building, casually lighting a cigarette, before flicking the still-burning match onto the tinder-dry straw, strolling nonchalantly away as the flames take hold, whistling in satisfaction of a job well done. Leaving the building, he notices a large black spider on the outer doorframe, engaged in the mummification process of webbing a struggling, loudly buzzing bluebottle fly, whose desperation to escape sends the web springing back and forth like a busy trapeze wire.

"Sorry to disturb your lunch, my friend," Calum apologises, lifting the spider and setting it down carefully in the field opposite. Without a backwards glance, he walks on towards Thruxton, whilst aptly belting out a passionate rendition of the number one chart hit by Authur Brown, "Fire! I'll take you to burn. Fire! I'll teach you to learn. Fire! I'll see you burn." Just as he crests the brow of Stanbury Road a dark blue MG Midget sports car speeds his way. The pretty girl in the passenger seat turns and waves. 'Just like in one of those period MG sales posters...' he recalls, 'with the sun glinting off the spinning silver wire wheels... hey!' Calum does a double take, turning round, as they speed by, realising, 'It's Coral... with Lambert driving.' A brief griping pang of regret grips him, but he lets it go. 'That's all in the past. After all, it's down to me not making a move on her when I had the chance. That's why she's with him,' begrudgingly allowing, 'can't blame them... it's my choosing'. He smells burning and turns to see a massive billowing plume of dense smoke rising up like atomic bomb fallout above Fyfield Village. He feels proud of his ambassadorial role in serving the Great Spirit, before casually ambling away, feeling fulfilled, at one with Nature, as sirens wail urgently away in the distance.

CHAPTER
THIRTY-NINE

Summer 1970.

The long school holidays beckon invitingly for Calum.

His self-imposed hermitage is now just a fading memory as he sets off one Friday evening for the White Horse. The last of the day's sun still warm on his back, with just a refreshing hint of cool breeze. Feeling upbeat, positive, he strides purposefully to the pub.

Frank is behind the bar and greets him warmly. "Hi son, not seen you for a while."

"No, been keeping my head down, Frankie boy, thought I'd give it a break from here for a while..." He cringes at the memory... "Especially after that embarrassing business with the biker chicks."

"Yeah, I get that kid," Frank concurs, "understandable... good to see you again though," he nods encouragingly. "And looking well... barley wine, is it?"

Calum goes over to the jukebox, grinning, "Yeah, go on then, I'd like to think my credit's still good with Mr Moray for a while yet." He chooses T Rex's, 'Get It On,' from the playlist. 'Very apt', he reckons, as two attractive young girls walk in, with him noting pleasingly, 'Mmm, both lookers,' as he casually scrutinises their vital statistics. The shorter girl of the two is around five foot five, with curves in all the right places, short auburn hair, tight blue denim jeans, green leather jacket and bright red heels. The other is slightly taller, long glossy dark hair, full red lips, and dressed to impress in silver chiffon blouse, short dark pencil skirt, finished with patterned nylons and black ankle boots. 'Slimmer, but just as sexy,' Calum determines, concluding his dutiful assessment in aroused anticipation.

The girls order cokes, before making for the jukebox. Frank glances over and winks, giving him the thumbs up. Calum smiles back in agreement as the girls start bopping beguilingly in time to 'On the Bayou' by Creedence Clearwater Revival, every so often glancing over in his direction, all sparkly eyes and coy whisperings. He grins and waves back, before ordering another drink. "Play your cards right," Frank advises as he pours, "and you're in there, son."

"Really, you think so, Frank?" Calum's feeling unsure and a little insecure after the upsetting debacle with the greaser girls. It has knocked his confidence big time, especially being so raw and recent.

"Yeah, sure of it, kid. Those young lovelies are more your type. Similar age, I'm guessing, nice lookers too. Go for it son, fill your boots." Calum takes heart from the barman's positivity and sits back down, his old bravado returning as the girls slink over and sit close, one either side of him.

"Hi, I'm Hazel."

"And I'm Karen... we're sisters, y'know."

"Well well, is that so girls?" Calum beams, graciously accepting, 'Christmas has come early... Santa Sex is in the house... and bearing gifts'. He's liking this good vibe going down, as the girl's identical musk perfume wafts seductively about him. 'The scent of wild abandon', it seems to him. The zen-like discipline of his recent hermitage experience waning rapidly. "Allow me to introduce myself, girls, my name's Calum... Calum Connor. I've not had the pleasure of seeing you young ladies here before... where you from, then?"

"Andover, we live with our parents... unfortunately," Karen moans. Hazel leans in close to him, her hand lightly brushing his. "How about you, babe?" The tingling sensation from her touch feels so exquisite he temporarily loses the thread of reality. "Mmm... uhh... come again, sweetie?"

"Where do you live?" He's bewitched now, and struggling to regain his composure, his thoughts all of a sudden turning to so much jumbled mush, replying falteringly, "Me... where do I live? Umm... oh... not far from here... Dauntsey Lane... just up the road a ways. Hazel giggles at his stumbling incoherence, well aware of her wily sexual power. "Oh yeah, hon, know it well. We walked down that way earlier, after we got off the bus." Karen cuddles in close, resting a warm hand on his thigh. He feels the rhythmic throb of her pulse through his jeans. Cautiously evaluating and validating all key credentials before making any rash moves, and despite his racing desire, he asks prudently, "How old are you young lovelies, then?" Hazel smiles, "Sixteen... almost."

"Seventeen," adds Karen. "I'm only fifteen," Calum smirks, "so it would seem I'm the underage impressionable one in this possible ménage a trois," he laughs. "Hope you older women ain't gonna lead me astray?" Hazel's eyes widen as she whispers enticingly. "What... innocent young schoolgirls like us?" He coughs, trying to dispel the tell-tale nervous tremor in his throat, but failing annoyingly. "Tell me, girls, what brings you gorgeous creatures to this part of the world then?" He squirms inwardly as his intended manly baritone comes out as an embarrassing high-pitched squeak.

The infatuated sisters seem not to have noticed. Karen smirks, tilting her head alluringly. "We heard say that this was a cool pub for talent."

"Yeah, well, they got that bit right sis," Hazel sighs, resting her head on Calum's shoulder and breathing softly in his ear. He's hooked now, and wants to know, "What time you babes got to be back home then?"

"Maybe we'll go when you do, mister," Karen nuzzles his neck, "then you can walk us to the bus stop."

"Yeah, you can be our protector Calum," Hazel coos, baby doll voice oh so vulnerable, and smiling wickedly. "Cos we need protecting by a big strong lad like you."

"Sure thing, ladies," he volunteers eagerly, not believing his luck, "you can count on me to take real good care of you."

The next two hours speed by for the teenagers, lost in their own make-believe reality, relegating time and other people to just nameless bit-part players, with the pub just another cardboard cut-out prop of life. Confident in their sexuality, oblivious to shame or embarrassment, senses heightened by excitement, fixated on lust, whilst eagerly participating in the preening flirtatious foreplay of the young.

Calum clocks the time… coming up to nine forty-five, aware the last bus to Andover stops at Whitey House, Weyhill at eleven-twenty. He's aiming to get to know these sisters a little more intimately before they go home, so he gulps down his drink and prompts, "Well girls, what say we all drink up and be on our merry way then?"

Hazel jumps up eagerly, "Thought you'd never ask, babe." The girls smile telepathically self-assured at each other as they link arms with him. "Hey Frank, can you lay a quart of dry cider on me?" Calum asks. "Square you up tomorrow, mate?" Frank grins as he hands over the bottle. "On the house, son… look, hang on a mo, guys." He turns to the optics and pours three double shots of Martell brandy. "On me, kids, this will warm you up as you go, y'all have a good time now, you hear." He winks at Calum. "Be sure to look after these young lassies mind." The girls giggle, and in tandem, they knock the strong spirits back in one. Calum grins, like the proverbial cat who got – or in his case, may get – the cream. "Will do, Frank," he downs his shot, "see you later mate, cheers."

Karen giggles as he opens the door for her. "A gentleman is this one sis, and hot to boot."

"Not too much of a gent though, I'm hoping," Hazel purrs. "Cuz I'm feeling so so horny tonight." As the excited trio leave the car park Karen tugs Calum's sleeve. "Hey mister, give us a swig of that cider then."

"Hmm…" he frowns, mock seriously… "not sure if I should, with you both being underage."

"So are you, matey," Hazel laughs, playfully attempting to snatch the bottle. Holding it tantalisingly out of reach above her head, he asks, "What's it worth?"

"You'll find out soon enough, lover boy," Hazel promises, pressing her warm body against him. He hands the bottle to Karen. She looks him daringly in the eyes as she takes a long slug. Hazel snatches it from her sister and gulps greedily. They walk on unsteadily up the steep footpath that runs alongside the A303. The way ahead well lit by a big bright moon...

By the time they reach Dauntsey Lane, the cider has been guzzled, with the empty bottle thrown and smashed on the road some way behind them. They stagger along, laughing and singing, the girls holding on tight to Calum, the effects of the alcohol freeing up any lingering inhibitions. "Just so you know, handsome... Hazel and I share everything together," Karen forewarns him, "and that includes boyfriends."

"Oh yeah, is that so?" He chuckles expectantly. "Well, best be gentle with me then babe, I'm not as experienced as you young ladies."

"Don't you worry none, honey," Hazel squeezes his hand and grins, "we'll look after you good... real good."

They arrive underneath the railway bridge above Dauntsey Lane, and Karen orders, "Let's sit here awhile," pulling Calum close to her. Hazel joins them on the ledge of the cold brick underpass. "What times is it, sis?" Karen peers at her luminous Timex watch. "Just coming up to... ten-thirty, so we've got a while yet then for some naughty fun. Gonna give me a kiss goodnight then, young man?" She doesn't wait for an answer and snogs him greedily. He responds willingly to her warm eager lips. Hazel wants in on the action, her hot breath and warm tongue soon tickling and probing his earlobes. He moans as her teeth gently nip his neck. These girls are expert partners in passion... one either side of him now... nuzzling... nibbling... kissing... tugging at his clothes... buttons popping... zippers zipping... before the feverish unclasping of skirt and bra... licking... caressing... snarling and growling guttural, fighting over him... the girls seemingly driven to a frenzy by his wild feral essence. Karen presses his hand to her silky sex, pushing herself against him, chuckling at his surprised gasp, whispering in his ear, "No lover, we never wear panties." These insatiable sisters are determined to have their way with the captive plaything. Too far gone for restraint and decorum, wanton sexual gratification is the overriding desire. Accepting his lot, knowing there is to be no escape from these ravenous creatures of the dark night... trapped, all resistance futile... struggling pointless... he surrenders submissively to his fate, sighing contentedly as he is enveloped in their delicious musky teenage conquest.

Time ceases to exist... planet Earth's orbit slows... the universe has stalled... the climax is so nerve-tinglingly intense... he needs them to stop... now! But so consumed by lust, they don't let up, until finally he can stand it no longer and has to push them away. Reluctantly releasing their prey, backing away, the girls stand brazenly naked before him, eyes luminescent with lust, heavy breathing slowing... gradually regulating to a soft synchronised panting. Calum's heart beats fast as he gazes up at the girls smiling moonlit faces. The flushed, fulfilled expressions confirming that their ravenous sexual appetite has been temporarily sated by this latest tutorial of constantly craved carnal knowledge.

No one speaks. No need of words. They know each other intimately now.

CHAPTER
FORTY

The sisters dress quickly, their duty accomplished, before ordering, "Come on, Calum," linking arms with him, "we've got five minutes to get the bus." He feels weirdly disorientated, hurriedly putting on his jeans and shirt, trying to remember where the bus stop is, where he is... "Uhh... yeah... sure... come on then, girls, allow me to escort you." Karen laughs saucily, "You mean... like we just did for you... sir." He stiffens... 'Escort! Now why did I say that... was it some kind of Freudian slip? And what does she mean... "Like we did for you?"' Cleeve's biting remark about the biker girls being 'prossies' comes to mind, but he swiftly dismisses this crazy unfounded notion. 'No, now don't be ridiculous, fool.' He berates himself for his irrational paranoia, but Karen's droll reply only confirms what he thought earlier, just after the sex, 'this was not these girls' first time. They were just too slick, too in control, too professional... professional?! There you go again, you mug! Stop now! Enough already, stop beating yourself up, just because they were enthusiastic and up for anything doesn't mean they're prostitutes, they're just sex-mad young girls... out for fun... so enjoy, dummie.'

His first full sexual experience has been so mind-blowing, though, he couldn't care less. 'So what if they turn out to be ladies of the night? At least they are young, sexy, fit as fuck ladies of the night! But no... cut it out, now, enjoy the moment, idiot! Don't over-analyse all the fucking pleasure out of it.'

Hazel seems to read the conflict in his mind. "How was it for you, babe... for your first time? As good as you were hoping?" He beams. "Better! Much, and then some... fantastic, girls... I've had the best time, really I have." Karen pouts up at him. "Well, that's all good then, now we've broke you in... we'll have to do it again... soon... very soooon! We've got lots to teach you," she says, slyly sliding her hand inside his jeans and gazing into his eyes, "just you remember though... we're exclusive now, lover... an item," squeezing tightly. "Get it?"

"Yes, sure thing," he squeaks.

"Bus coming, sis," shouts Hazel. He gasps as Karen removes her hand to delve into her handbag, slipping him a note as the bus pulls in. "Our address and phone number, come visit, be sure to phone first, though. After nine." They kiss and cuddle him, bringing him back to lusty arousal, before running upstairs to the top deck, laughing at his befuddled state as they wave and blow kisses from the back seats. Calum sighs, waving back long after the illuminated upper deck disappears into the distance... Walking home, on cloud nine, he discounts Cleeve's jealous scaremongering, realising he has something special going on here, and only his first time... a hot threesome... with two sexy young sisters... probably most men's dream fantasy come true.

He has difficulty sleeping... replaying the evening's highlights over and over. Trouble with this entertaining mental playback is, by next morning, he is practically gagging for it again... waiting, frustratingly, until the designated time... "after nine, after nine", he murmurs, "yes, yes, omg, yes, after nine, after nine". Before jogging down to the red telephone box at Weyhill, calling their number... the phone rings... and rings... Lighting a cigarette, he pleads aloud, "Come on... pick up... pick up," whilst pushing the heavy door half-open with his foot to let out the smoke.

Karen eventually answers. "Yes... who is it?" She sounds monotone dull... subdued even... 'Hmm... strange...' he ponders. 'Totally different from the vivacious vixen of last night?' Calum intuits, 'Ahh well, no worries, give her a break, she's just obviously not a morning person.'

"Hey babe! Calum Connor here, ready and willing, at your service girls, do you want to—"

"Oh... it's you... You fucking woke me up! What do you want?" His heart sinks at the lukewarm reception... chuckling awkwardly, "Haha... What do I want? What do you think I want, babe... what we all wanted... last night, remember?"

"We're not bloody sex machines you know!" She sullenly informs him. "Besides, we're going out with our parents today, can't get out of it... wish we could, but—"

"Aww, come on Karen, I'm missing you already babe, surely we can—"

"I said no! Just stop being so fucking needy... but yeah, yeah, really missing you too, much much." She sounds bored to tears. "Come round tomorrow... after nine... parents will be at work then." He's sure she just yawned? "Are you OK, Karen?" Suspicious now, wondering, 'has she got someone else there?'

"Yes, yes, sorry, just tired, didn't need to be up this early, Cal... look.... tomorrow's better, we'll have the house all to ourselves, be sure to save yourself for us, you'll need all your energy, lover boy." He sighs in relief, feeling better. "OK, will do babe, looking forward to that, can't wait to get hold of you and—"

"Save it." Karen cuts him dead. "We don't do phone sex." Click, the line goes dead... "Hello... hello?" He taps the connector repeatedly before slamming down the receiver. "Yeah, bye bye to you, too... fucking prick teaser!"

He's mad as hell... doesn't get it... 'The vibe was so different from last night... she still obviously wants sex,' he hopes, 'but the fun and spontaneity had gone from her... as if sex was just another bodily function that had to be attended too... like she knew she had to do it, but the act was so impersonal that when the urge came over her she would have fucked anyone.' Calum swings the phone by the cable, whacking it against the side of the call box again and again, smashing the Bakelite reciever and several glass panes into hundreds of tiny fragments before storming home, angry, deflated, frustrated. He spends the rest of the day listening to music in his room. His optimism and positive thinking return by early evening though, and so he heads off for the White Horse. He's looking forward to meeting up again with the sisters tomorrow... only another night to wait. He accepts their limitations, allowing graciously, 'after all, you ain't gonna get sex like that from normal girls.'

He grins when he sees Frank behind the bar.

"OK son, spill... chapter and verse now... how did it go last night then?" Calum laughs, hoping he's not blushing. "Well... I'll keep the intimate details to myself, Frankie boy, but let's just say, my friend... coke ain't the real thing."

Next day, Calum's up at dawn, washed and dressed and on his way to his raunchy rendezvous before Jim and Janet rise. He decides to walk the four miles into town. It's a cold morning, but the sun's coming up quickly. Pausing to pick the sisters a bunch of wild flowers on the way, it's eight-thirty when he knocks on their door. Tingling with excitement, he peers close up through the frosted glass door, just making out the sexy silhouette of a curvy female form coming down-stairs. "Fuck yes!" he murmurs in aroused anticipation.

Karen opens the door dressed in a flimsy nightie and looking sexily drowsy. "Mmm... hello, lover... christ, you're keen, Hazel's still in bed, come on then, you'd best come in." Hazel suddenly comes bounding down the stairs, all smiles and oozing enthusiasm. "Oh Calum, so good to see you, Karen said you might be round... didn't expect you this early though." She leaps into his arms and gives him a wet sloppy kiss, before sliding off him like a sticky pole dancer, taking his hand, and pleading, "come upstairs then, hon."

"Yeah, love to, babe." He reaches inside his jacket and proudly produces the wildflower bouquet... But first... I got you these." Karen grabs the flowers and slams them into his chest. "Soppy bugger. Look, I'm gonna level with you, Cal, let's get this straight from the get go... We don't want fucking flowers, tacky presents or naff cards. All we want is sex, sex, and more sex, we'll teach you all we know, and you can be assured our repertoire is extensive." Calum drops the drooping blooms and nods eagerly, he's not arguing. Hazel presses up close behind him, moaning and writhing in impatience. "Mmm, I'm ready for our next lesson now, honey." Karen grabs a rough handful of his crotch. "Yes, me too, sis... but first... let's get one thing straight, mister." Her wet tongue flicks across his lips, pale grey eyes close up, searching his. "Just so's you know, you belong to us now... exclusively, understand?"

"Yes, I get the picture... no romance, no love, no niceties... just full-on no-strings sex." He laughs. "So be it, girls... hey, after all, I'm an adaptable kinda guy." Karen slaps his bum. "That's all good, then... now get yourself up them fucking stairs."

Calum meets up with Hazel and Karen regularly during the following weeks – always at their house, whenever their parents are out. The sex spree had begun in earnest, and he soon comes to the conclusion that these sisters are insatiable nymphomaniacs.

These are exciting times. No school, just the long summer holidays stretching ahead of him. Six weeks of fun and frolics ensue with these ever-willing girls. Sex is always on offer and the menu choice comprehensive. If their parents are at home when he phones, they meet in town, before fornicating on the parked-up buses late at night in the station, or in summer-warm cornfields. Village bus shelters and hay-filled barns are also favoured venues... pretty much whenever and wherever the fancy took them, with Calum recalling proudly, 'once even standing up in a phone box'.

It was great fun to begin with, this sexual liberation, the sex on tap. He couldn't get enough. Calum was gulping from the fountain of youth with an unquenchable thirst. But, as with all sure things, the novelty eventually began to wane. Problem was, try as he might, these girls could never be satisfied. Calum now realised that the 'Sinister Sisters' (as he had affectionately nicknamed them) would always need extra attention... more than he alone could ever provide. He was acutely aware now that less is never more, and more is never enough, in the world of the nymphomaniac.

There was never any real conversation with them, unless it was talking dirty about their favourite subject... fucking... which was fine when he was aroused and up for it, but one could have too much of a good thing, as was quickly dawning on him. Desperate for a break, he starts making excuses so as to swerve the girls, or just fails to turn up for their pre-arranged dates. This indifferent attitude only serves to makes them desire him even more. The relevance of barman Frank's advice, 'Treat 'em mean, keep 'em keen,' certainly applied to the sisters. The last thing Calum wants now though, is to 'keep 'em keen.' What he yearns for is some space and distance.

He had also begun dating other girls, assuming correctly that variety is the spice, but naively believing that these new girlfriends would be less high-maintenance. Calum was disappointed. Granted, these latest flames were not full-on sex addicts like Hazel and Karen, but they still expected something in return for their love and attention, not to mention any relinquished favours.

On reflection, after this sexual saturation, Calum realises he's not into the females as much as they are into him. He loved the thrill of the chase, for sure, and the most enjoyable passionate reward at the moment of capture, but the anti-climax and clingy aftermath left him reaching for his boots and ready to run for the hills. Calum comes to the conclusion he is more feral than human in this respect. After all there was no romance, no agendas, no recriminations or mind games involved when animals had sex, the brief moment of pleasure was Nature's canny enticement, ensuring reproduction so as to continue the species.

The six-week summer holidays became one hectic social whirl. At one time he has seven girlfriends on the go, with him smugly reflecting, 'one for every day of the week,' sometimes even two a day, when he met up with the Sinister Sisters. He is a boy in demand, but beginning to find it increasingly tricky to juggle and satisfy his adoring female fans. The well-worn phrase, 'be careful what you wish for,' often niggles prophetically.

But tough shift as it is, the holidays pass far too soon for Calum. He detests the return to school and is now even more determined to leave, especially since coming across this new exciting lease of life. He can't wait for the chance to escape, so he stubbornly refuses to learn, embarking on a strategy of non-involvement, taking no interest in lessons and giving no respect. Calum would switch off from the droning school teachers, who he saw as just perverted pedlars of the past. Punished regularly for this lack of reverence towards the great human institution of dogmatic doctrine, if his work did not meet their educational standards, then he would receive the slipper, cane and/ or detention. 'Isn't that always the way of it with most tutors in this school,' Calum thinks, 'if a pupil does not bow down to their conventional institutional teaching, then there is always that old standby, corporal punishment, to fall back on.'

Being whacked on the backside with a slipper was the least of the bare-knuckle reality at Andover Secondary School. Most disobedient scholars could stand the stinging pain of that degradation occasionally; it was expected, accepted as an occupational hazard, a given of being in such close proximity of sadistic egotistical teachers. Punishment with the cane was a different matter, though. Six sharp lashes with a bamboo cane – or sometimes even a flat wooden chair leg – to the unfortunate pupil's backside or legs was the norm. This painful thrashing was dispensed with such force and gusto that the victim's skin would often be raised in blood-clotted weals and welts, or severe blue-black bruising. Sometimes the skin would be broken, and the boy would have to endure the pain and bleeding until that glorious reprieve, 'home time.'

The term used for this legalised violence was 'six of the best.' Calum knew he had the cruel enforcers' number when he heard the cane lashing so described. He wondered, 'why is such a brutal beating not called "six of the worst"? Or even "sadistic six"? Why?' Because these abusers so loved the power of control and dominance over the meeker and weaker that was why the tormentors called it, 'six of the best.'

As self-confessed masters of the English dictionary, the teachers knew only too well that the meaning of 'best' in the English language is 'to get the better of,' 'one's maximum effort,' 'excelling all others.'

And this they duly did in the name of discipline, the perverted punishment sanctioned and condoned by government and society. 'Karmic or what?' Calum deduces. 'That the next word to follow 'best' in the dictionary is bestial, described therein as, 'of beasts, marked by brutal or inhuman instincts or desires, sexually depraved.' The word 'bestial' articulated and depicted so eloquently before being entered into the thesaurus by the humans themselves, and clearly evaluated and translated beforehand with much due diligence and consideration, until becoming their own self-fulfilling raison d'être, so leading by example these cultured abuse specialists.

'School teachers, those sadistic, gloating practitioners of pain.' Calum has them sussed and is not fooled by the sly insertion of 'in,' before 'human,' in the grand Lexicon's description of bestiality. 'Ah ha! So now we're getting to the heart of the matter!' His interpretation being, 'fact is, this depiction is *all* about the human, and not at all inhuman.' He is well aware from painful experience that causing the weak or meek, child, man or beast, pain, anguish and humiliation was how some humans got their kicks. He was strongly of the opinion, 'you can dress it up how you will, use as many Freudian terms as you can muster, site all the repressed psycho-babbling nonsensical reasons why the oppressor would wish to inflict such degrading treatment on another living being, but bottom line... always the bottom line, is that some cowardly individuals get their pleasure by dishing out pain and cruelty to the meeker, weaker, frail, feeble – in fact, any being more vulnerable than themselves. They enjoy it, it's that bloodlust thing again... like the fox hunting, "for the sport, sir," oh and let's not forget conservation... of course, that ridiculous excuse for cruelty, death and the abuse of innocent animals, or the beating up on their women. Inflicting pain and punishment, that's what turns them on, abusing someone who cannot defend themselves. Even the British police force turn a blind eye to this violence towards women, known throughout the force as a 'domestic'. What these teachers and law enforcers are stating, no, ordering, the young and impressionable is, "like it or not, you will learn the ways of our world, our macho controlling way, or else!" The UK government is in control, fully aware and complicit in condemning the masses to legalised brutal cruelty. This hand-me-down doctrine was inherited from and reinforced by the enslaving rule of Great Britain's Empire.' Calum smiles to himself at the absurdity. 'Hey, after all is said and done, it was not that long ago that Britain ruled the world and used our fellow homo sapiens as slaves. Now there's a tradition for them to be proud of.' He is not fooled by the brainwashing methods of school education, remaining unmoved by the egotistical posturing used to protect the offenders. He is convinced the only true lessons – any real meaning of life – is to be gleaned from the Great Spirit's hidden laws of Nature. Knowing from the core of his soul there is no other authentic or relevant teaching.

CHAPTER
FORTY-ONE

The bullying and harassment of first year pupils continues relentlessly at school. Calum abhors this unjust situation and knows he will never condone any form of cruelty and injustice. He keeps a look out for the poor kid thrown down the stairwell, but there is no news of him until, at assembly one morning, when the headmaster tells the congregation, "A pupil of this school fell down the stairs during a fire drill evacuation. The careless boy is being treated in hospital for head injuries, but he can remember nothing of the incident, a most unfortunate accident... but let this be a lesson to you all. Do not run in the school corridors, or up and down the stairs." Calum snorts, muttering under his breath, "yeah, how very convenient," glowering at the guilty RI instructor, standing up there on stage, next to the headmaster. 'As if butter wouldn't melt.'

The simmering resentment finally comes to a head the following Friday morning. Calum and four classmates – Eddie, Hoody, Cleeve and Pete – decide to take matters into their own hands. Bored out of their minds with the maths lessons, and grown big-time weary of the frequent corporal punishment doled out by Eli, they bind and tie the maths teacher with his own steel measuring chains before bundling him, screaming, up into the loft space of the wooden classroom. After warning the rest of class to keep schtumm, the boys go running off to Andover town centre, spending the rest of the day in the Mason's Arms, a pub notorious for the elderly landlord's tendency to allow underage drinking.

In the meantime, after great deliberation, a thoughtful and deeply reflective process, which is aided by smoking all the absent form teacher's cigarettes, the rest of the class decide they had best set Eli free, albeit two hours later, lest they be blamed for aiding and abetting his incarceration.

Calum, upon his belated return to school, is summoned to the headmaster's office to find that he has already been tried and condemned as the ringleader, accused of the physical and mental abuse of a teacher. His sentence is to be the dreaded 'six of the best' caning. "And that's just for starters," Mr Grantham informs him, appearing excited, flushed and breathing heavily as he prepares to deliver the beating.

"I get it now, you dirty bastard!" Calum accuses, realising the sickening truth. "This is how you get your rocks off, isn't it? By caning young boys. Well, you're not getting your perverted satisfaction at my expense." He makes for the door. "I'm outta here, mister."

"How dare you, you insolent brat. If you leave this room, then do not bother to come in to school tomorrow." Calum laughs as he walks out, with Grantham shouting after him. "You are hereby suspended for a fortnight with immediate effect, Connor. A letter will be in the post, informing your parents of my decision." Calum turns back and points accusingly at the headmaster. "Talking of letters in the post, sir... if you're not careful, Mr Pervert, I might just be posting a letter to the authorities concerning your accomplice... Mr Coezens? And the matter of the kid he threw down the stairwell." Grantham looks shaken. "What do you mean, boy? That's nonsense, and you know it."

"Oh yeah... I think the witness may disagree... you might just want to think on that, sir... before you go making any rash decisions." Calum slams the door behind him, whistling as he walks along the corridor. He hangs around outside until school finishes, then joins the rest of the pupils on the bus home, before announcing, "well lads, that's me done here, head's suspended me, pending further investigations."

"Wow! Cool," says Stevie. "What happened?"

"Things kicked off big time with old Eli, looked like he was gonna seriously lose it and injure someone, or worse, so we tied him up in his measuring chains and then stuck him up in the loft." Pete high fives him. "Yeah, heard about that, you crazy buggers, that's the first step to getting expelled y'know." Calum laughs. "Duuhh... really? Well yeah... that was the plan, c'mon, keep up now, fellas."

But keeping the news from his foster parents? 'Hmm... finding a way around that was going to be complicated.' Heaven forbid being grounded and housebound with the Browns for two weeks, 'perish the thought of that nightmare scenario'. He would rather the shadow beings came for him, every night, and even prefer to endure the living hell of school, than waste quality time cooped up with that dismal pair of preconditioned robots.

Calum continues to leave for school each morning as usual, but is sure to check the post first, in case there is written confirmation of his expulsion. He doesn't want the Browns finding that. Invariably, he would then spend the day in town, hanging out with the other lads who are suspended, or enjoying pleasurable daytime liaisons with one... or two... of his current girlfriends.

A week later, he finds a letter from school in the wooden post box and tears it open. The official-looking document states that the perpetrators who abused their form teacher, Mr Ellison, had caused him to be treated for a suspected nervous breakdown, further statiung that Calum Connor is forthwith suspended from school for two weeks while enquiries are ongoing. Criminal proceedings are being considered. He smiles as he rips the letter to shreds before stuffing it out of sight under the hedge.

Calum keeps up the pretence of attending school until the date of his official reinstatement, returning to Andover Secondary, with his foster parents none the wiser. Upon their readmission the guilty boys are immediately rounded up and hauled by prefects to appear before the headmaster. Mr Grantham informs them that they are only being allowed to resume their schooling under the strict proviso that they must all be on their very best behaviour, or else they will be sure to face certain expulsion. The reprimanded pupils are escorted to their form class by the deputy headmaster.

Ellison is back on duty for the first time since his nervous breakdown. After the deputy head leaves, he walks slowly past the line-up of pardoned boys, his eyes radiating menace as he warns them, "I can assure all of you moronic reprobates that forthwith, your lives will not be worth living whilst you remain under my tutelage." Smiling with relish, he continues, "every opportunity that arises for me to punish you, then I shall… and most harshly. The slightest transgression will bring a battering with the chair leg, atlas, or whatever else I can lay my hands on. In fact, anything that will cause the most pain and distress possible. You will regret what you have done to me. The suffering I have endured will be returned tenfold." Chuckling, gloating over his intended revenge, he continues, "your lives will be so miserable from this day forth." Gesturing to the desks, he orders, "Now, sit down and start writing out the multiplication tables. When you have finished… guess what? Then you will resume the very same times tables, performing all day, the exact same task, over and over, with no variation, and no playground or break times for you good-for-nothing wasters."

Eddie speaks up bravely. "You can't do that. It's against our human rights." Eli storms up the aisle, waving his fist threateningly. "Can't I? You just fucking watch me, boy, you relinquished any semblance of personal privileges the day you bastards crossed me."

Calum realises now that Ellison has lost it, big time, and decides – in the interests of self-preservation – to terminate his own contract with the school tomorrow. The teacher has gone stark raving mad, is his analysis, determining that Eli is now a serious danger to any kids entrusted to his care.

Calum awakes early the next morning, with a leaving plan formulating in his mind. 'Sod damage limitation, if I'm going out, then I'm sure as hell going out with a bang.' "Yes, literally," he murmurs, smiling, whilst fondling the smooth wooden stock of the Webley177 air pistol nestling snugly in his coat pocket. 'This relic from the gang days is going to come in handy after all.'

Determining to dress appropriately for this special occasion, he hides his ripped Levi jeans and a psychedelic inspired multi-coloured Ben Sherman shirt in his tatty duffle bag. Leaving the house, he is nervous, but also extremely excited. He recalls the old western film, thinking, 'Yes, this is going to be my *High Noon*'.

Although his stomach is churning, the overriding emotion coursing through him is one of overdue relief, now that events at school are set to finally run their course. This has been a long time coming. 'But hopefully, freedom will beckon now, in full glorious Technicolour, after today's outcome.' Whatever happens, he knows this is to be his last ever day at school.

Skipping breakfast so as to dodge any unnecessary conversation with Janet, he sets off early, jogging down the lane, before going behind the hedge near the barn to change into his rebellious battle dress.

Calum is centre of attention on the school bus. The other pupils cheer and clap him, amazed at his bravado. It was unheard of in the history of Andover Secondary for anyone to dare wear such flamboyant dress code into school. On arrival he gets off the bus first. Head held high, striding ahead, bolstered by hero worship, followed in by his hushed and expectant peers, Calum's footsteps echo loud and proud throughout the corridor. He takes a deep breath before entering the classroom, the other boys whooping and cheering as he takes his seat. Some minutes later Mr Ellison arrives, sitting behind his desk, failing to notice Calum immediately... until a nervous tittering undercurrent causes him to look up. First thing to catch his eye is the loud shirt. The teacher gets to his feet, open-mouthed in disbelief, before exploding into apoplectic rage. "What are you doing here, Connor! You... you have been suspended, boy?"

"No, 'fraid not Eli," Calum replies calmly. "Suspension ended yesterday. I was recalled to resume my schooling by Mr Grantham, the head, no less. I attended your class yesterday. Don't you remember man... or have you completely lost your mind?" Several kids laugh out loud, infuriating the teacher even more. "I don't care what you've been told," he splutters, "I will not have you in my class again. Never,

ever, do you hear? Not after the distress you have caused me. You're the ringleader. The one that had me tied in chains... I remember that, you bastard."

The rest of the previously hushed class are sniggering and giggling now, growing in confidence as Calum holds his ground. Shaking his head in pity he sighs. "That's all in the past, Eli. I think you, my man, are still suffering somewhat from your recent nervous breakdown."

"You are soon going to be suffering, boy, really fucking suffering, and what the hell are you wearing? How dare you come in to my classroom dressed like a goddamn hippy."

"I wear what I like these days, teach, you dim-witted pleb." Suddenly galvanised by fury, Ellison screams, "Out! Out, you retarded oaf, get out, I want you out of my classroom. Now!" Calum sneers, "the feeling's mutual, I can assure you. You don't think I want to be here, do you? In fact, I've decided this is to be my last ever day at your pox-ridden school."

"You... y... y... you... you've decided, have you now?" Ellison stammers in disbelief at Calum's nerve. "Does your insolent audacity know no bounds? This will not go unpunished, mark my words boy, you will pay for this... I'm going to brain you... finish you off good and proper this time," fumbling in his desk, rummaging for a weapon, anything with which to beat and bludgeon. He mumbles, "pay you will boy, pay, pay, pay," until his pudgy hand grasps the chair leg. He growls and goes for Calum, huffing and puffing, his bloated face turning a deep crimson, breathing coming laboured and rasping as he holds aloft the chunky wooden club. Calum knows there is no choice but to defend himself, so he pulls the pistol from his bag, aiming it two-handed steady at the advancing teacher, before shouting a final warning. "Drop that chair leg or I'll drop you, you bullying git." Ellison is now muttering incoherently, his eyes bulging, and a strange gargling sound coming from his frothing mouth as he keeps on coming.

Calum knows that if the deranged tutor reaches him and lands a blow with the heavy chair leg he could be seriously injured, or

worse. It's not a chance he's prepared to take, so he opens fire...
Phutt! A lead pellet hits Ellison in the right thigh. Shock registers
suddenly and he squeals, weirdly high-pitched, like a girl, yet still
he advances, stumbling on, blind rage making him even more determined. Calum deftly reloads and pulls the trigger again... Phutt!
The pellet embeds deep into Ellison's hand this time. Screaming
shrilly and dropping the chair leg, he collides heavily with a desk
before collapsing in a moaning, sobbing heap upon the floor. A loud
cheer erupts from the watching boys. Grabbing the chair leg, Calum
makes as if to land a blow on the cowering teacher, before leaping
over him and running fast for the door, with Ellison whining, "come
back here, you fucking coward."

Calum laughs. "Haha, fuck you, Eli, this coward lives to fight
another day." He then sprints full pelt along the square connecting
corridor, sliding and skidding expertly slalom-style on the polished
tiled floor, skilfully negotiating the tight corners, throwing the chair
leg to go clattering against the wall, before emerging victorious into
sunlit freedom, running as fast as he can from the school grounds...
past the girls' school and away... the scary but exciting adrenaline
rush stimulating his senses, engendering a feeling of empowerment as he heads off down London Road, towards the sanctuary
of Andover town centre. Calum slows to a brisk walk as he enters
the town. Breathing hard as he passes the King's Head pub, his
fast-fading exhilaration now tinged tangibly with nervous pangs of
regret. The seriousness of what has just gone down at school only
just hitting home. Any remorse, however, is short-lived, as a heightened sense of self-preservation kicks in. Sneaking a glance behind
him, he's apprehensively expecting a posse of teachers and prefects
to be closing in on him at any moment... Calum smiles with relief.
There's no one following.

A pulsating purple neon sign flashing ahead advertising MIKADO
CAFE offers him a 'dive in here quick, kid' refuge opportunity. The
heavy glass door swings open to his urgent shove. Walking swiftly
past some dozy diners, he skips the last three steps up into the back

room of the café and orders a coke. Sitting down with his drink in a corner of the room, as 'Whiter Shade of Pale' by Procol Harem plays out in tinny monotone from the jukebox, the relaxing melody helping his heart rate to slowly return to normal. Breathing regularly now, the tension evaporates as he absentmindedly watches the punters playing the row of four pinball machines.

The Mikado is busy today, the gamblers consuming a steady intake of strong coffee and well-done bacon sarnies, as they shoot the silver balls in the hope of winning cash prizes. The brightly backlit legend 'SEA ISLAND' illuminates the colourful glass screen of the favoured pinball machine. The aficionados of this game would aim for what was the ultimate score, the five in line, which paid out 108 points, and could be cashed in at the café counter for a penny a point. Some regulars were so adept at pinball they could eke out a reasonable living from playing these machines on a daily basis. The unemployed were always first in the queue early morning, huddling together outside in a grey cloud of tobacco smoke, waiting patiently in single file, in all weathers, early doors, at least half an hour before opening, to ensure having first shout on the best machines.

The same sacrosanct rituals were always adhered to pre-play. Firstly, the essentials that would sustain the gambler throughout the long twelve-hour shift were organised and set up. Most important, to aid concentration, was the tobacco tin, accessorised with green Rizla cigarette papers, petrol lighter, brown Bakelite ashtray and strong black coffee. Last, but not least, several bags of threepenny bits were placed close to hand on the plate-glass surface of the machine, or just dumped in the ashtray for convenience. The more experienced players possessed the skilful (though strictly management-forbidden) knack of wedging a folded cigarette packet beneath the iron legs on the right-hand side of the gaming machine. This improvised technical adjustment served to slant the roll of the silver ball, having the desired effect of influencing the trajectory to the left, therefore making the run of the five balls true to the five in line. Skill was still needed to win, as the machine was prone to TILT (game over) more easily with this canny alteration. But it made the game far easier and the subsequent payouts more frequent.

The two other pinball machines, 'CIRCUS QUEEN' and 'RIVER ISLAND,' were much less profitable to play due to their aged condition and poor mechanical reliability, and were usually occupied by those less skilful, so these inferior individuals were naturally relegated lower down the pecking order.

Sat behind these dedicated pinball fortune seekers is a group of five pale-faced longhaired hippies, all wearing raggedy-assed patched jeans and long grey greatcoats. They could be found here most days, these permanently stoned regulars, spaced out on a variety of illegal substances, huddling together, their shaking hands cradling black coffee or Coca Cola, and repetitively playing Santana's 'Black Magic Woman,' or anything by Hendrix, Pink Floyd or Deep Purple from the playlist of the big Wurlitzer jukebox. This cadaverous-looking quintet patiently appraised the continuous flow of human traffic, seeking to entice any gullible or vulnerable prey into their clutches. These gaunt, emaciated-looking guys are the local heroin addicts, sleazy dealers and pushers of a varied menu of drugs, but mostly poor-quality hash and adulterated amphetamines, Mandrax sleepers (aka mandies) and various uppers and downers. They were always geared up, and not fussy who they ensnared, prepared to foist their narcotics onto anyone so as to pay for their next fix, which, when regularly injected, temporarily anesthetised them from the hopeless monotony of their everyday lives.

A haze of blue-grey cigarette smoke drifts lazily throughout the room, clinging doggedly to the café ceiling, discolouring the once pristine white polystyrene tiles to a sticky nicotine-yellow. Contributing generously to this swirling chemical fug is a stoic gang of tough Irish groundworkers, hard men, aka 'navvies', who sit, chain-smoking around the long plastic dining tables. With Old Holborn roll-ups, Senior Service, or Woodbine cigarettes smouldering perpetually in the corners of their mouths, body clocks primordially set for pub opening time, warming up for the main event by surreptitiously slugging shots of cheap whiskey or brandy into mugs of strong black coffee.

The one-armed bandits are cranked noisily by two young skinheads. Posing resplendently in their mob uniform of Levi jeans and Sta-Prest trousers, the 'strides' are accessorised with the obligatory braces and worn just above highly polished Doc Martin 'bovver boots.' The taller of the two 'skins' is wearing a pale blue pin-striped Ben Sherman shirt and a black Abercrombie overcoat. The other shaven street soldier is immaculately attired in a red Fred Perry polo shirt, finished with a pork pie trilby hat.

The Mikado is a haven for a cosmopolitan selection of criminals, dossers, dropouts, dealers, thieves, tough guys, rebels, has-beens, never-weres and never-would-bes. All and sundry found sanctuary in this café. Despite this edgy mix of culture and cloth, an uneasy coexistence prevailed. It was unlikely anyone could say exactly why they were all drawn together here. But no one tried too hard to analyse the whys and wherefores. As with most strange phenomena, it just seemed to happen that way. 'Maybe,' thinks Calum, 'this fragile truce exists because of the current ensuing global uncertainty, with everyone being unsure of the future and their place in the world order.'

Indeed, the general public seemed more than a little jittery, and thrown, by the preceding worldwide events of the past decade. The year 1966 had seen the USA's first major space exploration end badly with the Apollo 1 disaster. This was followed by an undercurrent of violence running through America in 1967 which seemed to go under the radar somewhat, as this was also the year the first human got to travel around the moon. 1968 was a far more openly brutal year, with race riots and the high-profile assassinations of Martin Luther King and the politician Robert Kennedy. There were riots all across the globe. Particularly prolonged were the violent student riots in France. Some light relief was provided musically, by the Rolling Stones releasing 'Jumping Jack Flash' and the Beatles' offering of 'Hey Jude.'

The following year, 1969, heralded 'the summer of love.' It was also the year of the Woodstock festival and Greenpeace's Amchicta anti-hydrogen bomb concert. As Bob Dylan prophetically observed, 'The times, they are 'a changing.'

The hippy movement seemed to arrive from nowhere. All Afghan coats and spiritual ideals amid a fanfare of tinkling peace bells. 'Make love, not war,' 'ban the bomb,' 'peace and love,' went the hippy slogans, 'free love, man,' and 'wear a flower in your hair,' especially 'if you're going to San Francisco.'

Coming out of the sixties into the seventies promised a wild old time of it for a non-conformist free spirit, with plenty of sex, drugs, and rock and roll on offer. Free love, psychedelic art, bohemia, the peace movement, all threatening the staid status quo. 'Could that be why everyone seemed to accept each other in the Mikado café, were they all subconsciously tuning in, and dropping out to the hippy ideal of peace and love going down at this time? Hmm... won't hold my breath,' Calum elects, 'as this harmonious vibe seems not, as yet, to have infiltrated the killing fields of Vietnam, the oppressive brutality of the Native American reservations, the Charles Manson family, or indeed...' he reflects ruefully... 'much closer to home, Andover Secondary Modern Boys' School.'

Although in his core essentially a loner, Calum blends in seamlessly with the café's motley crew. The Mikado is a non-descript unremarkable little place, albeit with a strange pulsating heartbeat, a moody, edgy asylum for the damned and discarded in this small English market town.

A painfully thin, balding hunched man comes in and orders tea before taking a seat. He blows on his spectacles, furiously rubbing them clear with his handkerchief before sipping his brew. As he writes, head down, in a bright red notebook, Calum checks out his look... tweed jacket, beige tank top and green corduroy trousers... assuming unkindly, 'pleb,' before immediately regretting the harsh judgemental assessment. 'Must stop doing that,' he determines, recalling that old Native American wisdom from Laughing Fox Wells... 'Oh Great Spirit, help me never to judge another, until I have walked two moons in his moccasins.'

One of the pushers leans over and whispers up close in his ear. "Ya wanna score, man?" Calum waves away the offer dismissively. "Best watch it, man," the sick-looking hippy continues, pointing at the plebeian like he's lower class, "that's old Ernie, oracle of the town, used to work as a reporter for the *Evenin' Echo*. Knows everything there is to know about Andover town, and just loves spouting off about it, until you is bored to tears and your ears start to bleed."

Calum smiles at the irony of the bedraggled pusher's moral high ground warning. He's casually interested in what Ernie has to say, though. It could be a free opportunity for him to learn something of the area, especially as he is now a fugitive on the run in the vicinity. 'After all, knowledge is power, had not some savvy guy once declared?'

"Hi Ernie, I hear tell you're all clued up on this rundown two-bit old town." Calum smiles, and offers his hand. "Just moved in, friend... care to enlighten me a little on my new surroundings?"

"Why, yes, certainly, young sir" Ernie offers enthusiastically, accepting Calum's handshake, appearing overjoyed to be asked. "My pleasure, be glad to." He adjusts his spectacles. "Hummmf," clears his throat, and takes another sip of tea. "Well now, where to begin?" Smiling broadly, he gestures expansively about the room. "What better location than where we now repose, the Mikado Café. This eatery is owned by husband and wife team," pointing to the busy couple behind the counter. "Peter and June, they also own a similar place in Bridge Street called the Cabin Café. Andover is a small market town, being most famous for the Angel Inn, the oldest public house in Andover, known to have been standing since Saxon times. King John, and latterly, Catherine of Aragon, both stayed in the inn as they passed through the town..." Ernie pauses to take breath, and more tea, before continuing. "The Angel Inn was the premier hostelry of the day in 1642. Its landlady, a Mrs Marie Pope, was also the great grandmother of the famous poet Alexander Pope. Records of the period show that she was once fined twenty old pence by the Andover magistrates for selling bad beer."

Calum is struggling to keep up with the droning monologue, spiritually drowning in this dull torrent of historical information, and isn't the damned hippy wearing a 'told ya so' smirk. He sticks with it though, as Ernie gushes forth.

"Andover is also infamous, because it is the only town in England that has moved its war memorial from the designated pride of place in the town centre to the relative obscurity of a church graveyard. This strange – and indeed illegal – decision by the local town council in 1956 was challenged by a petition from the townsfolk, but to no avail. The call for the memorial's return to its rightful place has been vehemently championed by several people down the years. The latest and most vociferous of these has been the local surrealist, author, and ex-soldier, Russell Tarrant, also known as RT. An accomplished artist and writer... do you know, one of his books resides in the library of the famous Tate Gallery in London. In a literary sense, that is some achievement, I can tell you. He has also created his own post-modernist surrealist movement. Some people are of the opinion he is intellectually way ahead of his time, others state he is a madman... and there are those that say the truth lies somewhere in-between. But nevertheless, despite his detractors, he has frequently exposed corrupt local authority leaders and bumbling politicians time and time again, with his exhaustive altruistic gathering of facts and figures, which indeed, have the authorities bang to rights. He has proven that morally, ethically, and also in the legal sense, they have done a great wrong to the men who fought and died for England's freedom, but still they do not return the memorial. Those that care about such things cannot understand why. It is as if the powers that be have no respect for Andover's war dead."

"Seems an interesting fella, this RT geezer... still about, is he, Ernie?"

"Oh yes, as far as I am aware he is still campaigning strongly, even though the only reward for his diligent efforts thus far was to find himself sectioned in the Basingstoke Park Prewitt mental hospital."

"Why won't anyone listen to him then, Ernie? If all he says is true."

"He believes it is due to corruption in high places, filtering down to the local authority here. As Ghandi famously replied... and I quote, when asked what he thought of England's democracy, "yes... I think it would be a good idea." Calum nods in agreement, feeling that egalitarianism is there for the rich and privileged in English society but is apparently in short supply for anyone else.

Ernie continues. "Andover still has a large selection of public houses, but not so many as back in 1840, when fifty were recorded. There is also a varied choice of diners. Besides the Mikado and Cabin Cafés there is the Wimpy Bar Grill, a burger outlet in Bridge Street, and at the top of the high street is the Milk Bar, which is the rough and ready haunt of bikers and hippies. Then there is the Gorge, a café in the modern shopping precinct, the hangout of suedeheads and skinheads, constructed to look like a plastic Cheddar Gorge cave." He shakes his head, "God knows why! Cheddar Gorge...! In Andover, I ask you?" Ernie pauses to draw breath, aiding this vital survival process with several gasping puffs on a blue asthma inhaler, before elaborating further. "Located on the outskirts of the town, near the railway station, you will find Joe's, a greasy spoon café, early morning haunt of the wild Irish tree feller Maxie Lane and his gang, and also of local builders and Irish groundworkers; then there's the 'Linga Longa' coffee bar on Weyhill Road; a few hundred yards on and one will come to Gills transport café. This establishment essentially is the truckers' choice of greasy spoon, boasting bed and breakfast rooms to boot."

He slurps more tea, before continuing. "Andover boasts a mainline railway station to London and Salisbury, plus good road links to the West Country and the capital city of London. There are large expansion plans for Andover in this year of 1970, aiming to provide affordable local housing for thousands of London overspill. The building work is in the early stages of development by a large contingent of Irish subcontractors who have come to Andover following the scent of work. These gaffer men, followed by hundreds of labourers, predominantly Irishmen, will travel anywhere in the country seeking out ground-working vacancies in the construction industry."

Ernie stops to finish his brew and seems about to resume the sermon. Calum holds his hand aloft in surrender. His head hurts and he feels like he's losing the will to live after being bombarded with this overdose of local narrative. "Thanks pal, but that will do me fine for now, methinks... I need time to digest this little lot first."

Ernie looks disappointed at being cut off in his prime and can't resist providing one last snippet of information. "Oh, and let's not forget the royal murder in Harewood Forest in medieval times, that was so—"

"Whoa!" Calum raises his voice sternly. "Didn't you hear me? That's it my friend, I'm done, finito... no mas... thanks all the same." Ernie looks downcast. "Of course... sorry, sir... but don't hesitate to ask if you wish to know more... perhaps a history of the railway, or maybe the local memorial hospital. I also have a pictorial record of Andover at my home, just around the corner, should you ever feel like perusing a slide show. I am in here about this time, most days."

Calum laughs, and then wonders if the reporter is some kind of dodgy pervert. "Yeah, you got it Ernie... slides, hey? I'll be sure to bear that in mind, can't wait," he sniggers, but on reflection, he realises he's learned a lot from this dull reporter. 'These are certainly happening times for Andover,' he acknowledges, as he gulps down the remainder of his coke.

"Hiya dude, how goes it?"

Calum spins around to find hippy Harvey grinning at him. First impressions ain't good. His long, dark, dreadlocked curly hair is matted and in dire need of a wash, he has dirty long fingernails and his shirt collar is grimy and worn. He's wearing multiple sparkly necklaces, tiny brass bells hang from his neck, and several brightly coloured bangles loosely adorn his wrists. Hundreds of multicoloured beads are sown on to his tie-dyed clothes. Harvey, although only seventeen, always seems high on marijuana – a habitual user – and with his permanent stoned dull-eyed stare he bears a striking resemblance to Rasputin, the famous mad Russian monk. Calum had first met him here in the café some weeks previously, when suspended from school. Harvey has a pathological aversion to working for a living, so being a naturally gifted musician he would often busk and beg on the streets, playing his guitar or mandolin as a poignant soundtrack of his destitution.

"Diggin' the shirt man," Harvey strokes Calum's psychedelic Ben Sherman, drawing hard on a spliff before offering it up. "Toke, dude?"

"No, you're OK, Harv," Calum refuses, knowing he must keep his wits about him. "I'll have a tailor-made though... if you've got one going?"

"Sure thing, man." Harvey delves in the pockets of his crumpled blue velvet jacket and offers a Kensitas filter tip. Calum accepts gratefully. "Cheers bud, got a light?" Harvey draws hard on the spliff and mates the glowing tip with Calum's cigarette. He looks up at the café clock. "So what brings you here fella, "at this time of day, skiving school again, dude?" Calum takes a long draw, the nicotine immediately calming his nerves, "No, not playing truant Harv, it's far more serious than that, mate. I'm done with school, won't be going back again. They wouldn't have me now anyway... not after what's just gone down."

"How so dude?" Harvey asks resignedly. "What you gone and done now?"

"Oh, no biggie really," Calum replies matter of factly, "just shot old Eli, the maths teacher, with me Webley air pistol." He proudly whips the gun from inside his shirt, grinning in anticipation of the reaction.

"You fuckin' what?!" Harvey takes a step back, a look of incredulous surprise on his face. "Shot him, man! With that? You mad crazy bugger you. Are you off your rocker or what? Oh jeez, ha ha ha, now I've heard it all!" Roaring with laughter, he slaps Calum on the back in salutary admiration before looking around apprehensively, "groovy man, come on then Jesse James, best we get yuh outta here dude, before the rozzers come lookin' fer ya. They'll 'ave yuh guts fer fuckin' garters fer this caper."

"Yeah, spose you're right," Calum agrees, as the seriousness of the situation slowly sinks in. OK, let's vamoose then, buddy."

"Where to, dude?"

"We'll high-tail it back to mine Harv, then we can have the craic down the White Horse pub tonight, whaddya say?"

"Yo, far out dude, diggin' that... they got sounds in that boozer?"

Calum laughs, "Do they got sounds? Only the latest chart hits, my man."

"OK, sounds like a plan, so lead on then, dude."

Leaving hastily by the back door of the café, they stride quickly through the rear car park of the Star and Garter Hotel, a 16th-century former coaching inn that's the main watering hole for many of the Irish labourers ensconced in the town. They pass through a black painted oak archway, formerly the old entrance for the horse-drawn coaches and dray wagons of the past. Coming out into busy Andover town centre, they find cars and vans parked all along the High Street. As they head for the bus station, Calum throws the gun into the slowly meandering river Anton. The Number 8 double-decker bus to Salisbury is parked up with engine running and just about to leave.

"Meant to fuckin' be," shouts Harvey, "fate be with us, dude."

Running for the bus, they dodge a swoop of scavenging pigeons before leaping aboard, heading for the rear seats up top, just as the old diesel grumbles lazily on its way. "I got me two acid tabs fer tonight," Harvey grins, "wanna try one, dude?"

"Dunno... what they like?" Calum is mildly interested, but buzzing enough due to recent events, without really craving any further chemical stimulation. "Yeah, right on mind massage my man, keep you going all night will these bad boys." Calum laughs and shakes his head. "Hold up there, friend... keep me going all night! Don't think so, not after the day I've had. I'm gonna need some shut eye later down the line."

"Sleep! Fuckin' sleep, whass wrong wiv yuh, man? You can sleep to your heart's content when you shuffle off this mortal coil. You'll 'ave all the time in the world to kip then, but in the meantime, in the 'ere and now, its serious party time, dude!"

The conductor clumps unsteadily up the stairs, leaning adeptly into the spiral staircase so as to keep his balance as the bus rocks and sways along. Calum requests "two singles to Whitey House." After punching out the tickets from his hand-operated silver machine, Calum pays him four shillings in return. The journey is full of jerky stop-starts as the bus lets off and takes on passengers. Some thirty minutes later they stand early, pushing the bell buzzer to request the next stop. The bus changes down though the gears as it rumbles along the long straight approach to Whitey House, before slowing and grinding to a brake-squealing halt, throwing them off-balance to grab desperately for the long chrome handrails. "Cheers, man," Calum thanks the driver as they jump off.

The sky is dark and overcast with threatening rain clouds as they walk down Dauntsey Lane. Harvey stops, reaching into his jacket pocket, pulling out a faded tobacco tin, and opening it to reveal two tiny transparent cellophane-encased pills. The tabs are imprinted with yellow zig-zag transfers and sat on top of a cache of several large marijuana joints. Harvey holds the LSD tabs reverently in his palm. "White lightning microdots my mate, bestest you kin get. No bad head trip or dodgy comedowns with these... gonna try one then, dude?"

Calum is a little intrigued. If this is to be his first time with hard drugs, he's hoping it will be as mind-blowing as his first sexual experience, reasoning, 'Besides, they're so small... can't be much harm to 'em... can there?'

"OK, Harv," he relents, "go on then, I've had a right day of it, so yeah, I'll give it a go... bit of chill-out never hurt no one, did it man?" Harvey slaps him on the back. "Groovy dude, this acid will sure take the edge off." Holding a tab carefully between finger and thumb, he places it on his tongue. Calum follows his lead. "Just let it rest there," Harvey advises, "it'll dissolve soon enough."

"How long does it take to work then, Harv?"

"It'll kick in in about half hour or so... give or take... it ain't no exact science though, man, affects everyone different like," he grins, "all will be revealed, takes its own sweet time though, yuh can't force it, dude. Trick is not to panic. Just stay cool with the good vibe goin' down." Harvey lights one of his home-grown joints. "We'll just puff out on this meanwhile and mellow ourselves into the scene," chuckling in anticipation, "we should be well and truly fuckin' trippin' by the time we reach your gaff, dude."

They walk on down the road. Harvey's eyes are wide and blood-shot, and he's giggling and laughing at nothing in particular as Calum leads them into the driveway of Meadow Bank. The rapid deterioration of Harvey's mental state is flagging up grave second thoughts in Calum about ingesting the LSD. 'Too fucking late now though,' he allows philosophically. "Best wait there, Harv," he points to the old Mercedes, "take a seat in the old motor, I'll go sort us some jam sarnies." Harvey gives the thumbs up as he staggers over to the car. "Cool dude, this hash always gives me a bad rush of the munchies."

Calum goes in to the bungalow, to be greeted by Janet. "Hello son," pausing from her washing up, "have you had a good day at school?"

"Oh, you know... so-so, Mrs Brown... pretty much same old same old really," turning his back and smirking, 'If only you knew, lady, if only you fucking knew.'

"Please try to be quiet dear, Jim is having his nap."

"Why yes... of course," Calum whispers in mock reverence. "Can't disturb the sleep of the righteous, can we now." He glares contemptuously at Jim as he dozes, snoring loudly. Every slobbering breath produces bubbly foaming dribble to trickle down his quivering chins. A lingering smell of stale body odour permeates throughout the room. Calum cannot recall the windows ever being opened since the day they moved in. He grimaces in disgust before turning to Janet. "A friend came back with me, so I'm just going to grab us a couple of quick sarnies, then we'll be off out for a while."

"That's fine, son, but your friend is welcome to sit down with us for his tea you know." Calum grins, thinking, 'how entertaining for her to have Rasputin to tea'.

"Thanks all the same Mrs Brown," he declines emphatically, "but we want to get out and about before dark."

"Very well dear, take care though, and please try to be quiet when you return." Calum nods, "Sure thing." Grabbing a jar of strawberry jam from the larder, he quickly makes two thickly spread sandwiches, before going back to Harvey, who's now sitting in the driver's seat of the Mercedes SL, pretending to drive. He grins at the fool and hands him a sandwich. "There you go mate, get that down your gullet."

"Cool as, man," Harvey chomps down ravenously on the food. "Groovy motor this, diggin' the patina... how old yuh reckon she is, dude?"

"Dunno... 1930s mebbe... I'm thinking."

"Shame to let the old girl rot away like this man... might be worth a shit load a dosh in the future," Harvey offers prophetically. "Besides, Kraut motor, innit? So yuh never know... it might just 'ave belonged to that evil old German git, Hitler?"

Calum suddenly remembers the deranged Hun invading the disastrous séance and giggles uncontrollably, the laughter building so hysterically his stomach begins to ache. Harvey looks at him pityingly, and with growing resentment, not sure if he is laughing at or with him. "It wasn't that fuckin' funny, yuh bleedin' saddo," but laughing himself now, doubling up with mirth, heaving with the crazy fun of the situation they find themselves locked into, but also recognising the tell-tale signs of chemical influence, "that's the old acid workin' its magic, my man."

"Oh fuck! Yeah," Calum recalls, "I'd forgotten about that bad bugger." Harvey suddenly leaps to his feet, throwing his sandwich crusts high into the air. "Hey man! What you doing, wasting food like that, you shoulda left it for the birds," Calum berates.

"I gave them flyin' fuckers a chance to pluck them crusts outta the air before they hit the ground," he challenges, "well... dint I... dint I man?" Calum laughs scornfully. "Call that a chance? You cruel git, you."

"Ain't my fault them feathered flappers is so damn slow, is it? Anyways, why cain't they eat from the floor? They will if they're fuckin' hungry, pal. You put them animals too high on a pedestal you does, fella. Truth be told I'm sick of birds, they flies about as if they owns the fuckin' gaff, but in reality, they ain't got the gumption to even catch a bit of bread. The little varmints ain't got the makins of a brain between 'em in their tiny empty little heads. Hopeless! The fuckin' lot of 'em, look, they had two chances dude," Harvey chuckles, a sardonic tone creeping into his voice. "Little and no chance... Now, let's get down to serious business... how far to the boozer?"

"Nearest one is the Fyfield Arms, just down the road, about a mile or so, bit of a dump though, miserable bitch of a landlady. We can go on a little further to the Kimpton Down Inn, run by Eric and his wife Kath, nice folks, or the White Horse, if you'd prefer?"

"Closest fucker, mate, I ain't into too much walking." Harvey sways unsteadily on the ripped red leather driver's seat of the Mercedes, licks a finger and holds it compass-like to face the breeze. Deducing no navigational inspiration, he attempts a standing jump out of the car, shouting as he leaps, "C'mon, let's hit the road then, dude." But snagging a trailing leg on the open door sends him sprawling heavily to the dusty hard ground. Calum laughs, "Haha, yeah, you sure hit the road, man. Fucking literally, hahaha." Getting groggily to his feet, and cursing the "fuckin' rust bucket," Harvey kicks the door shut and puts an arm around Calum's shoulder. "Let's make tracks then, my man."

'This acid buzz is cool as,' thinks Calum, as they jig and jive their way merrily up the driveway. That is until he is suddenly plagued by a large swarm of massive flies, buzzing loudly about him, altering his mood abruptly from fun to fear. "Never seen flies this big before Harv," he says, swatting at them fearfully with both hands.

"What you playin' at dude?" Harvey looms up close from out of a dense swirling red mist. His face is distending, stretching, as if elasticised, like one of those zany fairground mirrors that distort the features. Calum is horrified. The flies are becoming entangled now within Harvey's eerily elongated profile, the trapped insects struggling frantically within the grotesque grinning facial fusion.

"Don't you worry none about the flies," Harvey replies in a childish voice, "after all, they be only teeny weeny little creatures."

Calum forges on, dread terror spurring him as he tries to outrun the persistent insects. "You're having a laugh, Harv, those are true monster flies, eating away at your face man, don't that bother you none?"

"Nah, thems only midges, they ain't really that big. I've been 'ere before y'know. Yuh trippin' out is all, just go with the flow man, it'll all even itself out, always does, in the end game, you'll see."

"So you keep saying," Calum screams, dodging a bloated black fly hovering just ahead. He's transfixed with horror as its yellow-tinged eyes begin to expand, bigger… and bigger… larger than its head… now even greater than its body. A screaming mosquito suddenly dives into the eyes of the fly, splattering in a splash of blood and gore, merging into a gruesome mutation of both insects. A pincer-like curling green stinger slowly extends from the rear of this shape-shifting creature. Calum, sure it is about to attack, averts his gaze in an attempt to lose the terrifying vision. He looks to the sky, where bulging white clouds hover above a beautiful rich red and orange sunset, and then glances to his left, where moon and stars sparkle and shine in darkest night. The flies and mosquitoes have now transmuted into soft furry rainbow-coloured butterflies fluttering about him. He opts for this scenario in place of the terror, caring not whether it's real or no, allowing, 'It's a strange setup this, never seen anything remotely like it, but I'll go along for the ride as it's not so scary now.'

A deep echoing voice reverberates all around, cackling with surreal disdain, "Haha…Oh yeah…like you had any fucking choice. Hahahahaah. I'm coming to get you, hahahaha…"

Calum tries to dismiss the intrusive demonic entity by concentrating on gleaning whatever positives he can to negate the narcotic negativity, looking to the sky, to the cosmos for salvation. "The vibe feels better now, Harv. Wow man! Just look at outer space. There's an exact split of the sky. I'm in the very centre of two dimensions. In one there's pure daylight, while the other is deepest black night."

"Yeah really? Far out dude, I'm diggin' where you comin' from." Harvey puts a finger to his lips. "But hush now, I can't talk trivialities with you... not for exactly two minutes."

"Why's that, Harv?"

"Cos Pink Floyd's tryin' to get through to me, and the monks are all being murdered by Viking invaders on Lindsisfarne Island, as we speak, so all me neuron receptors gotta be tuned in to the exact frequency... so as to receive the wisdom... the message."

"OK, but you do know you're going crazy man," Calum giggles, "but best you keep on, keeping on. But why you moving so slow Harv, like a lazy old snail?"

"Say what, my friend?" Harvey's confused. "What's it all mean, dude? For sure, I'm just walkin' at the great god's pace... spiritual slow motion... thass wot yer always goin' on about, aint it, the zen stuff? Anyways, after all said and done, it's his universe, the Lord's, his alone, dont'cha know?" Calum laughs. "Did the Lord tell you to crawl along so, like some aged slovenly sloth?" Harvey sucks in a sharp intake of breath, appearing hurt by the cruel criticism. He answers slowly. "Well... yeah... no... but if you're gonna lay tech-nicalities on me man, then no... not God... exactly. It be the voices advisin' me mainly... more like Jesus... freakin' me out if I'm truthful with thee." He holds his hands over his ears as he walks on, glassy gaze fixed straight ahead. "Oh yeah, and now them disciples is givin' it some, bangin' on about some fuckin' dive called Damascus." Calum shakes his head in pity. "You sure got a bad case of bible-bashing going down, my man."

"Shhh!" Harvey stops suddenly and points to the heavens, "There's a guy channellin' through now... sez his name's Pontius... a pilot... must be an RAF guy, into flying planes or summat... He's inviting us to dine with him tonight, at his base, should be a good gig dude, Pontius says don't be late." Calum looks bewildered. "Why?"

"Cos' it's the last supper."

"Do they cater for vegans?"

Harvey turns and scowls, "How the fuck should I know, man. What am I... his brother already? Anyways, you ain't no vegan, pal... leastways not when I seen you scoffin' that bread 'n jam earlier."

Calum smiles. "I'll have you know sir, I'm one of the converted... anyways fool, what's not vegan about a little bread 'n jam?"

"Shush now, cut the crap," Harvey whispers, deadly serious. "I'm concentratin' on sendin' out two twin beams of light from me peepers."

"Why?"

"To light our way ahead in this cruel tempestuous world, I am the way... and the light." Calum chuckles. "Did the Lord Jesus tell you to say that."

"No, he gone now, but he left me the power, man."

"So you thinks you is Jesus now then, Harv?" Harvey raises his hands above his head. "All in the eyes of the beholder my friend, the beholder is key to all mysteries."

"But it's not even dark yet, so why do we need light beams... my Lord?"

"Cos' it's darkest night, black as yer fuckin' hat in fact, on your side of the dimension, you said so yourself, dude." Calum gazes skyward, seeing only clear daylight above. "No, no Harv, not now it isn't. Morning has broken... like... the first morning..." 'Must remember those lyrics,' he resolves. 'Got the makings of a good song going on there.' "Hang on... there's a strange sound I'm picking up now Harv... like a squealing... and rustling... and it's getting louder," grimacing at the high-pitched screeching, tapping his head. "The noise, it's boring deep inside my brain." Panicking, he shakes his head from side to side in an effort to rid himself of the persistent clamour. Harvey jerks a thumb over his shoulder. "Don't look behind you, dude."

Calum ignores the warning and spins around... suddenly quaking, feeling faint, as he sees thousands of rats, some big as cats, queuing impatiently, nipping and scratching at each other, hustling and bustling, as if vying for the best position from which to strike. "Did me a bit a natural history at school man," Harvey advises nonchalantly, "and I reckons them bad boys is black plague rats." The unblinking piercing red eyes observe the boys knowingly. Yellowy green pus oozes from the rodents' many rancid open body sores. Calum walks away smartly, nape hairs twitching, expecting to be attacked any second by the horde of vermin following him. The screeching is becoming ever-more intense. He feels the horror eating away at him and is sure the giant rodents are preparing to devour them alive at any moment. Harvey starts suddenly jigging from side to side, holding his fingers to his lips as if playing an imaginary flute.

"Come on now, Harv, don't fuck about man," Calum pleads, "this is serious stuff, stop antagonising them or we're dead meat. Let's just beat it the hell outta here." Harvey appears unconcerned. "Yeah, OK, gotta stay cool though, dude, and don't look back. Be a cool cat, yuh won't outrun them bastards." He starts singing, reggae style, "Evry little ting gonna be all right now, evryting' gonna be OK, cos I'm the pied piper, the pied piper of Fyfield." He dances on ahead, with Calum following up close, not daring to look behind...

Arriving minutes later in Fyfield, and finding 'TED'S' small grocery shop is open, Calum darts inside, sweating and breathing anxiously. Dropping to his knees, he peers fearfully out through the large plate glass window, mightily relieved to see that the rats seem to have disappeared.

Shopkeeper Ted, a short, stout, middle-aged man, sits on a tall wooden stool behind the counter eating a cream doughnut. He is immediately wary. Working as a shopkeeper is not a very lucrative business for Ted. His already low profit margin is constantly under threat by the daily pilfering of the hard-up locals.

As Harvey saunters through the door, Ted thrumms his fingers nervously on the counter. "May I purchase a pack of your finest Kensitas King Size cigarettes, my good man."

"Have you been drinking?" Ted asks, suspiciously noting the stranger's wild eyes and slurring voice. Harvey smiles benignly, "Nah, not yet dude, but I'm sure intendin' to be imbibing a few wee drams real soonish like, if yuh gets me drift." He drags up a mouthful of phlegm and is about to spit on the floor, but thinks better of it, as he catches the shopkeeper glaring at him with undisguised distaste.

"I have to go get your cigarettes from out back... sir... so sorry for the inconvenience. Please bear with me. I'll try not to keep... sir... waiting too long." Ted bows, sarcastically elaborate, before heading out to the storeroom... pausing, he turns back and points to Calum, who sits quivering, knees drawn up to his chin. "Oh, and while I'm gone for your ciggies... *sir*... perhaps you'd be good enough to help that retard up from the floor... he's making the place look untidy." Harvey chuckles as the shopkeeper disappears out back. "Bundle a laughs that fat little bastard, aint he just?" Calum jumps to his feet and reaches behind the counter to adeptly snatch a twenty pack of Gold Leaf cigarettes. "Who's retarded now, then?" he says, laughing loudly as he leaves the shop.

Ted hears the bang of the heavy plate-glass door closing. Immediately suspecting foul play he curtails his search for Harvey's Kensitas and rushes back to the counter. "Oi! Where's me fuckin' snouts then, dude?"

"Don't have none... awaiting stock delivery," Ted lies, panting, heart sinking as he scans the shop anxiously. "Where's your accomplice gone?" The whining tone to his voice conveys weary resignation, realising he's been robbed... yet again. "OK, what's the dirty little git taken?"

"Whoa there dude," Harvey throws up his hands in protest. "Now hold up my man, you cain't go round makin' them kinda accusations. We ain't fuckin' criminals, I'll 'ave yuh know." Ted comes out from behind the counter, angry and frustrated, his face reddening as he hustles Harvey towards the door. "Go on, get out of here, you dirty hippy, and be sure to tell your low-life friend to never come back into my shop."

"Fuckin' maniac," Harvey shouts back, gobbing the mouthful of saved up spit on the door as he storms out. "We wouldn't wanna come back 'ere anyways, yuh dozy little pleb."

He finds Calum a little further down the road, apparently deep in contemplation, leaning back against the old brick bridge over the village stream. "Yo, what's goin' down then, bud?"

Calum takes a long draw on his cigarette, staring intently – a little too intently – at the activities of a group of busy black ants at his feet. "Just taking a puff, man... whilst standing on the verge of this dusty old road."

"Ahah," Harvey laughs, "sounds to me like a line from a Steinbeck novel, does this mean ya could be standin' on the verge of greatness, my good man?" Calum smiles and tosses him a cigarette. "Yeah... digging what you did there... nice one pal, right on... 'spose I am, at that." Harvey fumbles the cigarette into his mouth. "Cheers buddy. You sure snaffled them fags a bit smartish dude. Respect, didn't know ya had it in yuh."

"No big thing, man, it's all in the reflexes, honed and toned, from many such adventures along one's journey of the Sacred Path." Harvey looks puzzled. "Far out... if yuh say so, man."

Calum points to the ground. "See those ants, Harv?" Harvey sinks slowly to his knees and peers down at the industrious insects. "Yass, sirree... surely do." He looks up... puzzled. "So what about 'em?"

"Well, for instance... did you know that ants have their own structured family life, with social integration and a programme of leisure activities? Even a form of class system, with a hierarchy of workers, soldiers and monarchy?"

"Ha ha... that's conclusive proof, if any were needed, that you've well and truly lost it... big time, matey. Fer fuck's sake, thems only bugs, and stingin' little buggers at that." Harvey stands and raises his foot as if to stamp. Calum grabs his ankle and twists hard, causing him to stagger backwards. Looking shocked and shaken, he glares accusingly. "What you think yuh doin', man? I nearly went over there... coulda been seriously injured, or worse." Calum snorts unsympathetically. "You'll live... this time... but don't ever harm any of the Great Spirit's creatures, or your days are numbered, my man."

"OK! OK," Harvey looks shocked and raises his hands, "cool it dude, let's just cool it now will yuh, didn't think youse were the violent type, sure seein' a different side to yuh bud, ain't we just." Calum smiles easy. "Not me, friend, I'm a pacifist... but I can always make an exception for animal abusers. But no, it ain't me you gotta worry about... Karma will be your judge. If you abuse the weaker and meeker, those that can't defend themselves." Suddenly feeling ice-cold raindrops falling on his head, he looks up. What had been clear blue sky just seconds ago is now one solid sheet of dripping ice, while soft choral voices sing about him, "It's only the sun rising, just the sun shining, now the night is past."

He feels Gaia close by, but is not reassured, just feeling more edgy and agitated now as there is clearly no sun to be seen. Tugging urgently on Harvey's sleeve he points to the heavens. "Look up there, Harv... see those cracks in the universe. The ice is melting fast. The whole roof of that sky is likely gonna come crashing down on us any time soon. Armageddon is near, my man."

"Hmmm," Harvey sighs, replying in his laid-back way. "The voices, they be telling me different, dude. They saying it be only rain... and that love is just a state of mind. You, my friend, is just havin' a bad trip, I've seen it so many times before. But the voices, they be assurin' me, that a rainbow will soon follow your paranoia."

Calum is feeling tense and disorientated now. "Whose... what voices, Harv?"

"Why, them geezers dat knows every little ting that goes on in de great big universe." Harvey chuckles, dancing on the spot, rolling his eyes and raising jazz hands to the sky. "Them words be comin' from de voice box of de main man, dude."

"Why you talking like Bob Marley, Harv?"

"Why, why..." Harvey thinks on this... for several... long... long... seconds... trying desperately to knit together the short-circuited reality connectors in his substance-damaged brain. "Because... because... Bob...Mr Marley to youse... he be only the most salubrious and celebrated exponent of that great musical genre, the Jamaican beat they call reggae, me dear boy, that be why."

"But you don't even like reggae!" Calum scoffs. "Ain't you always been a mandolin kinda guy?" Harvey ponders briefly. "Yeah... well... true enough my man, diggin' you got a point there, I guess... even if it's beside the point." Looking hang-dog hurt he walks away, pausing to call back over his shoulder "I ain't no one-trick pony though, I'll 'ave yuh know..." ...before suddenly oozing with positivity, "anyways, come on, let's split, o ye of little musicality."

Calum gazes up, relieved now to see a rainbow forming in the sky. "Wow, Harv! Will you just look at that arc rainbow." Harvey squints up at the sky. "Yeah, well, there yuh goes, told yuh it was comin'... 'spose it's cool man, in its own way, but I ain't familiar with any of them strange colours in it, though, dude." Flinching, he looks away, moaning, "it's hurtin' me brain just lookin' at the fucker."

"Yeah, me too man," Calum agrees, shielding his eyes, "never seen anything quite like it."

Suddenly a bolt of lightning forks down, embedding a massive discharge directly into a ploughed field directly opposite. A deafening thunderclap follows through, exploding into the atmosphere, triggering a cordite mist to rise slowly from the smote ground, engulfing the river and bridge and lingering in a fog-like shroud about their feet. The Great Spirit's voice resonates forth. "This rainbow is a gift created by Nature, a blessing for those who are discerning and appreciative of the wonders of the universe." Calum groans in recognition, "shoulda known you'd be involved in this madness somewhere along the line, Great Spirit, and yes, granted, wondrous this rainbow may be, but why can't we recognise any of the colours?" He holds his head in his hands. "Or even gaze upon it too long, before our brains start to ache?"

"This is a rainbow formed in another galaxy, so no Calum, you will not recognise the colour scheme. Your mind's eye finds it incomprehensible. Just as that which is real will be felt, but not seen, by the purest soul."

"Now 'ang on 'ere a minute, mister spirit man," Harvey speaks up. "I don't dig who you is exactly dude... maybe just a figment of me mate's LSD trip or such like, but the scientists say a rainbow is created by–"

"Ha ha ha," Harvey is cut off off mid-sentence by Gaia's disdainful laugh booming about them as elemental echo. "Don't talk to me of your scientists. The majority of humans are only interested in feathering their own nest. Whatever inventions or discoveries they lay claim to are mostly duplicitous egotistical conjecture. A smokescreen of conjurers' illusion, concocted for the benefit of the ego and the onerous multiplication and preservation of mankind. Their actions are always, and without exception, at the expense of Nature."

"Sorry I'm sure, Mr Spirit, if that truly be your moniker, geezer, but forgive me for thinking that this is a free country like, and as such we as individuals is entitled to us own opinion."

"Another illusion, Harvey, democracy and liberty are only afforded free rein if it suits the objectives and agendas of those that control the masses, those who rule over you... the government... the privileged, the entitled... Allow me to enlighten... scientists are not open to spiritual enlightenment – in fact, strive to deny – that animals, birds and insects are recipients of any profound thoughts and feelings. Their perceived wisdom is that the smaller size of a creature's brain prohibits any above-average intelligent thought process. But the truth is that Nature's spiritual messengers make no distinction of brain capacity. Size just doesn't enter the equation regarding intellect. The Great Spirit's offspring are not susceptible to the falsehoods of indoctrinated human education. Nature's creatures are receptive to happiness, to love, and to compassion. It is not a physical or mental attainment, but a soulful attribution of subconsciousness. Animals can show sadness, can give healing. They do not harbour evil intent, do not abuse their partners or offspring, physically, mentally or sexually. Left alone, Nature's creatures are satisfied with their lot. They crave not, nor yearn for anything more. There is no need for them to deviate from the Sacred Path. Unlike humans, all animals, mammals and insects manage to coexist – albeit in a primitive way – in the rapidly diminishing space remaining here on planet Earth. Inbred in these pure souls is a subconscious feral desire to uphold natural balance and harmony."

Covering his ears with his hands, Harvey protests, "I ain't listenin' to any more of this guff, Mr Spirit. Before you came along I was receiving my karma." He starts jigging on the spot and singing, "from the Dalai Lama, from the Dali Lama, my karma, my karma, came from, was from, is from, the Dalai La... la la... lama, la la... the Dalai la... la... Lama."

The Great Spirit chuckles, "I applaud the theatrical improvisation of your denial, sir... painful as its assault on the ears may be... but where do you think the Dalai Lama found his truth?" Harvey sneers, "In Tibet, ev'ry one knows that... near the fuckin' mountins... Everest, innit?"

"You're on the right track, realisation and realism comes from Nature, yes, authentic enlightenment, that's all one need search for, is it not? That's all that exists in the universe, the fundamentals of Nature, Creation and Truth. Why must your culture put so much reliance and belief on the words and teaching of scientists? These people, who by their very disposition will always doubt the omnipotence of Nature. To them the beauty of the natural world is something to be dissected and controlled by mathematical calculations and chemical experiments. They attempt to reduce and relegate spiritual wonder from unpredictable magnificence to mundane monotonous synthetic data. The irony is that Nature does not need man, but man could not survive without Nature. Scientists on this planet do nothing that has any profound positive benefits for flora and fauna. On the contrary, any so-called scientific breakthrough only tampers with the natural order, which then – paradoxically portentous – hastens mankind's own karmic demise. In short, scientists are to spirituality what your financial accountants are to surrealism."

Calum is surprised, and a little irritated, that Gaia is conversing with Harvey. Knowing it's crazy, really, to feel this way, he is embarrassed by his jealousy, and aware, of course, that he holds no monopoly over Mother Nature.

"OK then, dude, so what about space travel?" Harvey challenges confidently. "Scientists created the ability for man to explore the universe, did they not? Even you gotta admit, that's a far-out trip, ain't it, man?"

"Granted, human emissaries may have left planet Earth, but they have not travelled any significant distance, have they? Certainly not within range of any other inhabited planets. This is a positive truth. The Intergalactic Panel wish it to remain so. Besides, why would man need to escape from this beautiful planet if he were not destroying it? Why spend so much time and effort in trying to flee to another world, when humanity could expend the same endeavour taking care of the wonderful place they already inhabit? The natural order here on Earth was as near perfect as one could find. Only the humans have added destructive negative properties. There are not many places in the universe as magnificent as planet Earth, you know."

Harvey lights a cigarette. "OK, point taken... but even Stephen Hawking says we must soon go to live on Mars and create human colonies there."

"Ah yes," the Great Spirit allows. "Mr Hawking... even allowing for his great visionary intellect and expansive consciousness, he fails to realise, indeed does not know, that mankind has already populated Mars – trillions of years ago – in the crude human view of spatial existence humans call time."

Calum is amazed at this bombshell. "Wow! I didn't know that."

"Yes, man once lived there, but destroyed the environment eventually through his incessant meddling with the natural order, and so consequently the human race was wiped out on Mars. Yet scientists from Earth are now sending investigative probes there to try to discover potential details of any previous life form that may have inhabited the planet. But the irony is that humans were that previous life form."

"Mmmm... OK... sounds a bit far-fetched, but if you say so." Harvey is not convinced. "What about cryogenics then, man?

Scientists invented that option, did they not? So that we can be frozen at croakin' time, if we got the dosh like, then be brought back to life to populate other planets, should planet Earth go tits up in the future."

"To put it in your parlance Harvey, you're having a fucking laugh, dude... come on, get real. Do you really suppose that any form of intelligent life, observing the way man has trashed Earth – and previously Mars – would ever feel the inclination to resurrect humans, taking into account all their meddling with Nature, like spoilt kids with chemistry sets?" Harvey leans back against the bridge and lights a cigarette, looking up to the sky. "Don't know where the fuck you is, but I'm kinda gettin' the feelin' you ain't too keen on us humans, is you Mr Spirit?"

"On the contrary... some of you I love... but I, and other galactic like-minded souls are extremely wary of association, because of man's past record. It don't make good reading, man, but then again I can understand your antagonism... the truth, for a non-believer, always hurts, doesn't it... Harvey?" Harvey bristles, but does not dispute the observation. "OK, OK, but tell me this, then. Will aliens ever visit us... to sort things out, like?"

"Other life forms on distant planets will no longer contact Earth directly. They see humans as a parasitic sub-species, because of mankind's past and continuing criminal record against Nature. Why would they put themselves at risk of contamination? Karmic influence will always be in attendance though when–"

"Why doesn't God do something then?" Harvey interrupts. "Instead of standing by and allowing bad things to happen." The Great Spirit laughs. "Nature is God. If one is to coexist with the natural world then one is bound by moral and ethical cosmic truth codes. What some humans label as 'natural disasters' are in reality natural karmic eventualities unfolding. Remember... there is always payback... Karmic machinations can be extremely explosive or deceptively subtle, but one way or another karma always get the job done."

Light rain begins falling, refreshing and renewing. The rainbow disappears. The Great Spirit has gone. Harvey looks around. "Was he for real, Calum?"

"Yep, 'fraid so friend… and by the way, it's she… Gaia… Mother Nature… to you pal… although, granted, the Great Spirit can manifest as divine feminine or decidedly masculine at any given time. You could say androgynous in make-up, very unpredictable is Nature."

"Ok… whatever… but he… she … sure got a big chip on her shoulder that one, dude… ain't exactly life and soul of the party, is she?" Harvey shakes his head. "Heavy trip or what, man. Put me on a right fuckin' downer, this has."

"Gaia's just telling it like it is, Harv… telling it like it is." Calum walks on, leading the way towards the pub. They round a bend and just ahead, a rusting faded sign proclaiming 'Fyfield Arms' swings back and forth in the gentle breeze, creaking, gratingly, welcoming them like an out-of-tune violin. "What's the time, Harv?" He glances at his watch. "Comin' up nine-thirty."

"Say what! You're having me on, man," Calum gasps in astonishment. "We left home at four-thirty. If your watch is right, it's taken us five hours… to travel less than a mile?" Sudden rhetorical rhyme gate-crashes his thoughts like a painfully prophetic headache. "From LSD… one cannot flee… seeking to escape, in such frenzied haste… from the demons of your first Lysergic taste." Calum recognises the measured, mocking voice, realising now that the imbibed acid has distorted all sense of time and place. "Yes, Gaia, I understand. That's exactly how I feel, never again will I touch that vile chemical. I promise."

"Hey man," Harvey tugs his sleeve. "You hearin' voices too?"

"Yeah… the one true voice though, Harv… much clearer than any other… pure, authentic, and always speaks the truth."

"Oh yeah?" Harvey snorts. "That's what they all say. Don't go gettin' all evangelistical on me now, dude." Calum sighs. "Evangelical, my friend… I believe evangelical is the term you are looking for." Harvey looks insulted. "That's wot I fuckin' said, man!"

Sudden griping stomach cramps cause Calum to double up, feeling really rough, alternating between shivering with chill and hot sweating, totally out of sorts, coming over feverish and unsettled.

"Wots up wiv yuh, bud?" Harvey leans down. "Yuh ain't lookin' so clever." Calum glares up, pain creasing his face. "My guts are killing me... brain feels like mush... What the fuck was in that acid!?" Groaning, he slumps down on an iron bench fixed to the pub wall, head in hands. "Got me a storming headache coming on, man, you've fucking poisoned me!" Harvey chuckles. "Ya just comin' down from your trip is all, dude. The old LSD always throws in a curved ball at the end," he grins, confident as only the specialist can be on his chosen subject. "There ain't nothin' wrong with the gear, man... look at me, I'm sound as a pound, ain't I?" Calum glances up at the thin, pale as a ghost, crazy bloodshot-eyed maniac grinning down at him, and reserves judgement.

Lighting a joint, Harvey draws deep, before offering. "Here dude, yuh just need a toke on this lil' ole baby to mellow yuh out some." Calum waves him away, a look of loathing on his face. "No! Not for me, I don't need that shit no more... and I won't ever be doing acid again, either." Harvey laughs close up in his face. "Oh yeah? Heard it all before dude, besides, it ain't the gear, it's that fuckin' rainbow from yer Great Spirit crony that's done yer head in... so think on, man, next time yuh so keen to sing that one's praises," he smiles and points to the door, "we goin' in for a pint bud, or what?"

"Yeah, OK." Calum's hoping the alcohol might have some medicinal effect, taking the edge off the insidious narcotic comedown. "Just the one though, need to get me some kip soon, my head's banging." As they make for the bar, Harvey rubs out his joint with nicotine-yellowed forefinger and thumb, sticking the stub behind his ear, before rap-tap knuckle-rapping on the bar. The staccato summons brings a short, plump, middle-aged woman bustling to the counter, her cold dark-eyed gaze appraising the dishevelled pair with obvious distaste.

"Yes?" She asks, the curt tone, raised eyebrow, and surly body language clearly intimating her annoyance at this unwelcome intrusion.

"Two cold lagers, madam," Harvey orders, slamming down a handful of loose change onto the bar, "if it's all the same to you."

She pours the drinks in silence, glowering hostilely at these unwelcome strangers and suddenly hissing with venom. "Now see here, you two, drink up smartly, quietly with it mind, and then be on your way. I want no trouble in here tonight from your kind."

"Oh yeah! And exactly what kind would we be then, missus?" Harvey snarls, riled by her damning assumption. "Correct me if I'm wrong, but I was under the impression we wuz just normal payin' customers like?" She turns her back abruptly and disappears up the staircase. Harvey shouts after her. "Hey wait up, missus, yuh got any fuckin' pies? I'm starving." No answer. Shaking his head, Harvey moans, "miserable old cow or what?" He grabs the bunch of daffodils from the vase on the bar and begins chomping on the flowers. Calum laughs. "Yeah, that's Meg for you. She don't like customers interfering with their TV schedule."

"Yuh mean there's more like that old witch around this dive?"

"Yeah, she lives here with her old man, Doc." Harvey looks nonplussed. "Who'd marry a fuckin' harpy like her? What is he then, this Doc... like a GP or summat, man?" Calum laughs and points to the copper nameplate fixed above the bar, stating in brass capital letters:

'Megan and Robert Holliday. Licensed to sell intoxicating liquor.'

None the wiser, Harvey looks vacantly at the plaque. "Holliday... Doc... get it? Doc Holliday," Calum elaborates. "Gunfight at the OK Corral? Famous old Wild West shootout, between the Earp and Clanton gangs? Doc Holliday was quite matey with the then Tombstone Town Marshall, Wyatt Earp... Holliday fired the first shot that started the gunfight?" Harvey shakes his head, still chewing on the daffodils, clearly having no clue who these people were, and caring less. "Oh yeah, is that so, OK dude, whatever you say." Calum realises this is going nowhere and gives up on the history lesson, sitting down in the corner while Harvey goes over to the jukebox and feeds in some coins before choosing 'Grooving with Mr Blo' from the playlist and playing vigorous improvisational air guitar as he returns. He savours the cold lager, taking a long swig, nudging Calum as he leans back. "Needed this fucker, man."

"Yeah, it'll sure wash the flower petals down, Harv... don't ever chew on daffodil bulbs, though."

"And why ever not, dude?" Calum sips his beer before answering. "The bulbs are toxic... kill you stone-dead they will if you eat them." Harvey looks shocked. "Nah! Really, no, go on... yer 'avin me on dude... ain't yuh?"

"No, it's true mate, absolutely, trust me."

"Oh yeah," he derides, deciding it's a wind-up, "and when exactly did you become such an expert on fuckin' plant life." Calum pointedly appraises Harvey, "when I gave up studying fuckin' pond life." Harvey glances up sharply, unsure if he's just been insulted.

Before he can make up his mind, the door opens and a tall stocky blonde lad walks in. Calum recognises him immediately. He looks pale and out of sorts. "Hey Pete," he calls over, "how goes it, big man? This is Harvey. Pete's an old school pal, Harv, and a fellow member of our old gang, the Weyhill Wanderers." Harvey shrugs and offers a 'so what?' expression.

"Hi guys," Pete sounds drained of all emotion. "Spose you've heard the latest," he says, shaking his large head mournfully, "still can't believe it." Calum is instinctively primed for bad news. "No, what's gone down, bud?"

"It's our old gang leader, Mickey... he's only gone and snuffed it." A cold shiver flashes through Calum. "No! When... how?"

"Last night, at Kimpton... just down the road. Mickey was in the back of a motor, stoned on hash and speed, or so they says. Apparently he leant out the window to spew up, then the driver must have lost control and driven up onto the verge. Mickey's head hit them old iron railings with the pointed ends. He was impaled, and that was it for him. Killed, stone-fucking dead." He's gripping the bar so tightly the lack of blood flow turns his knuckles anaemic white. "Would you Adam and Eve it, mate... our old mucker, gone, just like that!"

Calum doesn't let on, but he has been expecting some form of karmic retribution for Mickey. The brutal finality of the punishment is a stark, shocking reminder nonetheless. "Yeah, who would of forecast that Pete? Thought he was immortal, did our Mickey."

The Great Spirit comes through to him. "Man is too fragile in his present incarnation to achieve immortality."

Meg comes downstairs, casting a disdainful glance over at Calum and Harvey, before asking, "usual, Peter?" She's already pouring his pint before he nods, "Yes, please." He downs his beer in one and moves to shake hands. "Well, best be off. Just wanted... needed... to tell someone. Glad I caught up with you, Cal... maybe see you around then, pal?" Calum grips his hand tightly and pats him on the back. "Yeah, maybe, Pete. You take it easy, my friend."

"Sorry about your mate," Harvey offers.

Calum can find no words to console shaken up Pete. He doesn't offer him a drink, reasoning, 'what's the point in prolonging the agony?' Futile to explain that Mickey's demise was not exactly unexpected. No point in explaining karmic stuff to Pete, he wasn't into all that.

Calum gets shakily to his feet as Pete leaves the pub, feeling suddenly exhausted, locked into this gloomy moment, wishing that he hadn't known the portents of the future in this instance, and wondering if being involved with the Great Spirit is as straightforward as he had previously thought. He suddenly feels even worse. Today's accumulated emotional wear and tear finally catching up. "Best be away myself, Harv... feeling really rough now... gonna get me head down... need to crash soon."

"Yo dude, I'll walk a ways with you," Harvey offers, "then I'll get the old bus back to town..."

Calum sleeps fitfully this night. There is some consolation though, in that his restlessness seems to prevent the nightmares from returning. He wakes around three, feeling jaded and depressed, due, he presumes, to the combination of LSD after-effects, the alcohol, and the shocking news about Mickey. He gets up, opens the curtains and leans forwards, forehead against the window, the cold glass soothing his fevered brow, peering out into pitch black nothingness, a deep dark void where no discernable shapes are even visible. 'Now this is heavy shit, man, desolation darkness, without any sound or movement.' Calum had never experienced morbid gloom as grave as this before. Imagining this must be similar to being held captive in a cosmic black hole. He falls back on the bed, the depressive intensity acting as a sedative anaesthetic against real life, but he realises life must go on, knowing, 'I need to snap out of this and plan my next move.'

Feeling more than ready to move on, desperate to find some joy, fun, happiness before he is consumed by this dark matter cloud of incessant doom, he muses, 'after all, there will be no more school now, not after the shooting of Eli, so I just need to sort my escape from the foster parents, and this dismal place, then total freedom will be mine.'

Mickey's untimely ending has only strengthened his resolve. He pledges, from here on in, that he will live only for the moment whilst treading the Sacred Path of his destiny alone. Pondering the prospect of this new exciting life ahead, he drifts back into welcoming, renewed slumber.

CHAPTER
FORTY-TWO

Calum is woken by loud knocking on the front door. Staggering from the bed he peels back a corner of the curtain and catches his breath... Hazel and Karen are outside! "Fucking hell," he whispers, whilst checking out the clock... nine-thirty. He is suffering a mighty hangover, the LSD comedown leaving him badly strung out, reeling around in panic, head in hands, feeling as if his brain is sloshing about unsupported in his skull. The last thing on his to-do list today was to see the Sinister Sisters. 'No way! I'm in no fit state to perform to their expectations.' But they knock on the door persistently. Searching the bungalow hurriedly, he's relieved to find the Browns are out, assuming, 'shopping perhaps, as it's Saturday morning.' A brief flash of devil-may-care opportunism dares him to let the girls in, but common sense (backed up by the sharp pin-like stabbing above his eyes) prevails, swiftly quelling the dim flame of desire. 'No, I'm not up to it,' he states adamantly to his goading inner demon, checking out the mirror and accepting, 'this ain't a good look, gotta recover first'. Slipping back to bed, he pulls the bedclothes tight over his head in an attempt to drown out the loud rat-tat-tat of the door knocker.

"Come on, sis," Karen has had enough, "he's obviously not in. Let's go back to town." Dejected, they mope away up the drive. The curtains of the mobile home twitch and part slightly. Jim Brown leers out, ogling the girls. Karen turns back to her dawdling sister. "Are you coming, Haze?"

"No! You go on." Hazel slumps to the ground, sitting cross-legged, lighting a cigarette. "I'm going to wait for him to come home." Pouting sullenly, angry at being spurned, she wonders aloud, "If he's not in, then what's he up to? That's what I'd like to know." Karen sighs, exasperated. "OK, please yourself, but you'll drive yourself mad, girl... I'm getting the next bus home. This is becoming boring. Look... I'll see you in town later, sis."

Hazel waves her away, going nowhere, determined to get to the bottom of Calum's absence. She gets up and starts walking along the road, pausing at the railway bridge... sighing, she starts fondling under her skirt, recalling the first time she got intimate with Calum here... needing him... ready for him... now... she moans softly, before clambering up the steep side path of the embankment. Once up on the railway track, she sweeps dust and dead leaves from her short black leather miniskirt before lavishly reapplying rouge lipstick. She walks on a short distance, until she's standing high above the bungalow, hoping to catch Calum unawares from this elevated vantage point... But there is only an old man in the garden below. Jim has seen her. He waves, and walks towards the fence, squeezing between the taut strands of stock wire before slowly ascending the sharp incline, and asking breathlessly as he approaches, "why, hello, missy, are you looking for Calum?"

"Yeah, course I am... I'm his fucking girlfriend, after all!" Hazel glowers defensively, long lithe legs planted defiantly akimbo, looking sexy rough in her creased leather miniskirt and laddered stockings. "What's it to you though, mister?" Hands on hips, wild, windswept hair falling over full sneering lips, she demands, "Is he in the fucking house or what?"

"No, I'm afraid not, dear," Jim lies, avoiding her searching gaze. "I saw him go out earlier... ahem... with another girl." This pushes Hazel over the edge. "I knew it! I just fucking knew it." Tears flowing, "how could he do that? I'm his girlfriend! How dare he cheat on me like this?"

"Now now, lovey, please don't take on so." Jim puts an arm around her shoulder. "He's not worth it, the bloody fool, if he can't see what he's missing with such a little cracker like you."

Suddenly an idea comes to her – how to get her own back – the only way she knows. "Well now then, mister," smiling deviously and swallowing her distaste, "You know what? This is your lucky day. Two can play at his dirty game, the two-timing skunk." She takes Jim's hand. "Come with me," leading him away along the railway track, until they reach an old ramshackle rail workers' hut. Holding open the door, she ushers him inside, unfastening and dropping her skirt in one fluid movement before kicking the door shut behind her with the heel of a scuffed green pixie boot.

CHAPTER
FORTY-THREE

Calum peeks out again. 'No sign of the Sinister Sisters.' He lets out a long sigh. 'Peace at last.' Needing a cigarette, he cautiously ventures outside, feeling edgy... can't put his finger on it, but something feels wrong... very wrong... worrying, he accepts the given, 'my feral instinct is never wrong.'

Finishing his smoke and returning indoors, he fully opens the bedroom curtains, and just at that moment catches a glimpse of someone stumbling down from the railway line. The shambling figure comes into the garden, heading for the caravan. 'It's Jim? That's strange... what's the dirty old bugger been doing up there? He never goes up on the railway line.' A few seconds later Hazel comes walking along the track, heading towards the bridge. 'This is more than odd...' He can't figure this out. 'Her too... what's she up to?'

Jim goes into the mobile home. Calum leaves the bungalow and runs to the foot of the railway bridge, arriving just in time to catch Hazel scrambling out, legs first, from the undergrowth. She leaps back, startled, surprised to see him there.

"For Christ's sake, you made me jump, you fucking idiot," she says, brushing off twigs and dirt and tugging down her skirt, "where were you? I've been waiting around ages for you to show up."

"Indoors... asleep... just... just got up," Calum replies warily, trying to work this out... 'Something's not right here.' Her rough and ready vulnerability makes him suddenly horny, wanting her, right now, but holding back... sensing trouble.

"Don't lie to me, you bloody wanker," she screams, "you've been with another girl. Jim told me so." He's baffled by her outburst. "Another girl... no... no, course not... who, when? Jim... what's he got to do with anything?" Suddenly she goes for him, raking her nails deep down his cheek. "Ow!" His hand flies to the stinging pain, feeling the warm ooze of freshly drawn blood. "You crazy cow!"

"Yeah, well, two can play at your dirty little games, you fucking two-timer!" Crying now, she gestures up towards the railway line, taunting, "wanna know what just happened up there, lover boy... do ya, do ya?" Bemused and disorientated by her wild attack, he laughs in bewilderment. "What are you going on about, you silly little bitch?" Hazel sneers confidently. "Glad you find it funny... cos I only went and let that dirty old man have his wicked way with me." Calum looks up towards the railway tracks, a grim realisation dawning, overriding the disbelieving expression on his face. She comes up close, triumphantly mocking. "Yeah, that's right, you cheater," crowing, "I fucked him... up there, in the shack." The image of them together is so, so wrong... so ridiculous, "You... you what? With him? That skanky old has-been?" He shakes his head in vehement dismissal. "No... no... you're having me on, girl... tell me this is a wind-up right? No... you wouldn't, Hazel... even you couldn't do something... something as vile and dirty... as that?" She stands before him, grinning, nodding yes. Head in hands, he falls to his knees, moaning, repulsed at the sickening scenario replaying over and over in his mind. "Tell me you have made up this nightmare, just to get back at me?" She scowls at him. "Nope, 'fraid not Calum, it's all true." He grabs her wrist roughly. "Yeah, that's it, isn't it? You're just saying this to get your own back, because I wouldn't open the door to you."

"Yes, vile and dirty, it sure was," she goads, "very dirty in fact. But then, wasn't it horrid, what you did to me, going off shagging with another girl? So now its payback time, matey," she twists free of his grip, "let's see how you fucking like it."

He wrings his hands in anguish and staggers to his feet. "But I haven't done anything. I was indoors all the time, you fucking fool."

Hazel jabs him in the chest with her finger. "You should know me by now, Cal... you know how it works... I had an itch, and it needed scratching. I wanted you though, you bloody fool, not some old deathbed letch slobbering all over me." She screams in his face, "but you were far too busy, weren't you? Playing away, having it off with some old slag."

"How many fucking times?!" He cries out in frustration. "You stupid, stupid girl. I've been here all night, and all morning, in my bedroom. He's lied to you, the dirty old pervert, just to lay you, and you fell for it, hook line and sinker."

Hazel bites into her quivering lower lip... reaching out hesitantly to him... uncertainty in her eyes, wondering now, with a sinking heart, if she may have made a big big mistake. Calum pushes her away, letting out a pent-up cry, "I haven't left here, or seen any other girl, you mental crazy cow."

"Oh yeah?" Hazel's voice wavering, faltering, unsure... still not convinced he's telling the truth, but serious doubts now creeping in to her confused mind. "If... if... that's true," she nervously chews a fingernail, "and I'm not saying I believe you mind... then why didn't you open the door? We were knocking for ages."

"I know you were... and yes... yes..." Calum looks to the ground "I admit... I should have come out to you, but I had a mad bad hangover and couldn't face anyone. That's why I didn't show."

"Well, it's you that's the fool then," she screams, feeling sick now, in the pit of her stomach, thinking of what she has just allowed the creepy old man to do to her. Reaching out to him, she tries to make things right. "I needed you, Cal... you know what I'm like. I always need the loving. You could've at least come to speak to me."

"Yeah, I know what you are," his voice rising as he shoves her away roughly. "Only too well, you're a fucking nymphomaniac. But even allowing for that... how could you have sex with a man old enough to be your grandad? How could you, Hazel? That's just plain despicable." Calum grimaces, feeling dizzy and nauseous. Suddenly, galvanised by righteousness, he grabs Hazel's arm and marches her forcibly along the road. "Right! You come with me young lady, we'll go to the police and get that perverted old child molester locked up. He raped you, Hazel. He's not gonna get away with that in a hurry. I'll look after you now."

"No Calum! No, get off, just let me go," she says, struggling and squirming, "please, let go," trying to break free from his grasp, "you can't do that see, cos I let him fuck me." She looks up into his eyes, mascara-infused tears trickling down into smeared lipstick, her wild-eyed gaze challenging him. "Don't you get it? I wanted it. He didn't force me. I let him, no, made him even." Her voice mocks Calum in scornful revenge. "Yep, that's right, it was all down to me, me, me, ME! I made him do it. You know how much I want it, need it. You let me down boy, the rest is history now."

"But he conned you, Hazel," Calum rages, fists bunching into tensed coiled weapons, the tendons and sinews of his forearms straining in taut fury as he grasps her wrists, pinning Hazel's arms to her sides, tightening his grip, shouting in her face, "Don't you get it, you fucking mug?! He made out I was with another girl, just so he could have his evil way with you."

Hazel's voice falters. "Well... yeah... so... I know that now... OK, I'm sorry Calum... but you still lied... now get off, you're hurting me."

Releasing his hold, he stands back from her, glaring, face creased with loathing... spitting out his condemnation, his sneering tone emphasising his disgust. "How could you, Hazel, that's more than depraved... even for a filthy little bitch like you!" She rubs her sore wrists, angered by his lack of empathy. "Oh yeah mister, is that so? Filthy, depraved, hey? Well you never complained before about how depraved I am, did you?! Not when you were getting what you wanted, I wasn't too filthy then, was I?"

"That's not the fucking point, that was normal, boyfriend and girlfriend stuff, this is... is... child abuse! Doing it with someone old... like..." His words trail off miserably, unable to speak Jim's name... "like... like him!" Hazel covers her ears with her hands and spins around, stamping her feet in confused exasperation. "Oh, just fucking shut up why don't you. I don't know any more... you lied... he lied... what does it matter now? You both took advantage of me. The pair of you led me on. You've got me all mixed up now." She looks him in the eyes, the messed up make-up lending her the appearance of a crazy face-painted clown. "I won't go to the police. I know that much, Calum... if my parents ever find out, they'll disown me. If you make me go to the law... then... then... I'll tell them, tell them it was you... yes you... who raped me." Weeping now in short little gasps, it's all too much for her. Hazel yearns desperately for the only thing that will make her feel better, the only thing that will make everything alright again. Moving closer, she cuddles into him, green eyes mistily sexual, gazing up, baby doll voice imploring, "how about you and me... we go back up there, to the shack, and do it properly, Cal. We can make up and get over this... together... let's just forget what happened before... it don't mean nothing, babe."

He stands back, looking at her as if she's insane, shouting despairingly, "Don't mean nothing?!" Struck incredulous by how she can dismiss this dark deed so casually. "Are you totally fucking crazy, Hazel, how can it not mean anything?" He slumps to the ground, sobbing, on his hands and knees, retching, close to vomiting.

"But I still need your loving, Cal." She crouches down with him, her arm around his shoulder. "You know you're still the only one for me, baby."

"No! No way," he pushes her off, wiping away tears, his anger subsiding, to be replaced by a rush of delayed shock. "You'd best go home, Hazel. I need time... time alone... some space to think this through... can't get my head round any of this, it's all too big a deal for me. I don't think I can ever see you again."

Trudging away forlornly up the road, she keeps looking back, hoping in vain that he will come after her. Calum stays put, slumped underneath the bridge, crying in anger and frustration, closing his eyes, hugging himself tight, rocking back and forth in pained grief, devising murderous thoughts of vengeance, vowing that Jim Brown will pay for this... big time... somehow... someday.

Opening his eyes, he immediately experiences a dramatic down shift surge of cosmic energy. A great rush of demonic dark power has suddenly transformed his world. No birdsong now, no blue sky, the sun has gone, to be replaced by a blustery wailing breeze, blowing in cold drizzling rain under the stark grey iron bridge. Planet Earth has been consumed by a wave of black melancholia. Calum realises that everything around him is now visible only in muted shades of black and grey, there is no other colour available. But he's welcoming these murky subdued hues; he can see and think much clearer without the distraction of bright uplifting colour. Depressive intensity and morose dark-mood clarity of thought is now ultra-defined. Exactly the right conditions for enabling karmic retribution... revenge is uppermost in his thoughts, before making good his escape, as soon as possible. The lyrics of the 'Animals' song, 'I gotta get out of this place, if it's the last thing I ever do,' fill his head, but cold calculating feral instinct is warning him to bide his time a while... a plan is formulating... he knows now what he must do to achieve universal justice. He unzips his boot, retrieving the pieces of worn card the old tramp had given him, scratching the dark matter symbols into the dirt floor of the underpass with his fingers, copying faithfully the ancient hieroglyph-ics until his nails start to bleed.

Calum stands unsteadily, trying to control the peripheral vertigo crowding in on him, staring at the hex he has created. He allows his breathing to regulate, commanding his heartbeat to slow, as he contemplates and meditates, envisioning the retributive scenario now set in motion within this dark matter vortex. Swaying back and forth, he sings the mad professor's song.

"Kill a cat, shoot a dog, squash a frog, burn a bat." Chanting the words over and over as a swirling grey mist gradually envelops him. "Squash a frog, burn a bat, shoot a dog, kill a cat. Bat, frog, cat...cat, dog, bat, squash, shoot, burn, kill, bat, cat, frog..."

The wailing crescendo builds in intensity, until he is whirling around and around, like some demented dervish flailing in trance, faster and faster, staggering, stumbling, dizzy, until he can no longer stand, eventually collapsing exhausted on the cold brick overhang beneath the bridge, drenching rain saturating his limp body, slowly losing consciousness. A grim smile of satisfaction plays on his lips as he knows with utmost certainty... Jim Brown is now condemned... by the dark matter curse.

TO BE CONTINUED.